LOUISE WESTLING

Sacred Groves and Ravaged Gardens

The Fiction of Eudora Welty,
Carson McCullers,
and Flannery O'Connor

The University of Georgia Press
Athens

© 1985 by the University of Georgia Press
Athens, Georgia 30602
All rights reserved

The illustrations in this book are from the
AMERICAN HERITAGE PICTURE COLLECTION.
On the title page and contents page:
drawings by Walton Taber, circa 1884.
Repeated on the chapter opening pages:
detail of a drawing by Harry Fenn, circa 1885.

Designed by Sandra Strother Hudson
Set in Mergenthaler Janson

The paper in this book meets the guidelines for
permanence and durability of the Committee on
Production Guidelines for Book Longevity of the
Council on Library Resources.

Printed in the United States of America

90 89 88 87 86 85   6 5 4 3 2

Library of Congress Cataloging in Publication Data

Westling, Louise Hutchings.
    Sacred groves and ravaged gardens.

    Bibliography: p.
    Includes index.
    1. American fiction—20th century—History
and criticism. 2. Women in literature. 3. American fiction—Women authors—History and criticism. 4. American fiction—Southern States—
History and criticism. 5. Welty, Eudora, 1909–
—Criticism and interpretation. 6. McCullers,
Carson, 1917–1967—Criticism and interpretation. 7. O'Connor, Flannery—Criticism
and interpretation. 8. Southern States in literature. 9. Landscape in literature. I. Title.

PS374.W6W4 1985   813'.5'099287   84-16434
ISBN 0-8203-0746-7 (alk. paper)
ISBN 0-8203-0831-5 (pbk.: alk. paper)

for my mother

Contents

Preface

W hen I was a young woman fresh out of college and sure my generation was going to correct all the world's ills, my Kentucky grandmother, a model of the old-fashioned Southern lady, asked me if my friends and I believed in free love. That old term was far from our ideal of sexual equality and frankness, but I didn't feel like going into a long definition of the theory we had gleaned from a *Time* essay on "The New Morality." So I said, "Sort of." She sighed and asked in a bewildered voice, "Then who will hold the banner?"

"What banner?" I said.

"For the men," she said.

That quaint idea made little sense to me for many years, though I puzzled about it as I tried to understand why the relations between men and women violated so many of my notions of cooperation. Gradually both life and fiction have helped me discover some of the reasons and see what my grandmother meant. Virginia Woolf's *A Room of One's Own* was a revelation to me, as was Ellen Moers's *Literary Women*. They showed how much responsibility men had placed on women while restricting their lives in ways that have caused special difficulties for women writers.

As I was reading Woolf and Moers, I was also discovering the fiction first of Flannery O'Connor and then of Carson McCullers, Eudora Welty, Katherine Anne Porter, and Caroline Gordon. Through them I began to rediscover my own Southern past. I began to examine the ways their fiction confronts the heritage of the Southern lady which my grandmother expressed in that poignant chivalric image of women holding the banner for their men. Ten years of questioning and reading have brought me to the conclusions in the following pages. I offer them in the hope that they will contribute to an understanding of how our literature illuminates the profoundest problems and possibilities of our present lives.

All along the way as this project unfolded, friends and colleagues have given encouragement, challenge, and aid. George Wickes is first among them, for he originally suggested that I write about Flannery O'Connor and since that time has suffered through every stage of the work with me. Important encouragement has also come from Ingrid Weatherhead, Esther Wagner, and Katherine Cudlipp. I am much indebted to Elizabeth Meese, Margaret Sullivan, Sally Fitzgerald, Ruth Vande Kieft, and Elizabeth Evans for challenging discussion about a number of major issues in this book. John Desmond has been a steady ally in the rather lonely pursuit of Southern literary studies in the Pacific Northwest, and Miriam Johnson and Rebekah Poller gave me a wonderful store of Flannery O'Connor anecdotes from their own experiences with her in Milledgeville. Ann Park of Milledgeville also contributed reminiscences. From my first trip to Milledgeville in 1976, when she opened her home as well as Flannery O'Connor's world to me, Sarah Gordon has been a most generous friend and discerning critic.

Steven Lowenstam of the University of Oregon Classics Department has advised me on many esoteric matters of etymology and Greek myth, knowing immediately where to find specialized information that I could never have discovered for myself. The strengths of my treatment of mythology are largely attributable to this generous colleague, who bears no responsibility for any of my missteps.

Some portions of the Flannery O'Connor and Carson McCullers chapters of this study first appeared in slightly different form in *Twentieth Century Literature*, the *Flannery O'Connor Bulletin*, the *Southern Humanities Review*, and *Modern Fiction Studies*. In 1981 Professor Alfred Weber of the University of Tübingen and Professor Dieter Schulz, then of the University of Stuttgart, gave me the opportunity to teach graduate seminars in their American Studies departments and thus develop the full scope of the book.

A Faculty Summer Research Award from the Office of Scientific and Scholarly Research at the University of Oregon allowed me to complete my writing and to consult original manuscript materials in Mississippi and Georgia during the summer of 1983. William Hanna, Michelle Hudson, and Virginia Sims of the Mississippi Department of Archives and History made my work in the Welty archives particularly rewarding. Gerald Becham first and then Robert Gorman and Nancy Davis, of the Ina Dillard Russell Library, similarly smoothed my paths in the Flannery O'Connor Collection at Georgia College.

Charles East and Karen Orchard of the University of Georgia Press have given this book a warm reception of the kind I never dared to expect. Anne Goodwyn Jones has given it the most generous of readings and valuable suggestions for improvements in the text, as have Gloria Johnson and Patricia Wooley Hutchings.

Finally I want to thank the office staff of the University of Oregon English Department, particularly Michael Stamm for his interest, astute advice, and great dispatch in the preparation of the manuscript.

Sacred Groves and Ravaged Gardens

Introduction

When a *Paris Review* interviewer asked Eudora Welty whether she ever felt part of a community of Southern women writers including her contemporaries Carson McCullers, Flannery O'Connor, Katherine Anne Porter, and Caroline Gordon, the answer was a gently qualified no. Welty explained that although she and her fellow writers knew and respected each other's work and some enduring friendships had been formed among them, she was not aware of any definite links or passing-about of influences.[1] Yet nowhere else in American literature is there a group of accomplished women writers so closely bound together by regional qualities of setting, character, and time. Because Ellen Moers and Elaine Showalter have revealed how much literary women rely on each other and on their own developing traditions, we now recognize the accuracy of Virginia Woolf's claim in *A Room of One's Own* that women need their own distinct heritage to nourish their art.[2] We can therefore assume that Southern women writers share a definite historical tradition, and we should not be surprised to find much closer alliances among them than Welty acknowledges. The three writers within this tradition who form the most coherent group and whose work is most richly illuminated by mutual comparison are Carson McCullers, Flannery O'Connor, and Eudora Welty. Although their birth dates are separated by neat eight-year intervals (Welty 1909, McCullers 1917, O'Connor 1925), the appearance of their major work falls primarily within the two decades from 1940 to 1960. McCullers and Welty published their first books within a year of each other—*The Heart Is a Lonely Hunter* in 1940 and *A Curtain of Green* in 1941—and continued to produce novels and stories regularly during the forties. Flannery O'Connor's first stories appeared in little magazines at the end of the forties, and during the fifties she joined Welty and McCullers as a highly respected Southern fiction writer. A vivid, pervasive sense of place and local color ties the work of all three writers to its regional source in the Deep South. These women grew up and drew their inspiration from towns not much more distant from each other than a day's travel. If she had wished, Eudora Welty could easily have driven to Carson McCullers's home town of Columbus, Georgia, in one day and then could have moved on to Flannery O'Connor's Milledgeville for lunch the next. The landscape would change gradually as she crossed Alabama and moved into the red clay hills and long-leaf pines of Georgia, but the social and cultural world would remain essentially the same. These matters of chronology and geography might be trivial if it were not for the profound function of place in the fiction of all three writers and, even more important, if it were not for interrelationships of theme, character, and symbol which give immense value to their collective work—a kind of richness and power which is far less apparent or affecting when they are taken separately.

Katherine Anne Porter and Caroline Gordon are not included in my focus even though each served as invaluable mentor and friend to one of the three writers I shall discuss. Their careers precede those of the writers they aided, and their work seems to me not as exclusively or profoundly identified with the Deep South. Some of Porter's work is set in the South, but it is the more cosmopolitan South of New Orleans or the peculiarly Texas South of her childhood. In some of the preoccupations of her Southern fiction, she shows herself a precursor for the later writers, but her work is not so vividly defined by local color and the middle-to-lower-class society which populates Welty's, McCullers's, and O'Connor's fiction. Caroline Gordon's South is Kentucky, Tennessee, and Virginia, the subtly different outer fringes of Dixie, and she does not seem to plumb her Southern landscape for meaning but rather to use it as graceful decoration for stories that could almost as easily be set in the Northeast or Midwest.

In a broader sense, however, all these women are the inheritors of a tradition of women's writing in the South which originated in letters, diaries, and oral histories. Scholars have begun intensive collection and study of these personal records in recent years, but one of the most impressive of them has been available in abridged form for a long time: Mary Chesnut's *Diary from Dixie*. A sophisticated observer with a satiric eye,

Chesnut was the Pepys of the Confederacy, watching the Civil War unfold from the center of the highest Confederate circles. (Southern historian C. Vann Woodward recently made the complete diary available in a new edition: *Mary Chesnut's Civil War*.) But by the time Chesnut was chronicling the Civil War, Southern women were already moving beyond private forms of literary activity and beginning to publish fiction. They began the public tradition of feminine letters which produced Augusta Jane Evans, Kate Chopin, Ellen Glasgow, and Elizabeth Madox Roberts. A valuable study of major writers in the tradition from 1859 to 1936 by Anne Goodwyn Jones has recently been published.

The fiction of Welty, McCullers, and O'Connor, seen as the natural contemporary product of this heritage, provides an unusual opportunity to examine the interrelations of a coherent, distinctively feminine literary tradition. Although these women participate in wider literary traditions than those of their sex and region, much of what is unique and most powerful about their fiction emerges from their experience as women in a society which officially worshipped womanhood but in its imaginative life betrayed troubled, contradictory undercurrents. We shall never properly value their work if we do not see it fully in this light; we shall be judging it by standards which do not quite fit.

More specifically, unless we look at McCullers, O'Connor, and Welty as women—and through them at the traditions of women's literature which they embody and send forth enriched—serious reading and scholarly discussion of their fiction will be shadowed by condescension. Most of their critics have been men, and even the enthusiasts among them sometimes patronize or offer unintentionally backhanded compliments. As an example, John A. Allen excuses Welty for placing female consciousness at the center of many of her novels. "Of course they present a feminine point of view; but this, in Miss Welty's work, is a matter of perspective which does not involve distortion. For Eudora Welty, showing the action of a novel through a woman's eyes is not an act of aggression but of illumination."[3] Distortion and aggression are the normal results, Allen assumes, when women write from their own experience. Leslie Fiedler is one of the most original critics of American culture as it is revealed in literature, a writer who has unveiled hostility between the sexes almost everywhere in American fiction, and particularly a negative attitude toward women. Yet he himself becomes an example of masculine contempt for women when he describes "a second Faulknerian line of descent in which women have rather consistently, though *quite improbably*, taken a leading part" (my emphasis). These he goes on to name "the first generation of distaff Faulknerians," such as Porter, Welty, and McCullers. In contrast to the "masculine Faulknerians" who are "tough, tortured, and, at their best, determinedly intellectual," concerned with the "complex moral and social problems at the heart of the matter of the South," the "feminizing Faulknerians" are weak, even decadent. "What tends to be dissipated in their fiction is the grossness, the sheer dirtiness, the farce and howling burlesque, all that keeps Faulkner from ever seeming precious." Fiedler's real point is that women have emasculated the powerful Faulknerian literary heritage by producing a feeble offspring: "the true Magnolia Blossom or Southern homosexual style."[4]

Although this kind of criticism fortunately does not dominate commentary on Southern women writers, it is disconcerting to realize that anyone should still describe these women as mere ribs and crooked pieces of their masculine contemporaries. Such attitudes are insidious enough to need the balance provided by a positive reassessment which assumes that women are capable of working within their own traditions; that such qualities as grossness, dirtiness, and howling burlesque are not synonymous with literary strength; that a female literary perspective does not automatically mean distortion or aggression. Anne Goodwyn Jones has begun this reassessment, and the pages which follow here will expand it by examining how Welty, McCullers, and O'Connor explore their Southern world, and through it, wider questions of human destiny, in ways men cannot.

I shall concentrate almost exclusively on their concerns as women: on their treatment of the problems of identity, on attitudes toward the mother, on the ways in which men are perceived, and on the distinctively female uses of place and symbol in their stories. At the beginning I shall try to establish the shared contexts of their lives and their literary apprenticeships. This means discussing what it is like to grow up as white women in the South, and what particular literary traditions nourished the development of their craft. But the real heart of my study will be an examination of each writer's distinctive contributions.

Eudora Welty celebrates the feminine, first in her portrait of the mother at the creative center of family life in *Delta Wedding*, a novel which I shall argue was inspired by Virginia Woolf's treatment of Mrs. Ramsay in *To the Lighthouse*. Welty's novel also dramatizes other stages of the feminine life cycle in the portraits of young girls and nubile maidens, as well as middle-aged matrons and tottering remnants of the matriarchal past. *The Golden Apples* and *The Optimist's Daughter* explore the situations of daughters seeking independent lives distinct from the example set by their mothers. Thus Welty pays tribute to the real Southern ladies who stood behind the ideal so often invoked by their men, and she also tells the story of her own generation who needed to question the traditional complacencies of Southern domestic life and find alternate possibilities for fulfillment. As critics like Peggy Prenshaw have pointed out, Welty's fictional world is matriarchal in its sources of power. That authority is strengthened in the novels by richly articulated mythic patterns from our collective past.

If Welty celebrates womankind, Carson McCullers and Flannery O'Connor struggle against it. In McCullers's case, we find again and again the tomboy heroine suddenly confronted by society's demands that she subdue her behavior, accept the facts of adult sexuality that she has tried to deny, and start acting ladylike. In one story the heroine refuses to submit to this diminution and is destroyed by an alliance of vengeful males who punish her impertinence. Similarly, Flannery O'Connor tells story after story of strong mothers who must be punished by masculine authority for their attempts to control the world around them. The sour and resentful children of these women stand as emblems of their mothers' debilitating power. Daughters set themselves at odds with their mothers in resistance to femininity, one by seeking to escape her mother's fate of childbearing and others by deliberately wearing ugly clothes and acting rude. One twelve-year-old girl escapes the whole issue of sex differences and adolescent courtship by identifying herself with a hermaphrodite. None of the daughters in these stories is at ease with her feminine self except the retarded Lucynell Crater, whose dumb innocence protects her from dissatisfaction. Virginia Woolf's description of Charlotte Brontë fits both McCullers and O'Connor: "One sees that she will never get her genius expressed whole and entire. Her books will be deformed and twisted. . . . She will write of herself where she should write of her characters. She is at war with her lot."[5]

Despite obvious differences, all three of these writers share preoccupations with feminine identity which are shaped by the traditional Southern veneration of the lady. My final chapter will comment on some of the major interrelationships in their treatment of this common heritage which are revealed in the symbolism of place. Houses, city streets, and pastoral landscapes all carry momentous symbolic force in the fiction. Because these writers are women, the depiction of houses takes on special importance. As Virginia Woolf said, "Women have sat indoors all these millions of years, so that by this time the very walls are permeated by their creative force." Not only do domestic buildings embody feminine creativity, but they also function almost like clothing or a second body, as in one of Flannery O'Connor's stories, where a frightened girl peers out of the upstairs windows of her farmhouse, as from large protected eyes, at a group of invading boys. In McCullers's *The Member of the Wedding*, a crazily decorated kitchen comes to symbolize the mad prison of Frankie Addams's adolescence. Or Miss Amelia Evans's cafe can grow into a symbol of her psyche by the end of *The Ballad of the Sad Café*, somewhat like Poe's House of Usher. For Welty, however, houses are temples of family life, whose shapes and colors embody the accretion of clan history and symbolize family character.

Beyond houses, the Southern landscape has traditionally been associated with woman and has special bearing on the question of feminine identity in each writer's work. The gardens, bayous, rivers, and forests of Eudora Welty's Mississippi world quiver with the very life forces of her fiction. Unlike the natural world of O'Connor's stories, which seems to function only as rigidly stylized setting for grim dramas as classically restrained as Greek tragedy, Welty's nature is varied, shimmering with its own myriad life apart from human concerns yet at the same time full of meaning for the cycles of ordinary life which have always occurred within the larger scheme. The pattern of meadow and wood in Flannery O'Connor's fiction is much more specialized, gathering tremendous sacramental significance, with woods protecting vulnerable pastures from invasion. The land, the trees, the sky, and the relentless eye of the sun are so powerfully charged in her fiction that they become some of its most powerful characters. McCullers's landscapes are much more confined than those of either Welty or O'Connor, for action is almost always limited to one or at most a few interiors—kitchen, bar, or cafe—and the streets and sidewalks of the Southern town where the story occurs. Interiors are the scenes for community, and sidewalks are paths of exploration for adolescent heroines. Even though Miss Amelia Evans of *The Ballad of the Sad Café* is reported to work in her fields, to travel around the countryside on business, and to operate a still hidden in the woods, we never see her in those places. Instead we see her almost always inside her cafe.

The function of place reveals something paradoxical about the fiction of Welty, McCullers, and O'Connor. Entrapment seems to be the preoccupation of the one writer who appeared to have escaped both her region and the restrictions of her gender. McCullers's heroines in *The Heart Is a Lonely Hunter, The Ballad of the Sad Café*, and *The Member of the Wedding* are all ultimately defeated, forced to accept imprisonment by the sexual conventions of their world. Thus Carson McCullers, who left the South and lived a sexually unconventional life among artists and intellectuals in New York and Paris, wrote stories of tomboys who failed or were punished. Flannery O'Connor's landscapes are wider and involve ancient connections between human life and the organic world, but they are often threatened farms where women owners struggle desperately to provide a safe haven for themselves and their children but are usually chastened by male invasion. The overwhelming sense we have in her pastures surrounded by protective woods is that of fortresses under sinister but hidden siege.

How differently Eudora Welty envisions place for her characters! The landscapes of *Delta Wedding* and *The Golden Apples* are celebrated for their beauty and the joy of life in their midst. Mystery and danger may lurk in the bayous, as poisonous snakes or semidivine visitors or water where one can drown, but on the whole the teeming natural world is a dreamy Eden for children, where they wander at will in unity with natural forces and where adults must return for renewal. Life and death coexist, interweave, and form the natural backdrop for human affairs. Is it possible for Welty to celebrate the land and the fecundity and independence of the world of nature so comfortably because she feels the same way about herself as woman and understands the ancient identification of the land as feminine? I think the answer must be yes.

This is not to assert Welty's superiority over the other writers, for each has her particular excellences. McCullers looks hard in the face of the painful choices forced on many lively and ambitious girls, and O'Connor writes the most intense and classically crafted fiction of all three. O'Connor's major concern is with problems of human pride and ultimate spiritual destiny, but she also illuminates more specialized problems of family relationships, sexual identity, and the social and moral subtleties in the racial climate of her world. Welty herself writes comedy of manners which celebrates the lives of women as it dramatizes many issues of kinship and community in small-town Southern life. All three add important fictional experiences to American literature, and they do so by investigating the identity and the experience of women in their unique Southern world.

Finally, it should be obvious that my study does not pretend to tell the whole story of women's writing in the South. It is only one chapter of that story, examining three related contemporary writers who belong to the privileged class of educated white Southerners. Black Southern women are creating an increasingly powerful literature depicting their own distinctive experience of Southern life. Although it touches on the white world occasionally, it grows primarily from its own sources in slave narrative, in oral traditions of black folk culture which often have African origins, and in the work of early published practitioners such as Zora Neale Hurston. A full understanding of Southern literature will not be possible until the work of all Southern women has received the close attention it deserves.

Chapter One

The Blight
of Southern Womanhood

lthough Southern belles enjoyed an enviable reputation from the middle of the nineteenth century through the early decades of our own, their traditional position has come under increasingly critical scrutiny in recent years. More and more we understand that Southern white women carried a distinctive burden as the darlings of their world. Their case is in many ways an especially long-lived version of the Victorian situation of women, with all its attendant ironies. Special difficulties arose, however, from the South's peculiar racial institution. The Southern lady was supposed to embody the ideals of her culture, but that culture was torn by profound contradictions and forced into a defensive position by wider national pressures. Thus the white female representative of Christian virtues was lauded in public to divert attention from problems of slavery and racism, but the scope of her activities was severely limited. "Enforcement of gender and family conventions was community business," as Bertram Wyatt-Brown explains in his book *Southern Honor.* "All ranks of men agreed that women, like other dependents upon male leadership and livelihood, should be subordinate, docile. As Dr. James Norcom of North Carolina put it, 'God in his inscrutable wisdom, has appointed a place & a duty for females, *out of which* they can neither accomplish their destiny nor secure their happiness!!' "[1] This proprietary restriction of women's lives is of course typical of patriarchies, but it gained special urgency in the traditional world of white supremacy. The Southern lady had to represent a racial purity which was required by her men for the maintenance of their caste but which many of them regularly transgressed in their own sexual behavior. Further increasing the weight of responsibility carried by the Southern woman in her ideal form was the traditional view of the land itself as feminine. Southern gentlemen loved their land and fought a disastrous war to preserve what they felt was their honor and their proper stewardship. Yet they knew they had abused its integrity with greedy and destructive methods of husbandry. Their attitude towards its fecundity was often as ambivalent as their attitude towards the females with whom it was associated.

Into this tangled feminine heritage Eudora Welty, Carson McCullers, and Flannery O'Connor were born. Any study of their imaginative lives must begin with an understanding of the traditional attitudes their culture imposed upon them.[2] Even if old-fashioned definitions of feminine virtue were losing their grip in the modern era, no section of the nation clung more fiercely to its past than the South. Popular national tastes seemed in fact to conspire with the Southern myth of the Lost Cause and the image of the enchanting ladies who epitomized the antebellum world, as evidenced by the remarkable success of Margaret Mitchell's novel *Gone with the Wind* and the even wilder triumph of the film version, which had its premiere in Atlanta in 1939. Welty, McCullers, and O'Connor were formed by the same world which produced Margaret Mitchell; they had to define themselves and their destinies against the same ideal of the Southern lady.

In 1915, when Eudora Welty was six years old, Professor Edwin Mims of Vanderbilt University made the following claim to the graduating class of Randolph-Macon Woman's College in Virginia before advising them how to conduct their lives as educated Southern women: "If there is one thing upon which Southern people have prided themselves, it is their reverence for womanhood. Long after Burke had pathetically lamented the passing of the age of chivalry in Europe, we maintained the outward form and the inward spirit of chivalry—in our ante-bellum social life and more especially our chivalric attitude towards the gentler sex."[3]

This chivalric attitude required the veneration of woman as a sacred being in traditionally hyperbolic Southern terms which W. J. Cash paraphrased when he exclaimed in *The Mind of the South:* "She was the South's Palladium, this Southern woman—the shield-bearing Athena gleaming whitely in the clouds, the standard for its rallying, the mystic symbol of its nationality in the face of the foe. She was the lily-pure maid of Astolat and the hunting goddess of the Boetian hill. And—she was the pitiful Mother of God. Merely to mention her name was to send strong men into tears—or shouts."

As evidence he quoted the following toast presented at the Georgia Centennial in the 1830s: "Woman!! The centre and circumference, diameter and periphery, sine, tangent and secant of all our affections!"[4] Although the geometrical dimensions of this conceit are perhaps unique, the same general sentiments are echoed in public declarations throughout the nineteenth century and survive into the twentieth in the fiction of Southern apologists such as Thomas Nelson Page and Thomas Dixon, Jr. A number of recent historical studies have even argued that the South made a literary conquest of the rest of the nation which reversed the effects of the Civil War and Reconstruction, just as "Carpetbagger" Judge Albion W. Tourgee predicted in 1867.[5] Among the propagandists for the South, Thomas Dixon was particularly successful in gaining Northern acceptance for his favorable view of Southern civilization and the women who were its crowning symbol, because his own considerable popularity as a novelist was paralleled by the overwhelming national success of D. W. Griffith's film epic *The Birth of a Nation*, based on Dixon's novel *The Clansman*.[6] The white gowns and fluttering graces of Griffith's Southern heroines effectively convey Dixon's assertion that "the young Southern woman was the divinity that claimed and received the chief worship of man." Indeed, the whole treatment of women in the film echoes the following sentiments from the novel's tribute to the Southern hero's mother: "Never had he seen his mother so beautiful—her face calm, intelligent and vital, crowned with a halo of gray. . . . Her whole being reflected the years of homage she had inspired in husband, children, and neighbours. What a woman! She had made war inevitable, fought it to the bitter end; and in the despair of a Negro reign of terror, still the prophetess and high priestess of a people, serene, undismayed and defiant."[7]

Not only was this woman seen as prophetess and priestess, but she was also identified with the landscape itself by traditional habits of thought, many of them originating with the earliest European explorers. Although the concept of earth as mother is an ancient one, the European explorers and settlers of the New World emphasized another, equally old feminine dimension in their view of the land as a virginal garden, as commentators on American culture have pointed out for many years.[8] The expression of this tendency is especially marked in the South and ultimately influences the culture's view of women. From the beginning the land was seen as female, and the Southern white male's stewardship of this rich possession reflected similar paradoxes to those in his relations with consorts and daughters. Uneasiness and guilt about his surrender to female seductiveness led him to severely subdue his public ideology. But the guilt lingered in the white male imagination, as perhaps some deeper sense of the land's independent power to withhold her fruits did also.

Virginia, named for the queen who presided over her nation's emergence as a Renaissance European power, was regularly described as feminine in the early days of exploration and settlement. Arthur Barlowe reported in 1584 that his ship was "allured" toward her shore by "so strong a smell, as if we had bene in the midst of some delicate garden abounding with all kinde of odoriferous flowers." Such imagery continued to be the basis for praises of the natural abundance of the new land, such as that of John Rolfe's *A True Relation of the State of Virginia* (1616). Rolfe stresses the temperateness of the climate, the fertility of the soil, and the hidden bounty in "the womb of the Land" which lies ready to be mined by man. His treatise was intended to refute gloomy stories about famine and pestilence among the Jamestown settlers which had found their way back to England, and he and other early Virginia colonists were ultimately successful in fixing the fruitful garden image in the imagination of the home country. This is a sharp contrast to William Bradford's account of the landscape which greeted his group of Puritans from Yorkshire upon their famous landing at Plymouth in 1620. Arriving in the cruel season of winter, "what could they see but a hideous and desolate wilderness, full of wild beasts & wild men?" The Northern landscape and climate could not sustain the hopeful Edenic visions of its first explorers once it was actually colonized, but the South continued to support sensuous feminine associations.[9]

These could be frankly erotic, as Annette Kolodny has shown, citing the mid-seventeenth-century protests of John Hammond, who felt obliged to defend his native Maryland from the kind of adverse rumors that John Rolfe had denied forty years earlier about Virginia. Hammond referred to Virginia and Maryland as Jacob's brides, entitling his tract "Leah and Rachel, Or, The Two Fruitful Sisters Virginia and Maryland" (1656). For Hammond, enough difficulties had arisen in the young colonies to lead to despair. He deplored "the general neglect and licensiousness" of Virginia, but saw more active vice in Maryland. "Twice hath [Maryland] been deflowred by her own Inhabitants, stript, shorne, and made deformed; yet such a naturall fertility and comelinesse doth she retain that she cannot but be loved, but be pitied."[10] Robert Beverley sensed the debilitating qualities of such a generous landscape, as is evident in his *History and Present State of Virginia* (1705).[11] Beverley catalogued the bounties of the country, but warned that "the exceeding plenty of good things" led to shameful laziness among his fellow colonists. The language of the following passage wallows in the sensuality which the habit of feminine associations excites in his mind: "Here all [people's] Senses are entertain'd with an endless Succession of Native Pleasures. Their Eyes are *ravished with the Beauties of Naked Nature.* Their Ears are Seranaded with the perpetual murmur of the Brooks, and the thorow-base which the Wind plays, when *wantons* through the Trees" (my emphasis).[12]

Because these implications are too dangerous to be long indulged, or because of general changes in taste, references to the Southern landscape focused increasingly upon maternal qualities as the eighteenth century progressed. Whatever the reason, the erotic abandon betrayed by Beverley was curbed and chastened. Throughout the next century, the South both as landscape and as culture would continue to evoke feminine images in the minds of her sons, but they would be pious rather than erotic, moving between the virginal and the maternal. In a defense of the Southern way of life during the troubled years before the Civil War, William Gilmore Simms protested to his audience in Buffalo, New York, "You would not, surely, have me speak coldly in the assertion of a Mother's honour." In 1867, after the South's defeat in the war, Virginia professor Robert L. Dabney sought to restore her honor by writing a defense of the South which he believed was personified in his native state. The purpose of his book, he wrote, was to "lay this pious and filial defense upon the tomb of my murdered mother, Virginia." Such poems as the following from an anthology published in 1872 established the conceit of the fallen South as a ravished maiden, in unconscious harmony with Hammond's view of Virginia and Maryland more than two hundred years before.

TRAMPLED TO DEATH

A fair young body trampled to death—
    This beautiful, glorious Lady of ours!
Bring spices and wine and all the spring's breath,
    And bathe her with kisses and shroud her with flowers.

O breasts whose twin lilies are purpled with blood!
    O face, whose twin roses with ashes are white!
O dead golden hair, at whose far splendor stood
    Millions of true souls entranced with delight!

Wailing in silence, as brave men wail,
    An army of lovers around her stands,
With fierce bitten lips and brows all pale,
    With broken swords and with manacled hands![13]

Orator and editor Henry W. Grady traveled to Boston and New York in the 1880s to paint the same benign picture of the emerging New South that filled his editorials in the Atlanta *Constitution*. Central to the peace and order of the awakened region are hallowed visions of pure wife and noble mother who inspire men of the South on their mission.[14] Similarly, Thomas Nelson Page's novels celebrate radiant maidens who grace old mansions and symbolize continuity with the best of the antebellum world.

Thomas Dixon goes a step further in *The Clansman*, extending standard maternal and maidenly associations for the South to embrace all "Anglo-Saxon civilisation" by the end of the novel. *The Clansman* is Dixon's attempt to convince a national audience that Reconstruction unleashed a rapacious horde of emancipated Negroes upon the South, whose "wounded people lay helpless amid rags and ashes under the beak and talon of the Vulture." As "An Historical Romance of the Ku Klux Klan," the story seeks to justify vigilante action as a chivalric crusade to save white civilization personified in the women of the South. Leslie Fiedler argues that here Dixon revived the archetypes of Spotless Maiden and Holy Mother which Harriet Beecher Stowe had used so successfully in *Uncle Tom's Cabin*, but for very different didactic purposes. Whereas Stowe had associated the violation of pure females with the oppression of Negro slaves, Dixon's "anti-Tom" novel reiterates the traditional Southern insistence on exclusively white and aristocratic connections for the ancient mother/daughter pair and empha-sizes their status as white male property.[15]

The climactic turn in Dixon's plot comes when a mother and daughter who represent the most radiant qualities of antebellum life commit suicide to escape the shame of the daughter's rape by a black man. Marion Lenoir, though only sixteen, carries the knowledge of her defilement with courage and resolution. She rallies her stunned mother to their joint duty, leading her "down the dim cathedral aisles of the woods" to a cliff called Lover's Leap above the river. Dixon presents their death as a *liebestod*.

> A fresh motionless day brooded over the world as the amorous stir of the spirit of morning rose from the moist earth of the fields below.
> A bright star still shone in the sky, and the face of the mother gazed on it intently. Did the woman-spirit, the burning focus of the fiercest desire to live and will, catch in this supreme moment the star's Divine speech before which all human passions sink into silence? Perhaps, for she smiled. The daughter answered with a smile; and then, hand in hand, they stepped from the cliff into the mists and on through the opal gates of death. [p. 308]

When the white male leaders of the town learn of the event, they see it as the ultimate degradation of their culture. The novel's hero, Ben Cameron, scion of the town's leading family who has just recovered from his Civil War wounds, discovers evidence of the suicide atop Lover's Leap and knows that the fate of Mrs. Lenoir and Marion involves all white society. "Now, Lord God, give me strength for the service of my people!" he prays (p. 310). He hurries to acquaint his father with "the hell-lit secret beneath the tragedy" and to assemble the local Klan members and apprehend the rapist. The symbolic importance of the rape is so great that Dixon repeats the scene at a huge nocturnal Klan gathering in a cave, by having Ben's father, Dr. Cameron, hypnotize the black prisoner so that he can enact the crime again. What follows is a cherished Southern nightmare.[16]

> Gus rose to his feet and started across the cave as if to spring on the shivering figure of the girl, the clansmen with muttered groans, sobs and curses falling back as he advanced. He still wore his full Captain's uniform, its heavy epaulets flashing their gold in the unearthly light, his beastly jaws half covering the gold braid on the collar. His thick lips were drawn upward in an ugly leer and his sinister bead-eyes gleamed like a gorilla's. A single fierce leap and the black claws clutched the air slowly as if sinking into the soft white throat.
> Strong men began to cry like children. [p. 323]

These men dedicate themselves to revenge in a strange ritual substituting the blood of the dead women and the water of the local river for the blood of Christ. A boulder in the cave serves as altar, and Dr. Cameron places upon it a crude cross, a candle, and the silver cup of blood and water. Lifting the cup, he says, "Brethren, I hold in my hand the water of your river bearing the red stain of the life of a Southern woman, a priceless sacrifice on the altar of outraged civilisation" (p. 325). This sacrifice rouses the assembled host to execute justice upon the rapist and ultimately to restore order and virtuous prosperity to the region. The novel ends with Ben Cameron's exultant claim that "Civilisation has been saved, and the South redeemed from shame" (p. 374).[17]

Such a close association of the South's integrity with that of white women continued to nourish the regional imagination until fairly recently. As Kolodny reminds us, the Southern Agrarians saw their filial duty to be the defense of their region's female honor against the harsh masculine industrialism of the North which threatened to destroy traditional virtues.[18] John Crowe Ransom was explicit about the distinction in *I'll Take My Stand*.

> The masculine form is hallowed by Americans, as I have said, under the name of Progress. The concept of Progress is the concept of man's increasing

command, and eventually perfect command, over the forces of nature; a concept which enhances too readily our conceit, and brutalizes our life. I believe
there is possible no deep sense of beauty, no heroism of conduct, and no
sublimity of religion, which is not informed by the humble sense of man's
precarious position in the universe. The feminine form is likewise hallowed
among us under the name of Service. The term has many meanings, but we
come finally to the one which is critical for the moderns; service means the
function of Eve, it means the seducing of laggard men into fresh struggles
with nature. It has special application to the apparently stagnant sections of
mankind, it busies itself with the heathen Chinee, with the Roman Catholic
Mexican, with the "lower" classes in our own society. Its motive is missionary.
Its watchwords are such as Protestantism, Individualism, Democracy, and the
point of its appeal is a discontent, generally labeled "divine."[19]

By now most readers probably find *I'll Take My Stand* archaic in tone and
reactionary in purpose, but the attitudes expressed by Ransom, Tate,
Warren, Davidson, and the others were common among traditional Southern families during the childhoods of Eudora Welty, Carson McCullers,
and Flannery O'Connor. Muted echoes continue to be heard in the writing
of Southern journalists like Russell Kirk (whose books Flannery O'Connor
had in her personal library) and James Kilpatrick.

However sentimental or extreme the traditional Southern veneration of
woman may have been, however much at odds with the actual hardships
and unromantic responsibilities which Anne Firor Scott shows to have
been the realistic lot of most Southern women, the worshipful stereotypes
remained the standards by which women were ultimately measured. Scott
demonstrates how difficult they were to emulate. Southern women's diaries and letters of the nineteenth century were full of self-deprecation,
prayers for greater purity of spirit, and admonitions to live up to all the
ideals their men held for them.[20] Unlike other ideals of behavior which
have all been impossible to achieve, however, this one was undercut by a
sort of moral and political schizophrenia. It was extreme, socially elite, the
creation of a patriarchy whose power was far less secure than it pretended.

Though Professor Edwin Mims of Vanderbilt University urged the
Randolph-Macon graduating class of 1915 to preserve the "social charm
and the pious devotion which come to us from a former generation," he
did admit one of the obvious limitations of the ideal. Mims quotes fellow
Southerner Walter Hines Page, then ambassador to England, on "The
Forgotten Woman" of the South.

Both the aristocratic and the ecclesiastical systems made provision for the
women of special classes—the fortunately born and the religious well-to-do.
But all other women were forgotten. Let any man whose mind is not hardened

by some worn-out theory of politics or of ecclesiasticism go to the country in almost any part of the State (North Carolina)—to make a study of the life of the women. He will see them thin and wrinkled in youth from ill-prepared food, clad without warmth or grace, living in untidy houses, working from daylight till bedtime at the dull round of weary duties, the slaves of men of equal slovenliness, the mothers of joyless children—all uneducated if not illiterate. . . . Some men who are born under these conditions escape from them; a man may go away, go where life offers opportunities, but the women are forever helpless.[21]

The image of the Southern lady was thus perceived early in the century by some observers to be hopelessly inappropriate for any but the privileged, who of course were white. Most women in the South were not members of the fortunate group; as far as the myth of Southern culture was concerned, they did not exist.

Even for the "aristocratic" women who were acknowledged to participate, the patriarchal focus of their culture made their exalted position ironic. Educated and propertied white men were of course the chief architects of Southern patterns of life and thought; they wielded direct political and economic power. All the declarations we have seen of reverence for Southern womanhood, and the original fictional embodiments of the type, came from them. Women were the *objects* of worship, the muses or guiding saints for these men who saw themselves as having established a chivalric and cultured world. Their patriarchal vision, legitimized by Protestant reliance on the Old Testament and the teachings of St. Paul, dominated nineteenth-century Southern discussion of regional social patterns,[22] and Richard King's recent study of the so-called Southern Renaissance of the 1930s and 1940s continues to assume the patriarchal structure of plantation life and of the traditional culture which grew from it. King attributes the blossoming of Southern literary and intellectual life after World War I to the ferment caused by an Oedipal struggle between the sons of the New South and the heroic traditions of their fathers and grandfathers. The Southern imagination as revealed in the writings of the Agrarians, William Faulkner, Thomas Wolfe, James Agee, and William Alexander Percy is thus dominated by a patriarchal family romance in Freudian terms, a myth centered on the father. No matter how important the Southern lady might be in fact, "she was distinctly subordinate in the romance to the powerful and heroic father." As time separated the Civil War heroes from their descendants, the heroes grew in stature to legendary proportions impossible to emulate. "Further, though many Southerners embraced the gospel of progress in the post-Reconstruction years, this optimistic stance was shadowed by the strong suspicion that the age of heroes lay in the past. Decline was an integral part of the Southern family romance."

King marshals compelling evidence for the obsession with paternal heritage expressed by Southern writers of the "renaissance." He seems to have accurately interpreted their view of the past and its debilitating grip on Southern intellectuals of the 1930s and 1940s. Theirs was the same culture, however, which had elevated white woman to sainthood for a century and continued to pay lip service to her veneration. King has trouble explaining this paradox.

> If the Southern family romance placed the father-son relationship at its center, the white woman was expected to play the role of the mother. As mistress of the plantation she was the lady bountiful, caring for the wants and needs of her family, both white and black. . . . The Southern woman was caught in a social double-bind: toward men she was to be submissive, meek and gentle; with the children and slaves and in the management of the household, she was supposed to display competence, initiative, and energy. *But she remained a shadowy figure, always there and ever necessary, but rarely emerging in full force. She was "queen of the home."* [my emphasis][23]

Not only is there a contradiction in the qualities expected of the Southern woman, as King recognizes, but there is also a logical problem in the movement of his description. He begins with the mother as "lady bountiful" but ends by calling her a shadowy figure whom he tries to revive by the final epithet of "queen of the home." Presumably, home is the scene of family life, yet in a cultural myth centered in the family, the queen does not really exist. Something is askew.

The truth is that the patriarchy of the South never really liked or fully believed in its custom-made goddess. The white Southern male might offer her ecstatic toasts or use her as a divine reference point, but he also betrayed a paradoxical condescension which sometimes revealed hostility or contempt. The chinks in his chivalrous armor are already visible in antebellum days. George Fitzhugh seems to protest too much when he demands weakness and frivolity of the Southern lady in 1854: "So long as she is nervous, fickle, capricious, delicate, diffident and dependent, man will worship and adore her. Her weakness is her strength, and her true art is to cultivate and improve that weakness. Woman naturally shrinks from public gaze, and from the struggle and competition of life. . . . A husband, a lord and master, whom she should love, honor and obey, nature designed for every woman. . . . If she be obedient she stands little danger of maltreatment."[24] The whole statement is an implied threat. If the Southern woman were the paragon her men claimed in their paeans, she would need no such coercion. Furthermore, if the lordliness and mastery of the husband required that she cultivate and improve her weakness, there must have been serious danger of feminine strength.

A series of articles that appeared in the *Southern Review* (Baltimore) from 1869 to 1872 is even more revealing. The journal was written almost single-handedly by Albert Taylor Bledsoe, a former University of Virginia professor who dedicated his publication to "the despised, disfranchised, and downtrodden people of the South." In order to elevate their spirits and instill new strength for the rebuilding of their land, Bledsoe vigorously defended the Lost Cause and argued against Yankee civilization in agrarian terms that anticipated the position of the Vanderbilt Fugitives in the next century. Bledsoe also sought to encourage Southern intellectual life by reviewing important current books in science, philosophy, art, literature, and politics. Although his journal lasted only eleven years (for two years after Bledsoe's death in 1877 it was edited by his daughter Sophia), it is an important voice expressing the tenaciously cherished values which would seduce the entire nation by the time of Woodrow Wilson's presidency. In a four-year period during which his review treated Darwin, "Recent Researches in Geography," German philosophy, and an anthology of Southern verse, four essays are devoted to the subject of woman. Is one to suppose that he wrote them out of chivalrous veneration? He claims to entertain it, as, for instance, when he begins an article on "The Education and Influence of Woman" with an attack on "those poor forlorn misogynists" who attempt to elevate themselves by insulting the gentler sex. In defense of women, he ends by quoting St. Paul's familiar assertion that "the head of the woman is the man," but goes on to produce another declaration from the same epistle, that "The woman is the glory of the man," because she embodies love, the major attribute of God. "In conclusion, then, man is the superior animal, and also the superior intelligence, but woman is the superior being, 'the cunningest pattern of excelling nature,' the paragon of all God's works."

More specifically Bledsoe examines woman's capacity for friendship and for artistic achievement, pronouncing her too personal and concrete in her responses, too weak in intellect, for either. "She must have a personal God, a personal religion, a personal honor, and a particular love, which are her own, to touch, to hide, to lock up, it may be, for her own private uses and enjoyment." Generous but not liberal, she "can give but does not know how to share." This renders her incapable of friendship.

On the question of artistic achievement, Bledsoe begins with characteristic gallantry toward the fair sex, intending to make a serious attempt to recover neglected geniuses. Men have always been willing to hope for female art, he says, for

> even in the darkest periods of woman's history, there has been instinctive
> recognition of the apparent relation between her chaste, flexuous, subtile orga-

nism, and the delicate grades and refinement of art-work, and no less an eager appreciation of all that she has done or tried to do in that regard. Even in this hypercritical and sceptic age we are always ready and ardent to welcome a poem by a woman, whether it be poetry or not, as if there was a certain consciousness at the bottom of our minds that the poet *ought* to come from that side of the house, whether he will or not.

Such phrases as "apparent relation," "all that she has done or tried to do," and "whether it be poetry or not" erode Bledsoe's assertions, and, most telling of all, he uses the masculine pronoun "he" to refer to the poet who *ought* to emerge from the distaff side of the house. Whether Bledsoe is unaware of his condescension or means to be snide, it is clear that he does not seriously expect art to issue from female hands. His researches lead him reluctantly to conclude that the whole sex is defective in the artistic sense, and in the strength necessary to sustain an aesthetic or moral idea. "The man, having reserved forces and discretion . . . can go to the mountain top and return safely; the woman, out of breath at the start, must abide at a low level, or succumb from exhaustion in an atmosphere too rare and chill. Hence, her art-work is almost invariably petty, inadequate, mean."[25]

Despite the certainty in Bledsoe's assertion of woman's innate inferiority, in his 1871 article on "The Mission of Woman," he acknowledges a problem which turns out to have been threatening on the Southern male horizon since around the middle of the nineteenth century. Anne Scott describes the slow growth of the suffrage movement in the South after the Seneca Falls Declaration in 1848, suggesting that male opposition below the Mason-Dixon Line betrayed deep fears.[26] Even before the Civil War, Southern men felt the need to defend themselves from "strong-minded" Northern women in the Abolition and Temperance movements. In 1853 John Hartwell Cocke, liberal Virginian, friend of Thomas Jefferson, and advocate of the emancipation of slaves, described the struggle for power at the World Temperance Convention in New York, where the "strong-minded" women asserted themselves. He bragged that the men "gained a perfect triumph, and I believe have given a rebuke to this most impudent clique of unsexed females and rampant abolitionists which must put down the petty-coats—at least as far as their claim to take the platform of public debate."[27] His self-congratulations were premature, for after the Civil War the disease crept South, at first in secret but gradually moving more into public awareness.[28]

Already in 1871 Bledsoe sensed the danger, fearing "the great and increasing multitudes" of strong-minded Northern women whose emancipation would bring Anglo-Saxon civilization to collapse, just as the independence of Roman matrons destroyed the grandeur of the Empire two thousand years before. There is still hope, however. "Our Southern women have, thank God! shown, as yet, but little taste for such forbidden fruit" but instead still grace "their own hallowed sphere" and thus remain sacred and inspirational. His essay concludes with a stirring exhortation:

> Be this your glory, then, O ye blessed and beautiful women of the South!— not that you can vote, or beat a negro for Congress, but that you can point to your sons as *your* jewels, and as the ornaments of the human race. Be this your glory, not that you are "the head," but that you are "the glory," of the man. Be this your glory, not that you can equal man in the might and the majesty of his intellectual dominion, but that you can surpass him in the sublime mission of mercy to a fallen world.

Women are further urged to soften and subdue man's rugged nature with Christian meekness, "to enchant the home circle" with their loveliness, and "mould the future Washingtons, and Lees, and Jacksons of the South, to protect and preserve the sacred rights of woman as well as of man."[29] Bledsoe is a representative spokesman for the traditional Southern point of view, as Scott's survey of responses to the suffrage movement shows.[30] Southern men wanted their women kept in cages, peripheral, submissive, inert. Any movement towards independence was grimly opposed.

Regardless of male resistance, more and more Southern women of the privileged class were feeling sympathy for the "strong-minded" activists in the North and beginning to seek glory outside the "hallowed sphere" of the home. The disruption of normal life during the Civil War and Reconstruction necessitated Southern women's active participation in areas formerly the exclusive preserves of men, but as the patriarchy gradually reestablished itself in the hands of the war's survivors, most of these women receded into domestic life. The old habits of deference to men were diminished, however, partly because of the recent experiences of responsibility, partly because "the Lost Cause lost a great deal of its lustre upon close observation of the ex-heroes," and partly because of pressures for change from the North and from Europe.[31] Two exemplary cases are those of Mrs. Cornelia Phillips Spencer of North Carolina and Mrs. Caroline E. Merrick of New Orleans, both born in 1825 and both beginning with traditionally deferential attitudes toward male superiority but ending in defiance. Mrs. Spencer treated the issue of suffrage in the Young Ladies' Column of the *North Carolina Presbyterian Standard*, gradually evolving from strong opposition to sympathy in the 1890s. After conforming for most of her life to masculine dominance, Mrs. Merrick grew flippant by the 1850s and became an active worker for the equality of women. Her answer to chivalry is the following parody of 1881:

Lest they should feel overlooked and slighted, I will say a word to the men. God bless them. Our hearts warm towards the manly angels—our rulers, guides and protectors, to whom we confide all our troubles and on whom we lay all our burdens. Oh, what a noble being is an honest, upright, fearless, generous, manly man. How such men endear our firesides, adorn and bless our homes. How sweet is their encouragement of our timid efforts in every good word and work, and how grateful we are to be loved by these noble comforters, and how utterly wretched and sad this world would be, deprived of their honored and gracious presence. Again I say, God bless the men.[32]

Times were changing. Professor Mims described the emergence of vigorous new economic and intellectual life in *The Advancing South* (1926). In a chapter called "The Revolt Against Chivalry" he chronicles the liberating descent of Southern ladies from their pedestals, he advocates higher education for women, and he heralds their entry into the professions. But even he is ambivalent about the kind of independence expressed in the radical intellectual life of Frances Newman, with her brash championing of Freud, Joyce, and Sherwood Anderson. He praises her learning, her acquaintance with the most challenging modern literature, and the incisiveness of her criticism, but he ends by saying, "Miss Newman has certainly gone a long way from Georgia! Too far, I am inclined to think."

Mims closes his chapter by evoking the same comforting scene he had used ten years earlier to end his Randolph-Macon commencement speech. He describes the exemplary life of a cultured Southern matron who lives among books in a country home "of the Elizabethan type" surrounded by huge oaks and pastures full of sheep. Here is a cultured mecca for the fortunate in the neighborhood who are invited to afternoon garden parties. The husband is a prominent lawyer of intellectual habits, and the woman herself, "a social leader in her younger days, is president of the Drama League and the friend of every cause that promotes the culture of the community." She is mother of four children: "three boys, who are honour graduates of the university, and a daughter, who is a student at Bryn Mawr." This new image of the Southern lady reminds him of the best of antebellum life.[33]

Although Mims champions women's education, he seems happiest in thinking its product will be an elegantly cultured Southern matron. In this preference he is really not terribly far from Bledsoe's notion of the proper destiny for Southern white women. Evidence that Southern men in general did not go even as far as he comes from his own criticism of the refusal of men's colleges and universities to support coeducation.[34]

What distinguishes the Southern attitude from the wider, Western European chivalric heritage of reverence for women is the complicated relationship of the Southern white woman to blacks. As William R. Taylor observes, the first published appearance of antebellum plantation myths "coincided not only with the appearance of militant abolition in the North but also, and I think just as significantly, with the first stirrings of the movement for women's rights, which occurred at about this time and appealed to—as well as alarmed—many of the same people."[35] Traditional defenses of slavery were intimately intertwined with declarations about the veneration and protection of white women. Yet these women in fact shared inferiority and powerlessness with blacks as subjects of the ruling patriarchs. "There is no slave, after all," commented Mary Chesnut with some bitterness in 1861, "like a wife." Throughout her diary Mrs. Chesnut sympathizes with the slaves and connects their sufferings with the plight of women. She describes the Southern gentleman as jovial and courtly when in a pleasant mood but ultimately "as absolute a tyrant as the czar of Russia, the khan of Tartary—or the sultan of Turkey." Under such masters African slaves must certainly suffer, and with them, all women, for "all married women, all children, and girls who live on in their father's [sic] houses are slaves."[36] When the suffrage movement became a serious political force, white male leaders resisted it in terms which support Mary Chesnut's connection of sexual and racist subordination. In Alabama, for instance, while suffragists prepared for the 1915 legislative session, a defensive pamphlet circulated around the state, warning of the chaos that would result from enfranchisement of women: "It is the avowed purpose of leaders among Northern advocates to break the 'Solid South' by means of votes of Negro women and break down race and sex distinction. Is this in keeping with the traditions and civilization of the south?"[37]

Southern white men—many of them—had been breaking down these distinctions from the beginning, but their picture of the graceful plantation world never betrayed the miscegenation which blighted their pretensions of Anglo-Saxon purity. The illicit recourse of white men to black women was far more frequent than is commonly acknowledged, and it had understandably painful effects. Black men and white women shared the deepest kind of sexual humiliation, and black women were denied control of their own bodies and forced into concubinage. Black women were somehow able to retain a sense of wholeness despite these conditions, perhaps because their essential identity was never denied. They knew themselves to be sexually potent and desirable, and they were the hyper-mothers of the South, nursing not only their own children but also those of their white masters and mistresses. The strength of popular stereotypes testifies to their power; though the 1960s banished the Mammy from popular view, she remains in the national imagination, and other strong black female images have convincingly taken her place in television specials chronicling the lives of Miss Jane Pittman, Wilma Rudolph, and Harriet Tubman.[38] Black men have proven themselves in national culture as the supermen of sports, seeming to fulfill the worst fears of white Southern folklore which had compensated for political (and sometimes literal) emasculation by fantasizing heroic black virility.

All along, the white Southern lady had been left in chilly isolation on her pedestal, for the facts of miscegenation spelled rejection and rendered chivalric tributes a painful lie. In 1941 W. J. Cash stressed the depth of this betrayal, though he described it primarily from the white male perspective of shame in the presence of white women: "And even though she feigned blindness, as the convention demanded she should—even if she actually knew or suspected nothing—the guilty man, supposing he possessed any shadow of decency, must inexorably writhe in shame and an intolerable sense of impurity under her eyes." And so Cash agrees with the 1924 assertion of Frank Tannenbaum's *Darker Phases of the South* that the idealization of white women was an unconscious compensation for male frailties. Lillian Smith claims that this behavior created a sexual schizophrenia in white men and made the lives of white women "only a shameful sore."[39]

Lest these reactions seem excessive, let us gauge the accuracy of the charges. The facts of racial mingling were evident to anyone in the South who chose to recognize them. Even an innocent young visitor from the North could not help noticing, as Lucius Verus Bierce did on his walking tour of the South following college graduation in 1822. Pausing for three months in Waxaw, South Carolina, to earn money teaching school, Bierce had occasion to observe the social life of the community. His diary describes the disparity between the lives of the planter class and the demoralized lower class of whites, comments on the layout of the plantations, and then describes the character of the inhabitants. "The virtues of the higher order," he writes, "are a love of liberty, hospitality, charity, and a nice sense of honor. The vices are drunkenness, indolence, and *among all classes of males, an indiscriminate connexion with the female negroes. This evil has extended so far that more than one half of the slave population are mixed with the whites*" (my emphasis).

Later, in Alabama, Bierce finds even more riotous habits and hears a remarkable story about a former governor of the state.

> The country around here is delightful, but the people devilish. Duelling and fighting the chief diversions, Gambling and drinking pastimes, *and an uninterrupted, common intercourse with the negroes the virtue of all the men*. . . .
> Governor Pope, of Huntsville, a wealthy respectable man of a family, formerly

Governor, notoriously kept a mulatto girl with whom he associated as freely as with his wife. His wife finding them in each others embraces made so much fuss about it that he sent the girl on to his plantation near to Mooresville where he then spent more of his time than he did at home. His wife complaining of his neglect, and knowing the cause, would consent to nothing short of the girls being sent to New Orleans and sold, which was done, when a merchant of Mooresville sent to his agent in Orleans, purchased the girl, and brought her back to Mooresville for himself. This but a specimen of manners in that respect. [my emphasis][40]

Reports of this kind were vigorously denied by Southerners, especially when Abolitionists began using them to prove the immoral consequences of slavery. But in a modern study of slavery, historian Kenneth Stampp concludes that "sexual contacts between the races were not the rare aberrations of a small group of depraved whites but a frequent occurrence involving whites of all social and cultural levels." Members of the slaveholding class could be expected to have superior advantages. "Indeed, given their easy access to female slaves, it seems probable that miscegenation was more common among them than among the members of any other group." Even though Eugene Genovese assumes the greatest frequency of interracial intimacy to have been in the cosmopolitan cities and slave-trading centers rather than on plantations and farms, he agrees that miscegenation "had a profound and in some respects devastating effect on southern life." *Roll, Jordan, Roll* richly documents the complexity of the problem. Nevertheless, Southern denials of "mongrelizing," as Southerners liked to call it, continued to appear even after the Civil War had put an end to the slaveholders' free use of their human property. Professor Robert L. Dabney refers to the problem in 1867. "It is the delight of abolitionists to impute to slavery a result peculiarly corrupting as to sins of unchastity," Dabney admits, but he challenges both the factual basis of the charge and its psychological probability. Temptations of the flesh between young men and female domestics are greatly diminished by racial differences, "while the very sentiment of superior caste would render the intercourse more repulsive and unnatural." Dabney recommends the example of white women as further evidence of Southern morality in domestic affairs. "If then, slavery is morally corrupting, Southern ladies should show the sad result very plainly. But what says fact? Its testimony is one which fills the heart of every Southern man with grateful pride; that the Southern lady is proverbially eminent for all that adorns female character."[41] We return to chivalric rhapsodies upon the familiar feminine theme.

But suppose Dabney had phrased his appeal a little differently, asking "What say the ladies?" to Abolitionist charges of unchastity among their men? Plenty of Southern ladies had ready answers, as Anne Scott shows, but most kept them within the pages of private letters and diaries. Mary Chesnut's voluminous running commentary on life in the social and political center of the Confederacy is especially outspoken. She would probably have answered Dabney to his face if he had tried to deny the hypocrisy which so disgusted her. In March 1861 she reports taking opium to quiet her nerves and then releases a flood of bitter indignation.

> I wonder if it be a sin to think slavery a curse to any land. [Charles] Sumner said not one word of this hated institution which is not true. Men and women are punished when their masters and mistresses are brutes and not when they do wrong—and then we live surrounded by prostitutes. An abandoned woman is sent out of any decent house elsewhere. Who thinks any worse of a negro or mulatto woman for being a thing we can't name? God forgive us, but ours is a *monstrous* system and wrong and iniquity. Perhaps the rest of the world is as bad—this *only* I see. Like the patriarchs of old our men live all in one house with their wives and their concubines, and the mulattoes one sees in every family exactly resemble the white children—and every lady tells you who is the father of all the mulatto children in everybody's household, but those in her own she seems to think drop from the clouds, or pretends so to think. Good women we have, *but* they talk of all *nastiness*—tho' they never do wrong, they talk all day and night of [erasures illegible except for the words "all unconsciousness"] my disgust sometimes is boiling over—but they are, I believe, in conduct the purest women God ever made. Thank God for my countrywomen—alas for the men! No worse than men everywhere, but the lower their mistresses, the more degraded they must be.

Mrs. Chesnut then recalls her mother-in-law's veiled references to the mulatto children of her own husband, a subject to which she returns in a later entry of similar exasperation.[42] I quote her comments at such length because she explicitly draws together many of the themes I have been stressing: the connection between slavery and the position of women, black and white; the morality of white women and its relation to the behavior of white men; and the effect of miscegenation upon the interior lives of white women.

If white men's dalliance with slave women evoked this irate intensity in Chesnut's mind, it must have been so common that upper-class women all over the South suffered more terrible private anguish. Mary Chesnut, after all, was remarkably cosmopolitan for her region, gender, and era, so that she was not shocked by the normal quotient of vice and corruption she saw around her in the Confederate capital. She read widely in French and English literature and was a lively participant in the most intellectually sophisticated circles of Southern society. Few subjects in her diary excite the kind of passion this one does; miscegenation was worse than ordinary failings she assumed human nature to exhibit, because it violated the central racial caste system of her culture and it deprived the patriarchal authorities of honor in the domestic relations to which they claimed such pious allegiance.

One of Mary Chesnut's contemporaries, Laura Clay of Kentucky, expressed similar sentiments in 1874. "When I consider the unspotted chastity, the temperance, the unselfishness, the daily ruling of life by duty of women, and compare it to the sensual and selfish lives of men it seems to me marvellous that their virtue should be overlooked by the world and all the great revolutions in the moral world should be imputed to men."[43] And Katherine Anne Porter records a similar response to the situation in "The Old Order," as the matriarch of a Texas family in old age recalls her struggle as a widow to raise her children after her husband's death from a Civil War wound.

> Miss Sophia Jane had taken upon herself all the responsibilities of her tangled world, half white, half black, mingling steadily and the confusion growing ever deeper. There were so many young men about the place, always, younger brothers-in-law, first cousins, second cousins, nephews. They came visiting and they stayed, and there was no accounting for them nor any way of controlling their quietly headstrong habits. She learned early to keep silent and give no sign of uneasiness, but whenever a child was born in the Negro quarters, pink, worm-like, she held her breath for three days, she told her eldest granddaughter, years later, to see whether the newly born would turn black after the proper interval. . . . It was a strain that told on her, and ended by giving her a deeply grounded contempt for men. She could not help it, she despised men.[44]

Upper-class white women's entanglement in these problems continued in the New South, because white men's involvement with black women did not stop with Reconstruction. Lillian Smith makes a strong case for the natural attraction between the races by appealing to the emotional bonds formed in those whites brought up by black nurses who provided the formative experience of warmth and love.[45] No doubt there is considerable truth in this Freudian explanation, but the simple force of social traditions also played a strong part. Sociologist John Dollard found the old-fashioned erotic habits still very common in the anonymous town he surveyed in *Caste and Class in a Southern Town* (1937). His data are dispassionately presented, in the context of the universal human tendency to underestimate departures from public morals. Nevertheless, he lost all his friends in the town when his book was published. Dollard had violated the taboo he described as still surrounding the image of the white lady.

> This ideal image is passionately and even violently defended, and the danger of soiling it is one of the threats which brings out the fullest hostility of southern men. . . . It seems possible that this idealization has an effect on the erotic behavior of white men toward their own white women, and produces perhaps a feeling that they are untouchable, that sexual sentiments are unbecoming in relation to them, and that sexual behavior toward white women must take place, though, of course it does take place, only against a personal sense of guilt. . . . It seems possible that the image of the white woman is in part conserved against sexual thought and allusions, whereas the Negro woman tends to draw the full burden of unsublimated sexual feeling.

Thus many white Southern boys began their sexual experience with black girls, and many continued finding solace in later life with prostitutes or mistresses of the other race, sometimes fathering children whose resemblance to them was cause of gossip and humiliation for their white wives.[46]

By the time Dollard published his study of small-town Southern life, Eudora Welty and Carson McCullers were young women in their twenties, and Flannery O'Connor was just entering adolescence. The troubled racial and sexual relations of the South were enveloped in a cloud of charming fraud through which these young women had to grope their way to maturity. Certainly all traditions of courtesy involve deceit of a graceful kind and for generous purposes, but a profound betrayal yawned behind the special privileges for girls of their backgrounds. The old-fashioned ideal of the lady made demands of them, though in fainter terms than it had for their mothers, and theirs was still an apparently patriarchal world. But girls like Eudora Alice Welty and Lula Carson Smith and Mary Flannery O'Connor were too perceptive not to sense the emptiness of its pretensions. The men who claimed to worship white women secretly preferred their darker sisters in many ways, so that their chivalry masked guilt, and serious intelligence in women was a terrible threat because it might probe through the sentimental facade. The Southern world provided only a dishonest basis for a girl's identity as she grew into a woman, and dishonest grounds for relations with men.

Ellen Glasgow seems to have been the first Southern writer to consciously understand the problem, though she was never fully able to transcend it.[47] She wrote in her autobiography, "I hated—I had always hated—the inherent falseness in much Southern tradition." As a beginning writer she vowed to write "as no Southerner had ever written, of the universal human chords beneath the superficial variations of scene and character. I would write of all the harsher realities beneath manners, beneath social customs, beneath the poetry of the past, and the romantic nostalgia of the present."[48] In *Virginia* (1913) she achieved her first clear success. Not only does the heroine stand for the vanishing (and actually irrelevant) type of the Southern lady, but as Anne Jones remarks, "the state takes the body of a woman."[49] By extension the beautiful Virginia Pendleton, who is betrayed and abandoned at the end of the novel, represents the whole South, abandoned by her men in search of the almighty Yankee dollar. Glasgow even alludes to the problem of miscegenation, though by very careful implication. Cyrus Treadwell, the typical grasping new Southern industrialist, has managed to achieve an obliviousness to poverty and injustice in his single-minded pursuit of money, just as more old-fashioned citizens use what Glasgow ironically calls "idealism" to avoid seeing ugly realities. Early in the novel Treadwell looks out over the town from his bank office, toward his factory, ignoring the squalid view of poverty beneath his building. "Nearer still, within the narrow board fences which surrounded the backyards of negro hovels, under the moving shadows of broad-leaved mulberry or sycamore trees, he gazed down on the *swarms of mulatto children;* though to his mind *that problem*, like the problem of labour, loomed vague" (my emphasis).[50]

Later, in his own home, he absentmindedly greets "a coloured washerwoman, accompanied by a bright mulatto boy" as he goes up to see his embittered wife (p. 87). Taken together, these few details could easily refer to the intimate crimes of white men, perhaps even Mr. Treadwell's engendering of an illegitimate son. Indeed, later the identity of the father is revealed, in a stroke that is bold for Glasgow to make in such a fastidious age, but which she can hazard behind the veil of genteel and delicate understatement. Treadwell chances to meet the tattered washerwoman some weeks later in the garden, and casual conversation about her age moves into dangerous territory. We learn that Mandy had come to work for the Treadwells eighteen years earlier at the age of fifteen, that Cyrus's wife had discharged her before a year passed, and that a month or two later the mulatto boy Jubal was born. When Mandy tries to play on the past for a bit of sympathy by reminding Cyrus Treadwell of what a "moughty likely gal" she had once been and asking for a slight raise in wages from her four dollars a month so that she can raise her son, Treadwell is outraged at her effrontery. He refuses and orders her to get out. When she has gone, he congratulates himself for having resisted blackmail. "It's a pretty pass things have come to when men have to protect themselves from negro women," he thinks indignantly. Then he turns his thoughts to his legitimate white nephew's need for a job. Treadwell decides to offer the young man a position because "even if the boy's a fool, I'm not one to let those of my own blood come to want" (pp. 172–75).

In a much later chapter entitled "The Problem of the South," we learn

that Jubal has murdered a policeman in a nearby town and will probably
be lynched. Again his mother appeals to his father for help.

> "You ain' done furgot 'im, Marster. He 'uz born jes two mont's atter Miss
> Lindy turnt me outer hyer—en he's jes ez w'ite ez ef'n he b'longed ter w'ite
> folks."
>   But she had gone too far—she had outraged that curious Anglo-Saxon
> instinct in Cyrus which permitted him to sin against his race's integrity, yet
> forbade him to acknowledge, even to himself, that he bore any part in the
> consequence of that sin. Illogical, he might have admitted, but there are some
> truths so poisonous that no honest man could breathe the same air with them.

Treadwell hands her a fifty-dollar bill and orders her not to come whining
around him any more. "Black or white," he says, "the man that commits a
murder has got to hang for it" (pp. 367–68).

Glasgow has not explicitly defined Treadwell's sin, and she has made
only three widely spaced references to it in the novel where even Cyrus
Treadwell is a peripheral character. In this chapter Jubal's dilemma is deliberately merged with the larger racial issue, replaced in the foreground
by the gentle old Episcopal minister's defense of an innocent black man.
Gabriel Pendleton, Virginia's father, has been on his way to help Jubal
when he comes upon an innocent man being beaten by drunken whites. In
a battle with the drunks, the black escapes, and then the old man has a
heart attack and dies, returning us urgently to the central plot involving
the personal tragedies in Virginia's life. But for the attentive reader, Ellen
Glasgow has placed an unmistakable burden of guilt on the Southern
white man, and it is an important part of her exposure of the cruel ironies
surrounding the old-fashioned ideal of the lady.

Another subtle but important emphasis Glasgow makes in this novel is
Virginia's association with plants and the landscape. She continually identifies or contrasts Virginia's moods with the seasons and the growing trees,
flowers, and crops of her native state. In the days of her courtship, for the
young man who will become her husband, "the thought of Virginia lay
always like an enclosed garden of sweetness and bloom. To think of her
was to pass from the scorching heat of the day to the freshness of dew-
washed flowers under the starlight." When he goes to her in her parents'
garden the June night he proposes, "her breath left her parted lips as softly
as the perfume detached itself from the opening rose-leaves" (p. 181). This
is the traditional Southern habit of associating the white lady with the
landscape, which we have seen originating with the first English colonists
and running through the nineteenth-century mind. But Ellen Glasgow
embodies the tradition in a new perspective in the early years of our cen-

tury—the perspective of the woman herself who, like the land, has been beloved, exploited, and then abandoned. Anne Goodwyn Jones sees Virginia as representing, like the roses, "nature radically shaped by civilization," but also as inappropriately desiring "to stay in an eternally spring-like Eden."[51] But the proper place for a rose is exactly such a paradise. The problem is that Eden is a mythological garden of continual spring. All the flowers which Glasgow associates with Virginia should make us see that, like the land, she flowers in the real world of changing seasons. Her delicate beauty is short-lived unless it is cultivated artificially, one supposes, by a doting husband. Virginia obviously does not have such a husband. He abandons the garden he found in her, because it begins to stifle him. His being cannot endure enclosure, while Virginia's thrives on it. When she turns her absorbed attention from him to the fruit of their love—to their children—he withdraws and eventually leaves the South to become a successful playwright in New York.

Virginia's husband Oliver refuses to face unpleasantness or the process of aging. In his own way he is as romantic as Virginia, but, unlike her, he is selfish. Where she lives in a dreamworld of loving sacrifice, he seeks comfort and pleasure. He ceases to love her when she loses her youthful beauty, and he goes North to pursue the success and money which keep him youthfully vital. While Virginia is at the mercy of the seasons and the passage of time, Oliver stands outside organic nature and uses it for his own pleasure. Glasgow certainly means him to represent the dashing Southern gentleman in many respects, the white male who loved but betrayed his region's honor. He knows his guilt in abandoning Virginia, but his shame can be forgotten in a new life.

Southern writers in our own age have continued to emphasize the relation of woman to land, but most of them have been men. Thus through their writing we have been exposed primarily to Oliver's point of view rather than Virginia's. In 1941 Wilbur J. Cash expressed the ambivalence in the male perspective when he described the influence of the Southern climate and land upon the regional mind as "a sort of cosmic conspiracy against reality in favour of romance."

> The country is one of extravagant color, of proliferating foliage and bloom, of flooding yellow sunlight, and, above all perhaps, of haze. Pale blue fogs hang above the valleys in the morning, the atmosphere smokes faintly at midday, and through the long slow afternoon cloudstacks tower from the horizon and the earth-heat quivers upward through the iridescent air, blurring every outline and rending every object vague and problematical. I know that winter comes to the land, certainly. I know there are days when the color and the haze are stripped away and the real stands up in drab and depressing harshness. But these things pass and are forgotten.

The dominant mood, the mood that lingers in the memory, is one of *well-nigh drunken reverie*—of a hush that seems all the deeper for the far-away mourning of the hounds and the far-away crying of the doves—of such *sweet and inexorable opiates as the rich odours of hot earth and pinewood and the perfume of the magnolia in bloom*—of soft languor creeping through the blood and mounting surely to the brain . . . it is a mood, in sum, in which *directed thinking is all but impossible*, a mood in which the mind yields almost perforce to drift and in which the imagination holds unchecked sway, a mood in which nothing any more seems improbable save the puny inadequateness of fact, nothing incredible save the bareness of truth. [my emphasis]

Cash is partly in jest when he says the land is part of a romantic cosmic conspiracy. But he has chosen to abandon himself in the same overripe language of seduction we saw earlier in Robert Beverley's description of colonial Virginia. Still, Cash does not trust the drunken reverie, the opiates which subdue the rational mind. Violence lurks beneath the surface, ready to explode. "But I must tell you that the sequel to this mood is invariably a thunderstorm."[52]

It is William Faulkner, however, as so often in the affairs of the Southern heart, who gives this complex of problems its definitive expression. *Absalom, Absalom!* came out in 1936 and *Go Down, Moses* in 1942. Together these books provide the most astute embodiment of the guilty web of traditional relations between the white man and the land, white women, native Americans, and blacks. Isaac McCaslin is, of all of Faulkner's characters, the most fully conscious that the white man has violated the land by trying to tame it and control it and rape it for its riches. The ledger section of "The Bear" shows that in a parallel way the white man has corrupted the Indians by implicating them in the improper exploitation of the land, and has violated black women while betraying those of his own kind. The races are fatally entangled in blood kinship whose taint only the blacks are strong and virtuous enough to survive.[53] As a child, Isaac had accompanied his mother on a visit to her bachelor brother and witnessed the response of outraged Southern womanhood when she encountered her brother Hubert's black mistress. Hubert Beauchamp's moral dereliction is further symbolized by the state of the gift he gave his nephew at birth. When Isaac finally opens the burlap lump at the age of twenty-one, instead of the original silver cup filled with gold coins, all he finds is a tin coffeepot full of IOUs from his uncle and a few copper pennies. Hubert Beauchamp passed on a debt rather than anything of credit, just as all white men handed their moral debt to their heirs. Because Ike has been initiated by the Indian Sam Fathers to the knowledge that no man has a right to own the land, and because he and his cousin McCaslin Edmonds have understood their inherited guilt by reading through the history of their family in the ledger entries of two hundred years at the commissary store, both men repudiate their claim to their patrimony—ownership of the family lands. The feminine qualities of this land become apparent near the end of "The Bear" when Ike McCaslin's young wife tries to force him to claim it. For the first time in their marriage, she shows herself to him fully naked. She seems to him not the woman he has known, "but composite of all woman-flesh since man that ever of its own will reclined on its back and opened," and this archetypal female demands that he promise to settle on the land before he can claim his right to her naked body. She is the land, despite McCaslin Edmonds's description of "their ravaged patrimony, the dark and ravaged fatherland still prone and panting" (p. 298). It is a motherland, traditionally as we have seen in the Southern imagination, and specifically here in the symbolic terms of Faulkner's story. Ike's passion overcomes his resolve on the one afternoon in his rented room, and he answers "Yes" to his wife's demand for a promise to claim his heritage, the family farm. The ecstatic sexual epiphany which follows is to be his last. His wife laughs cruelly with her back to him, "And that's all. That's all from me. If this dont get you that son you talk about, it wont be mine" (p. 315). She knows he did not mean his promise, that he will never commit himself to the land. Thus no child can come from their union. Connection with the land is fraught with guilt, but it is necessary for both human and agricultural fertility.

Faulkner himself reveals confusion here, for Ike McCaslin's wife seems to be an evil creature who is trying to corrupt a saint. She is Eve to his Adam, enticing him to fall. Saintliness is associated with celibacy in the characterization of Sam Fathers too, and the only great good place in *Go Down, Moses* is an all-male hunting camp in the heart of the virgin wilderness reminiscent of Eden before Eve, Andrew Marvell's "happy garden-state,/While man there walked without a mate." The object of the hunters is to live as prelapsarian boys in noble innocent fellowship upon her bosom, hunting for the meat they eat but never defiling the wild spirit of the place, which is oddly represented by great male creatures—first a huge magical stag in "The Old People" and then Old Ben in "The Bear."

Leslie Fiedler points out Faulkner's ambivalent attitude toward the female attributes of the land in *Love and Death in the American Novel* when he discusses the suggestive names of Faulkner's women. Dewey Dell and Lena Grove and Temple Drake are ultimately horrifying characters, Fiedler believes; "Faulkner's dewiest dells turn out to be destroyers rather than redeemers, quicksands disguised as sacred groves." Why is Faulkner horrified as well as fascinated by these associations? Is it because white Southern men are guilty of abusing woman and land, or is it because women in any form are too dangerous to approach with security? Fiedler inclines to the latter explanation, asserting the Freudian/Jungian view that "the themes of self-punishment and self-destruction are inseparable (in the West at least) from the worship of the Female, who represents the dissolution of consciousness as well as poetic vision, the blackness of extinction as well as that of ecstasy."[54] This sounds very close to Cash's comment on the romantic influence of the Southern physical world, whose sensuous opiates drown the rational mind in dreamy bliss but will be followed by a thunderstorm of violence. Fiedler also thinks Faulkner is revolted by Southern woman's betrayal of her traditionally submissive role. I think Faulkner shares these views of the female but he also quite consciously blames his own white patrimony for its sins.

Faulkner could never really untangle the snarl of his love, his guilt, his fear, and his disgust for his Southern heritage, but he does explore and dramatize the bitter side of the Southern lady in *Absalom, Absalom!* In this novel an implacable old maid is the repository of her family's honor and its guilty history. Miss Rosa Coldfield, her very name suggesting forbidding and barren earth which should have flowered, is the only surviving white remnant of a family representing the Southern aristocracy in its questionable origins and its inevitable decline. She has remained inviolate, but her sister Ellen has been exploited in marriage by reckless Thomas Sutpen, Faulkner's archetypal "Southern gentleman." Sutpen in fact had tried to use Miss Rosa as he had her sister, but his dynastic ambitions fell into ruin because he abused land and woman alike as objects in his grand design. Furthermore, he is guilty of miscegenation more than once, repudiates a mulatto wife and son, and then refuses to acknowledge his paternity when the son appears again as a grown man. The mulatto son's name, Charles Bon, suggests that he is good enough to receive equal treatment from his father, but Sutpen will never accept him, and the ensuing tragedy of fratricide and incest between pure white and mulatto offspring destroys Sutpen's fortune and family.

This is Faulkner's intended point in the novel, but less often explored is the text's tremendous ambivalence about women. On one hand he describes the eternal female as "the eternal Who-suffers," and presents her almost reverentially as wiser and far older than infantile man.[55] But then he speaks of the dread and fear of females which men draw in "with the primary mammalian milk" (p. 265) and describes Charles Bon's nearly hysterical flight from his octoroon wife as escape "from that massy five-foot-thick maggot-cheesy solidarity which overlays the earth, in which men and women in couples are ranked and racked like ninepins; thanks to whatever God for that masculine hipless tapering peg which fits light and glib to move where the cartridge-chambered hips of women hold them fast" (p. 312).

At the end of the novel we are left with destruction presided over by two women and a spellbound adolescent Quentin Compson, white scion of the town's other prominent family. Quentin's father says Sutpen's mistake was a fatal innocence, but Miss Rosa doesn't agree. She sees him as Satanic destroyer, a cold-blooded Bluebeard who only uses women to produce offspring and abandons them if they are unsatisfactory. Miss Rosa, who successfully withstood his seduction, and Clytie, his illegitimate mulatto daughter, are triumphant witnesses to the burning of the family plantation, while the only male descendant to survive is a mulatto half-wit and grandson of Charles Bon rather than offspring of Sutpen's legitimate son Henry. These survivors, in other words, represent those whom Sutpen abused. They are all sterile, and only the women have their wits intact.

The novel ends with Quentin hoping some satisfaction can come from the tragedy—"that the one [Sutpen] cannot escape the censure which no doubt he deserves, that the other [the women and blacks he wronged] no longer lack the commiseration which let us hope (while we are hoping) that they have longed for" (p. 377). Quentin hopes for new life to arise in this blasted Southern land, but he seems unable to convince himself that he does not hate it as his college friend accuses him of doing. His masculine heritage has doomed itself, and he has to take the side of outraged womanhood. In *The Sound and the Fury* Quentin is finally unable to bear the burden of his past; he commits suicide, leaving behind an idiot castrated brother and his sister Caddy. She is the new woman of the South, soiled but fertile and defiant, having rejected the hollow code of her patriarchal culture. If Caddy represents new life, it is not the kind Quentin hoped for or Faulkner himself desired. Caddy produced a daughter named Quentin, who debases herself even more than her mother had and blames her only white male relative, her embittered and sterile uncle Jason.

Faulkner concurs with the female Quentin's charge, yet he seems to have been unable to think of a way to compensate the Southern woman for the betrayal she suffered. For one thing, as we have seen, he was profoundly disturbed by women's power. But he did give Quentin Compson's heritage to the women of the family, even sealing the bequest with the scion's Christian name. The male voice of the archetypal Southern family is dead, leaving the women to carry on and to speak for themselves.

They had begun telling their side of the story in letters and diaries before Mary Chesnut's time. Anne Firor Scott has recovered their testimony, C. Vann Woodward has edited a full edition of Chesnut's diaries, and Anne Goodwyn Jones has provided a close study of seven fiction writers, from Augusta Jane Evans in the mid-nineteenth century to Margaret Mitchell in the third decade of our own, who began a more public but subtly artistic exploration of the feminine experience in the Southern heritage. In general, Jones concludes, "the masks they wear as authors, the personae they create, half reveal and half disguise the truth within their fictions. Yet perhaps their ambivalence should be forgiven; it is quite a magician's trick, after all, to make a marble statue live and move, and then to make it speak."[56] Ellen Glasgow's self-sacrificing Virginia Pendleton and Margaret Mitchell's cynically capable Scarlett O'Hara are two contrasting examples of Southern women writers' indictments of the idea which had proved such an illusory example for their lives. The next generation of writers in the tradition would provide a deeper and more direct examination of the feminine self in the Southern landscape.

Chapter Two

Growing Up
in the Modern South

Virginia Woolf believed that before the American writer could achieve a distinctive identity he had to free himself from English attitudes, in order to know what he was *not*. The second step in the process would be far more difficult. "For having decided what he is not, he must proceed to discover what he is. This is the beginning of a stage of acute self-consciousness." The bitterness and touchy defensiveness she finds in American writers remind her of another group only recently freeing itself from historic bonds. "Women writers have to meet many of the same problems that beset Americans. They are too conscious of their own peculiarities as a sex; apt to suspect insolence, quick to avenge grievances, eager to shape an art of their own." Allen Tate suggests a similar problem for Southerners and argues that it generated a burst of creativity. Though he never mentions women, we should expect them to have experienced this acute sensitivity with a special intensity. Tate argues: "With the war of 1914–1918, the South reentered the world—but gave a backward glance as it stepped over the border: that backward glance gave us the Southern renascence, a literature conscious of the past in the present."[1] For Southern women, that past had been far less hospitable than for the men who controlled it and from whom Tate descended; the old traditions were perhaps even more hollow for Southern women than for men. If Tate is right, the backward glance for women must have revealed a host of ironies that could be exploited in literature.

Eudora Welty, Carson McCullers, and Flannery O'Connor represent the generation of women writers who grew up in the New South during the years Tate describes. Thanks to Anne Goodwyn Jones, we now understand some of the ways earlier Southern women writers explored their legacy from the antebellum world. The fiction of these writers manipulated, adapted, challenged, but all too often finally capitulated to the traditional expectations for the lady. Kate Chopin's Edna Pontellier gave up her quest for independence and drowned herself at the end of *The Awakening*, for instance, and Ellen Glasgow's Virginia was left a withered and disillusioned saint waiting dully to die. Where did their fates leave the next generation? The old image of femininity had been revealed as a mirage, but nothing very positive had been suggested as an alternative. The women writers growing up in the 1920s inherited an acute consciousness of what they could not be, of how the past had jilted their mothers and grandmothers. They would take the more difficult next step to discover who they were.

William Faulkner was already fascinated by the problem at the end of the 1920s, claiming that his purpose in *The Sound and the Fury* was to tell Caddy's story. "To me she was the beautiful one," he said; "she was my heart's darling. That's what I wrote the book about." Yet the novel always sees her from a distance, through the wistful or vindictive eyes of a brother. Faulkner explains his difficulties.

> It began with the picture of the little girl's muddy drawers, climbing that tree to look in the parlor window with her brothers that didn't have the courage to climb the tree waiting to see what she saw. And I tried first to tell it with one brother, and that wasn't enough. That was Section One. I tried with another brother, and that wasn't enough. That was Section Two. I tried the third brother, because Caddy was still to me too beautiful and too moving to reduce her to telling what was going on, that it would be more passionate to see her through somebody else's eyes, I thought. And that failed and I tried myself—the fourth section—to tell what happened.[2]

At first it may seem odd that Faulkner would find it "more passionate" to present his heart's darling so obliquely, but if we understand the traditional reverence for the Southern lady, we know that he could never have managed to approach more closely when she began to assert herself and peer boldly into the secrets of her family as she did when she climbed the tree to watch her grandmother's death. The enterprise was far too dangerous for a man. Only a woman could tell Caddy's story; only women could explain what led her to break the old code and her adoring brothers' hearts or what caused her daughter Quentin to go even further.

Actually Zelda Fitzgerald told one version of Caddy's story in *Save Me the Waltz*, and Katherine Anne Porter told another in *Pale Horse, Pale Rider*. Both rebellious young protagonists reject their traditional feminine destinies and leave the South as Caddy did, but both are disappointed. Zelda Fitzgerald describes the ultimate souring of the brilliant but dissipated life which she and her husband helped make famous. Porter's Miranda does succeed in finding a career as a journalist, but her achievement seems empty when death steals the young man, appropriately named Adam, who was to share her brave new world.

Eudora Welty grew up to suggest the origins and dramatize the emancipation of such young women within a positive, celebratory vision of the more traditional world that produced them, and Carson McCullers and Flannery O'Connor took closer, more problematic looks at the next generation, Quentin's, to explore the sources of their resentment. All three of these modern Southern writers drew their strength from a source which has not yet been fully appreciated—the matriarchal traditions of the South which Welty, McCullers, and O'Connor experienced in their personal development but also found stretching back to support them in the traditions of their literary foremothers, English and American as well as more specifically Southern.

They needed the support of other women, because their world was continually trying to ignore their existence as serious, distinct people. The problem lies with the patriarchal heritage of the antebellum myth which Richard King so effectively anatomizes in *A Southern Renaissance*. He is right about the power of the Southern family romance, but he has failed to see all of it. His Freudian thesis of Oedipal conflict excludes blacks and white women by definition, thus gravely oversimplifying a heritage that is far richer than he admits. Claiming to focus his examination of the Southern Renaissance on literary works which present the region and its tradition as problematic, he omits blacks because "for them the Southern family romance was hardly problematic." They rejected its relevance and concentrated on escaping the South altogether. He omits women because "they were not concerned primarily with the larger cultural, racial, and political themes that I take as my focus."[3] These excuses are contradictory. If cultural, racial, and political issues are the troubled areas of Southern tradition, black writers should have been included. Southern blacks like James Weldon Johnson and Richard Wright gave searching fictional treatment to those issues in *The Autobiography of an Ex-Coloured Man* and *Black*

Boy, exposing the region's social injustice as few had done before. Women writers are omitted by King for similarly peculiar reasons. The Queen of the Home may be part of the family romance, although only a shadowy figure, but King implies that women writers have no right to portray her function as, for instance, Eudora Welty does in *Delta Wedding*, unless they are also treating the political problems of the South. King surely has the right to choose his emphasis and to limit the number of writers he will discuss, but his reasons should be just and logical. The case he makes leaves him open to the charge that, as a Southern man himself, he is merely examining his own kind and excluding the two groups the Southern patriarchy has always suppressed in order to maintain its power. William Faulkner is King's quintessential dramatist of the Southern family romance, and although Faulkner does portray the Oedipal struggle in a culture with a heroic masculine past, blacks and women are absolutely central to the fate of white men in his fiction. The real Southern family romance is the one we examined in the previous chapter, the passionate and guilt-ridden story of romantic white men who idealized their land, their women, and a code of individual freedom yet enslaved another race and betrayed their own women by mingling their blood with that of the slaves for generations. All the novelists who take the South seriously are concerned with the whole tangled story, from Thomas Nelson Page and Thomas Dixon through Ellen Glasgow and James Weldon Johnson and Richard Wright, Katherine Anne Porter, Eudora Welty, Carson Mc-Cullers, and Flannery O'Connor. Nobody can carry quite as full a load as the Dixie Limited, to use Flannery O'Connor's famous nickname for Faulkner, but she was far too modest in characterizing herself and, by implication, most other Southern writers as mere horse-and-wagon rigs stalled on the tracks.

And Faulkner, for all his rich sensitivity to the region's life, could not tell the real story of the Southern lady. He tried in *The Sound and the Fury*, and he admitted that he failed. He said he felt he would reduce Caddy's beauty by letting her talk, but perhaps he was afraid of what she would say. For him as for other men of his heritage, women were perhaps too potent. Southern white men stood at a disadvantage with women because of the myth of chivalry which they had invented. They needed the vision of their inviolate women to sustain their elaborate fiction of aristocratic civilization, and when women like Caddy began to openly reject the game and live as independent warm-blooded beings who asserted their sexuality—New Women, Southern style—the loss of the myth was insupportable. It was really the loss of a goddess incarnate, the end of a religion which, despite their trespasses and hypocrisies, these men loved. Caddy had to smell like trees, to personify the virgin land, to be the fresh garden of Eden before the Fall. Then her men could believe that, whatever degradations had come upon the South, its spirit remained inviolate. Whatever unpleasant historical realities lay behind the myth of the Lost Cause, the ideals could still be articles of faith by which the South could recover her way of life. In order to function in this way, however, the goddess had to remain a static object of worship, the repository of passive virtues. Even then, she represented a threat because of enormous potency, both moral and sexual. If she should be allowed to speak, she would cease to be inert and begin to exercise her moral force. So Faulkner could not allow Caddy to tell her own story.[4] It was bad enough that she acted out her sexuality and thus destroyed the possibility that her brothers could worship her. When she lost her virginity, she ceased to smell like trees and forced her brothers out of Eden. When she became a living woman, the myth shattered, and her brother Quentin was exiled into the modern world of mutability and decay where flawed humans of both sexes would have to face their sins.

That was and perhaps still is the problem for the masculine imagination in the South. For women, however, the tradition of reverence for the lady had certain positive elements which corresponded to actual conditions of life and could be secret sources of confidence. The cliché of the passive, static goddess on her pedestal referred to an immense active force in every life. Celebrating it publicly in even the most sentimental terms legitimized it and freed it for use in the right hands. Patriarchies naturally celebrate the dominating power of the father, but the mother is the primary figure of strength for the early years of every person's experience, as even Freud will grant. The Southern habit of gyneolatry, as W. J. Cash termed it, continued to accord at least verbal recognition to the mother's power, which runs counter to the patriarchal scheme. Perhaps this was true to some degree in all late-Victorian societies, but it held on longer in the American South and served as a self-conscious and defensive religion to divert attention from obvious social and political problems from the 1830s through the early decades of the twentieth century. Thus at the Texas State Fair in October 1887 Henry Grady sought to rally his audience to a glorious vision of a New South emerging from the ruins of Reconstruction: "Every man in the sound of my voice, under the deeper consecration he offers to the Union, will consecrate himself to the South. Have no ambition but to be first at her feet and last at her service,—no hope but, after a long life of devotion, to sink to sleep in her bosom, as a little child sleeps at his mother's breast and rests untroubled in the light of her smile." Here Grady appeals to the same holy female power he pictured as the guiding spirit of the South in speeches to Northern audiences, where his purpose was to conciliate, to portray the South as contrite, humble, dedicated to building a just new society loyal to the Union. In fact his purpose was the same as that of his former mentor Henry Watterson, capable Southern apologist and nationally known editor of the Louisville *Courier-Journal*. Grady, as editor of the Atlanta *Constitution*, followed Watterson in working to persuade the North to relent in its postwar vindictiveness toward the South, to allow the former Confederate states self-determination and their own resolution of the "Negro question." The result, of course, was white supremacy and Jim Crow. In return for the solid support of white Southerners, the Democratic party averted its gaze from the gradual disfranchising of blacks and the nation began a long infatuation with Dixieland.[5]

Thomas Dixon is even more explicit in *The Leopard's Spots* (1906) about the mother deity who guides his hero Charles Gaston to overthrow Negro rule in his North Carolina town. "Every woman is something divine to me," Charlie confesses to his foster mother. "I think of God as a woman, not a man—a great loving Mother of all Life. If I ever saw the face of God it was in my mother's face."

Gaston's real mother is conveniently dead; there is no danger of her imposing female authority on our hero's life. Dixon makes sure we do not take the mother-deity's worship too seriously by providing Gaston with a spirited but ultimately submissive Southern belle for a wife. At the end of the novel, when Charles Gaston presides over newly restored white supremacy as governor of North Carolina, he promises his bride, "From tonight, my dear, . . . you will share with me all the honours and responsibilities of public life." Reassuringly she protests, "No, my love, I do not desire any part in public life except through you. . . . I desire no career save that of a wife—your wife." With a little sob she hides her face on his breast.[6]

But this is a male fantasy designed to remind Southern women of their men's conditions for love. Real women were not so quick to melt into the identity of their husbands, as we have already seen. William Taylor has explained the dangers of moral authority which the cult of chivalry created, and the consequent necessity of limiting the scope of women's activities: "She was given the Home on the understanding that her benevolence was to stop at the bounds of the family. Women were projected into the center of the plantation legend and the plantation became a kind of matriarchy. Nonetheless, behind the plantation portico there can frequently be heard, faintly but distinctly, the still small voice of an awakening Southern consciousness that wrong has been and is being done behind the complacent facade of the planter's social code.[7]

We have already heard that voice; it is the voice of women, which may have been still and small in the nineteenth century but which grew progressively more audible. When the moral authority of women began to be voiced outside the home in the early decades of the twentieth century, the greatest single achievement of Southern women reformers was the Association of Southern Women for the Prevention of Lynching (ASWPL). As Jacqueline Dowd Hall perceptively demonstrates in *The Revolt Against Chivalry*, a biographical study of the movement's leader, Jesse Daniel Ames, the work of this group drew a good bit of its strength from the enlightened "New" Southern lady's realization that her social position was closely connected with that of black men and women. Lynching and the threat of rape both functioned to keep subordinate groups in their places. The reformers used the unassailable logic of Christian morality to undermine the whole myth of rape and insist on the immorality of lynching. Lillian Smith described the process with her characteristic flair.

It was truly a subversive affair, but as decorously conducted as an afternoon walk taken by the students of a Female Institute. It started stealthily, in my mother's day. Shyly, these first women sneaked down from their chilly places, did their little sabotage and sneaked up again, wrapping innocence around them like a lace shawl. They set secret time bombs and went back to their needlework, serenely awaiting the blast. They had no lady Lincoln to proclaim their emancipation from southern tradition but they scarcely needed one. . . .

And then it happened. The lady insurrectionists gathered together in one of our southern cities. They primly called themselves church women but churches were forgotten by everybody when they spoke their revolutionary words. They said calmly that they were not afraid of being raped; as for their sacredness, they could take care of it themselves; they did not need the chivalry of a lynching to protect them and did not want it. Not only that, they continued, but they would personally do everything in their power to keep any Negro from being lynched and furthermore, they squeaked bravely, they had plenty of power.

They had more than they knew. They had the power of spiritual blackmail over a large part of the white South. All they had to do was drop their little buckets into any one of numerous wells of guilt dotting the landscape and splash it around a bit. No one, of thousands of white men, had any notion how much or how little each woman knew about his private goings-on.[8]

It would be wrong to attribute all feminine progress against injustice to whites, for after 1910 the National Association for the Advancement of Colored People had been working hard to combat racial injustice, and in

1922 it had formed a women's group called the Anti-Lynching Crusaders. White women, to their discredit, did not heed the Crusaders' urgent requests for support in sufficient numbers to give the organization a chance for genuine political success. But the Crusaders set the precedent and began the moral appeal that the AWSPL would follow.[9] The ultimate point to notice is that women's organizations challenged the terrorist tactics of white male supremacy and began to succeed. Educated people knew about these organizations, and their activities clearly demonstrated the strength which Southern women usually kept hidden or in reserve.

At its domestic center, out of the bustle of political and commercial activity, upper-class life in the South remained a feminine domain. Women were the traditional keepers of the family genealogies so proudly cultivated to demonstrate noble ancestry, and children grew up surrounded by imposing old ladies. Grandmothers, aunts, courtesy aunts, and elderly maiden cousins were the family storytellers. In the cool gloom of high-ceilinged nineteenth-century family houses children gathered about the old ladies, who always retained their virginal names. Cousin Mary Vee or Aunt Nita or Cousin Lil or Grandmother or the mysterious spinster aunt who never even came downstairs but flitted about her darkened rooms clipping "proofs" from the newspapers that the communists were taking over the country—any one of these could spin long tales of gallantry in the service of George Washington or Andrew Jackson or describe the exploits of children and handsome young people now long dead of consumption or war wounds. Children would hear how General Jackson rescued an eloping ancestral lieutenant and his bride from the wrath of pursuing in-laws and gave him a sword which somehow mysteriously later disappeared. They learned how great-great-grandmother sent great-grandfather to the University of Göttingen at sixteen to keep him from running off to fight in the Civil War. They heard grandmother sing the German songs she had learned on his knee long years after his return. Old cousins lent children books about lovely virgins rushing to save their missionary lovers who were dying of malaria in Africa. The children were dressed up and dragged off to have cambric tea with invalid widows who wore lace collars and complicated black dresses, or carted out to visit Cousin Jane's farm where she lived alone in the Victorian splendor of echoing rooms with polished black floors, antiques, and her rare doll collection. There she would preside over a feast on a summer noon that Northern cousins thought was Thanksgiving. And always in the kitchens where these miracles were produced, there were more women, black ones, who knew every family secret and condescended to their crotchety, aged mistresses.

This was the world where Eudora Welty was a child, though she has said that because her parents were both from outside Mississippi she had less absorption in such communities of kinship than some other Southerners.[10] Its upper-class form is dramatized in *Delta Wedding* and its lower-class version in *Losing Battles*. Lula Carson Smith seems not to have grown up in quite such a wide family network, and she has purposely omitted the matriarchal dimension of Southern life from her fiction but she too was well acquainted with female domestic rule. Mary Flannery O'Connor very clearly did grow up in the center of the kind of "old family" world I have described, except that it was not filled with children. She was the only child. She grew up in the O'Connor family home on one of the historic old squares of Savannah, next door to a household of female relatives: her mother's Aunt Annie Treanor and a Cousin Katie. When her family was forced to move back to her mother's family home in Milledgeville, it was a reentry into a familiar community for her mother. Regina Cline O'Connor installed her gravely ill husband and her daughter in the Cline House, built in 1820 and inhabited by her unmarried sisters. She continued to be referred to in the community as Miss Regina Cline according to small-town Southern custom, as if her maiden identity had never been seriously threatened by her marriage.

In her irreverent autobiographical reflections, *Southern Ladies and Gentlemen*, Florence King describes her childhood awakening to the matriarchal character of this Southern social world.

> Suddenly I realized, with that visceral instinct that children have, that I lived in a goddess world in which women reigned supreme according to a carefully worked out hierarchy. The various titles that came so naturally to my cousin and me were like the graduated obeisances of royal protocol; more, they were *heavenly* titles. If we had been well-to-do enough to have had black servants, I might also have grown accustomed to that well-known distaff triumvirate that has long abounded in upper-class Southern households: Old Miss, Young Miss, and Little Miss. . . .
>
> Southern men, black and white alike, are affected throughout their lives by the Big Mama Syndrome. The black woman's strength has been moral and quite often physical; the white woman's has been primarily social, but in their men's minds they both symbolize on an unconscious level an ancient matriarchy in full tilt.[11]

This description may be exaggerated, but in the early lives of Welty, Mc-Cullers, and O'Connor, women were powerful beings.

Eudora Welty's autobiographical sketches in *One Writer's Beginnings* recreate a childhood world centered in a protected family but set in a wider social milieu dominated by fiercely demanding women schoolteachers and librarians. Outside the charmed family circle little Eudora suffered occasional mortification at the hands of these arbiters of manners and learning. Miss Duling, the Jefferson Davis Grammar School principal dressed in black, whose brass bell seemed to grow "directly out of her right arm, as wings grew out of an angel or a tail out of the devil"; Mrs. McWillie, the stern Presbyterian fourth-grade teacher also dressed in black; and Mrs. Calloway, the librarian who would only allow two books a day to any patron, are only a few examples of this august group.

Within Welty's family, authority seems to have been balanced between father and mother, although her reticence makes it unlikely that we shall ever know much about her parents' specific influences upon her childhood. Christian Welty was an active business executive, president of a life insurance company, but he was also a tender parent. Miss Welty recalls that he was so worried about her safety that before she could wear new shoes he insisted on scoring their shiny soles with his knife to prevent them from slipping. Her mother was similarly protective and a central part of the daughter's life, and her sacrifices left a permanent sense of guilt.

> When my mother would tell me that she wanted me to have something because she as a child had never had it, I wanted, or I partly wanted, to give it back. All my life I continued to feel that bliss for me would have to imply my mother's deprivation or sacrifice. I don't think it would have occurred to her what a double emotion I felt, and indeed I know that it was being unfair to her, for what she said was simply the truth. [12]

Warmly returning her mother's gift, Welty gave up her life in New York City and returned home to help her mother when her father died in 1931. She has remained in Jackson ever since, taking care of her mother until Mrs. Welty's death in 1966.

Among her novels and stories, *The Optimist's Daughter* is unusually close to her own experience and thus provides some sense of her mother. The novel apparently gave her a way of confronting her mother's death and accepting her grief, a process reflected in Laurel Hand's painful reassessment of her mother's character. Welty has said that Becky Hand's West Virginia home and family are taken from personal memories of visiting her mother's family there. "The way my uncles looked coming home at night through the far-off fields, just white shirts showing down the mountain. And the sound of the horses. All the physical sensations were memories of about age three, when you really have very sharp sensory perceptions. I still recall this, and I just put it all in there." She also put in many details from her mother's life: the specific titles of books in the family library, her mother's experience as a young mountain schoolteacher, even her mother's trip down the river on a raft and then by train to Baltimore with her dying father. Like Becky Hand, Mrs. Welty married and moved south to Mississippi, was a pessimist in contrast to her husband, and lay blind on her deathbed reciting passages from McGuffey's Reader.[13] We can safely assume that the real and fictional mothers are similar in the positive example of womanhood they provided for their daughters.

The maternal influence was far greater in Lula Carson Smith's life. It could easily be described as overwhelming. By all accounts, her father Lamar Smith was a shy man who let his flamboyant wife prevail in the household. He seems always to have been outnumbered. In boyhood his mother had been the responsible parent, as his father was an alcoholic and often absent. Then when Lamar Smith married, he and his wife Marguerite moved into her mother's house, where they stayed for nine years. As the strong-willed mother-in-law had been widowed early and had raised a large family alone, she must certainly have continued to direct the affairs of her house until she died, when Carson was almost seven. Her property reverted to her daughter, who then sold the old house downtown and bought a newer one in a moderately fashionable suburb, keeping the title to the house in her own name alone.[14]

Virginia Spencer Carr's biography of McCullers clearly establishes her mother's almost smothering influence. Carson was the first of the three Smith children and remained the favorite whom her mother declared a genius and groomed for greatness. If Carr's account is accurate, the mother was relentlessly effusive about her daughter's talents. Carson McCullers's brother generously said, "Not only were we proud that Lula Carson had proved herself a genius in her writings, but we also believed that our mother was almost one herself for recognizing it in our sister." McCullers remained dependent upon her mother into adulthood, returning home to Columbus when ill for long periods of recuperation, and crying out, "Mother, Mother!" on at least one occasion when in the throes of frustration with her writing. The fact that there is no strong mother like Mrs. Smith in any of McCullers's fiction is explained by her brother as inability to deal with such a strong figure. He believed his sister "so utterly dependent upon Mother throughout her lifetime that she would not have dared strip herself that bare in her writing."[15] The one time she did try to depict a figure like her mother, in the mawkish play *The Square Root of Wonderful*, the result is a monster of treacly clichés and caricatured Southern manners. She dedicated the play to her mother, but all she was able to express for her was hostility. Lamar Jr. must have been right: her mother was too close for comfort.

Flannery O'Connor's fiction is the opposite of McCullers's in its direct, almost obsessive portrayal of dominant mothers, returning again and again to the setting of a small farm inhabited by a widow and one or two sour children. The widowed mother appears in several urban stories too; in all, a third of O'Connor's stories present such mothers. Flannery's father died when she was fifteen, leaving her mother as the only close person in her life. Throughout her college years she lived at home, and from 1945 until Christmas of 1950, when she lived away from Milledgeville, she wrote her mother every day. The return home at the end of 1950 was scheduled to be a holiday visit but became permanent when she was found to be gravely ill with disseminated lupus, the disease that had killed her father. Anyone familiar with published biographical materials and with the letters collected in *The Habit of Being* knows Regina O'Connor was central in her daughter's life from that time until its premature end in 1964. The tough little widow was clearly not a model for her daughter's own development, however. In the many letters to friends after the beginning of her invalid existence at home, O'Connor joked about her mother's use of clichés and her literary insensitivity, caricatured her mother's fierce efforts to maintain control of intransigent mules and employees on their farm, and referred to her as "Parent" or "Regina" in a bemused, distant way, as one might speak of a local curiosity. Nevertheless, Flannery O'Connor admitted to her friend Sally Fitzgerald that her mother was the most powerful and necessary person in her life.[16]

Nurtured by these strongly maternal families, Welty, O'Connor, and McCullers grew to maturity in the quiet backwaters of Southern town life, receiving the standard conservative education that the region offered. Flannery O'Connor's grammar school education differed from the others in being Catholic and thus suffused with Church doctrine, but otherwise the curricula were similarly focused on basic literacy and computational skills, literature, history, and the traditional physical sciences. All three were avid readers from their early years and had serious interests in other arts as well. Eudora Welty remembers her youthful reading as "a sweet devouring," and her friend Katherine Anne Porter wrote that Welty spontaneously began writing in childhood as well. She supplemented her reading with piano lessons and painting. According to Porter, "For a good number of years she believed she was going to be a painter, and painted quite earnestly while she wrote without much effort." Carson McCullers described her early efforts at playwriting and producing her dramas in the family living room with casts of neighborhood children, but at the same time she was practicing the piano five hours a day and hoping for a career as a concert performer. As a child, Flannery O'Connor wrote poems for her father, little surprises she hid under his napkin for discovery at dinner.[17]

"I suppose my father toted around some of my early productions," she told her friend "A," referring to his habit of keeping pieces of her work with him to show to friends. "I drew—mostly chickens, beginning at the tail, the same chicken over and over, beginning at the tail. Also occasional verse." Some of her childhood manuscripts were preserved in the O'Connor Collection at Georgia College and reveal that from the beginning her writing was characterized by a delight in the absurd and grotesque. In her teens she began imitating such serious writers as Proust, and by the time she was in college her sense of literary vocation was strong. She saw writing as a way to fulfill her father's literary ambitions. "My father wanted to write but had not the time or money or training or any of the opportunities I have had. I am never likely to romanticize him because I carry around most of his faults as well as his tastes. I even have about his same constitution: I have the same disease. . . . Anyway, whatever I do in the way of writing makes me extra happy in the thought that it is a fulfillment of what he wanted to do himself."[18]

The intellectual interests and literary aspirations shared by Eudora Welty, Lula Carson Smith, and Mary Flannery O'Connor made them oddities in a world which demanded beauty and charm for women but disapproved of intellect. What Ellen Moers describes as typical European and American emphasis on female beauty holds especially true in the South.

> From infancy, indeed from the moment of birth, the looks of a girl are examined with ruthless scrutiny by all around her, especially by women, crucially by her own mother. "Is she pretty?" is the second question put to new female life, following fast upon the first: "Is it a boy or a girl?" Whatever else may have changed in the experience of women, Maggie Tulliver is in this respect still with us, and George Eliot's memories of the ugly intellectual's girlhood still give us the horrors, Gothic or otherwise.[19]

None of our three writers was conventionally pretty, all were bookish, and two took special pains to rebel against demands that they grow up to be graceful ladies. Lula Carson Smith struck sullen tomboy poses in childhood photographs, and by the time she finished high school she was well known in her hometown as a deliberate eccentric who wore knickers or dresses that were too long, cut her own hair in unfashionable shapes, wore the wrong socks and tennis shoes or Girl Scout oxfords, had smoked cigarettes for years, and went across the river to "Sin City," Alabama, to drink beer in bars frequented by soldiers from Fort Benning. "After all, Little Precious has to gather material so she can be a famous author someday," said her mother when acquaintances criticized.[20] McCullers's adult preference for slacks and men's shirts became a trademark when she established her literary persona after the publication of *The Heart Is a Lonely Hunter*.

Flannery O'Connor also refused to be ladylike, deliberately accentuating clumsy physical traits much as her character Joy-Hulga Hopewell does in "Good Country People." In one letter to her friend "A" she recalled how, in her early days, she was "forced to take dancing to throw me into the company of other children and to make me graceful. Nothing I hated worse than the company of other children and I vowed I'd see them all in hell before I would make the first graceful move." Local boys groaned when their mothers made them dance with Mary Flannery out of politeness at the parties connected with the dancing school, and girls her age were warned by their mothers not to walk slew-footed and round-shouldered the way she did. One of O'Connor's contemporaries says the walk is described in "A Temple of the Holy Ghost," when the twelve-year-old protagonist goes upstairs to her room and paces "the long bedroom with her hands locked together behind her back and her head thrust forward and an expression, fierce and dreamy both, on her face." When other girls were making frilly clothes for home economics projects in school, Mary Flannery displayed her talents by dressing up a chicken and having it follow her into class. Like Joy-Hulga, she wore an ugly sweat shirt out of pure perversity. In another letter to "A" she recalled, "The only embossed one I ever had had a fierce-looking bulldog on it with the word GEORGIA over him. I wore it all the time, it being my policy at that point in life to create an unfavorable impression."[21]

The only clear path open to such uncooperative young women was education, but the Southern patriarchy's disapproval of feminine intellectual development was reflected in the poor quality of women's higher education in the years when Welty, Smith, and O'Connor went to college. Ellen Glasgow bitterly describes the traditional Southern view that knowledge should be kept from young women "as rigorously as if it contained the germs of a contagious disease." A woman's education was designed "to paralyze her reasoning faculties so completely that all danger of mental 'unsettling' or even movement was eliminated from her future." University education had been closed to women in Glasgow's day, and even as late as the 1930s most Southern universities excluded women. In 1930, when Eudora Welty was a student in a Southern women's college and Lula Carson Smith was the age of her adolescent heroines, a grim indictment of

Southern education for women appeared in the *South Atlantic Quarterly.* Eudora Richardson's "The Case of the Women's Colleges in the South" reveals that support for these institutions was almost nonexistent at the time. Since women had no regular access to male colleges and universities in the South, separate female institutions provided their only opportunity for higher education, yet only seven met the minimum requirements for membership in the American Association of University Women. The first women's colleges in the United States had been established in the South, but Richardson's account of their fate is disheartening. Lack of financial support left them to limp along with substandard facilities and pitifully paid faculties. Only one of these venerable colleges was able to meet AAUW requirements by 1930, although some newer women's colleges were certified. The situation was not much improved by the early 1940s when Mary Flannery O'Connor went to college. One thinks back to Virginia Woolf's comparison of men's and women's colleges at Oxbridge in *A Room of One's Own.* As she walked back to her inn from the bare and ugly women's college where she had eaten a supper of beef and prunes, she remembered the opulence and security of the male college where she had lunched and wondered "what effect poverty has on the mind." She thought of being denied access to the male college library earlier in the day, "and I thought how unpleasant it is to be locked out; and I thought how it is worse perhaps to be locked in"; and she went on thinking of "the safety and prosperity of the one sex and of the poverty and insecurity of the other and of the effect of tradition and of the lack of tradition upon the mind of a writer."[22]

Ultimately Welty, Smith, and O'Connor were not locked in the South or locked out of superior higher education. All three escaped to the North, where they immersed themselves in wider intellectual and literary traditions than they could have found in Georgia or Mississippi, two of the states with the lowest-rated educational institutions in the country. Both Welty and O'Connor started out in relatively neglected Southern women's colleges: Mississippi State College for Women in Columbus and Georgia State College for Women in Milledgeville. In 1927, however, Welty began her exodus, first transferring to Randolph-Macon Woman's College in Virginia, but having to leave after a few weeks because her previous college credits were not acceptable and the courses she had taken would have had to be repeated. Unable to afford an extra year of college, she bought a train ticket and "rode weeping across the James" on her way to the University of Wisconsin, where she had also been accepted.[23] There she finished her undergraduate education, afterwards moving on to Columbia University in New York for a graduate degree in business. Welty's higher education in

New York was not confined to university classrooms. "It was a good time for me. It was my chance, the first I had ever had, to go to the theater, to the museums, to concerts, and I made use of every moment, let me tell you. I was taking a business course, which meant I didn't have to study at all, so I went to the theater." It was a time of great cultural ferment in New York, and Welty's account of her time there reveals her lively participation.

> Everybody that was wonderful was then at their peak. People like Noel Coward, all the wonderful music hall stars—Beatrice Lillie, Bert Lahr, Fred Allen, both the Astaires, Jack Benny, Joe Cook, and Ed Wynn. Wonderful dramatic stars, even Nazimova! Katherine Cornell, the Lunts—if I sat down to it, I could make a list of everybody on God's earth that was playing. Martha Graham was dancing solo in a little cubbyhole somewhere. I would go and watch her dance. And Shan-Kar! Everybody was there. For somebody who had never, in a sustained manner, been to the theater or to the Metropolitan Museum, where I went every Sunday, it was just a cornucopia. We had a good group of people from Jackson there at Columbia to start with, so we had company for everything we wanted to do. We could set forth anywhere. We could go dancing in Harlem to Cab Calloway. We went a lot to Small's Paradise, a night-club in Harlem where all the great bands were playing then; whites were welcome as anybody else. [24]

Though her father's death and the difficulty of finding work in New York forced Welty to leave this heady urban world, the experience in Wisconsin and New York had freed her from Southern provincialism and put her in touch with the most innovative trends in American culture. Back home in Jackson, when she began traveling around Mississippi for the WPA, she saw her homeland afresh. [25]

Carson Smith dropped "Lula" from her name at the age of fifteen, and planned to dissociate herself from the narrow world of Columbus, Georgia, by seeking a career in the North. But she did not leave home immediately after graduating from high school at sixteen. Instead, she lived with her family another year, continuing to study the piano and undertaking an ambitious program of reading "the greatest literature in the world," which a local librarian cousin outlined at her request. Music may have seemed her major interest at the time, because she continued to practice five hours a day, but she had already begun to write. After writing a play starring Jesus and Nietzsche, she wrote a novel set in a peculiar New York City where houses had front lawns and there were conductors taking tickets on the subway. But she also wrote the short story "Sucker," which grew from the childhood world she knew and anticipated the concerns of her mature work. A year and a half after leaving high school, she set out for New York with plans to study music at Juilliard and writing at Columbia. By some mistake she lost most of her money shortly after arriving, but she managed to eke out a living with odd jobs and to take night courses at Columbia. Juilliard had to be abandoned. After surviving her first year of college in New York, she moved more easily through a second, this time studying writing both at Washington Square College of New York University and at Columbia. Her formal education ended with summer school that second year, but by then she had become a successful writer, publishing two stories before the end of the year. Though illness forced a return to Columbus in the fall of 1936, she would soon marry Reeves McCullers and leave Georgia for Fayetteville, North Carolina. Two years later she left the South for good.[26]

Like Carson McCullers, Flannery O'Connor began serious preparation for an artistic career with two alternative but ultimately complementary interests. Drawing and painting occupied much of O'Connor's time during adolescence, but she was also writing. One of her productions was a series of short books she described as "too young for adults and too old for children." When she went to Georgia State College for Women, O'Connor intended to major in English but apparently found the department lacking and changed her major to social science before graduation. With hindsight we might be tempted to regard the choice as a private joke; certainly she ridicules social scientists throughout her fiction. But whatever her motives, she abandoned neither her literary nor her artistic interests. She was art editor of the student newspaper, the *Colonnade*, and editor of the literary magazine, the *Corinthian*, during her senior year. She produced many cartoons for campus publications and tried unsuccessfully to have drawings published by the *New Yorker*. One of her college teachers thought highly enough of her writing in the *Corinthian* to submit some of her stories to the Writers' Workshop at the University of Iowa, and these won her a scholarship to the program. From the fall of 1945 through spring of 1948, she lived in Iowa City, matured as a writer, and began to form serious literary friendships which had never been available to her before. As she later admitted to friends, she never intended to live in the South again. "It's perhaps good and necessary to get away physically for a while," she wrote Cecil Dawkins, "but this is by no means to escape it. I stayed away from the time I was 20 until I was 25 with the notion that the life of my writing depended on my staying away. I would certainly have persisted in that delusion had I not got very ill and had to come home. The best of my writing has been done here."[27]

It was characteristic of Flannery O'Connor to make a virtue of necessity, most obviously in her uncomplaining use of terrible illness to focus and purify her life as a writer. Unless she had transplanted herself to richer soil, however, she could hardly have found the nourishment and encouragement she needed. In Milledgeville *Gone with the Wind* was considered the height of literary achievement. There she would always have been Miss Regina's daughter, who *ought* to act like a lady and never say or write anything "ugly" or unconventional. Instead she spent three years at Iowa with demanding teachers and scores of other aspiring young writers who were prickly, competitive, deliberately unconventional. Acting pretty was no one's idea of virtue there.

The fierce young woman with the unfeminine name of Flannery O'Connor was quick to establish her place in the literary community of Iowa City, publishing "The Geranium" in *Accent* in 1946 and winning the Rinehart-Iowa Fiction Award for a first novel with *Wise Blood* the following year. The award carried with it a commitment to publication by Holt, Rinehart and made possible O'Connor's acceptance at Yaddo in 1948. By the time she left the writers' colony in 1949, she was well launched on the mainstream of contemporary literary life.

Through close friendship with Robert Lowell and Elizabeth Hardwick, whom she had met at Yaddo, she met Robert and Sally Fitzgerald when she moved to New York City. Unlike Eudora Welty she lived a solitary life in New York which she later described as enjoyable. "I liked riding the subways and the busses and all and there was a church on 107th and I got to Mass every day and was very much alone and liked it." However, other comments on her life there lead one to suspect that she was too shy and too accustomed to a settled small community to be comfortable in the bustle of a city like New York. "I didn't see much of the city when I stayed in New York . . . I didn't go to a single play or even to the Frick museum. I went to the Natural History Museum but didn't do anything the least cultural. The public library was much too much for me. I did well to get out and get a meal or two a day. I finally ended up eating at the Columbia University student cafeteria. I looked enough like a student to get by with it, and it was one of the few places I suspected the food of being clean."

When the Fitzgeralds offered her a room with them in rural Connecticut, she took it gladly and settled into what must have been a much more congenial sort of life in a domestic routine with fellow Catholics of similar literary interests. Either Robert or Sally went with Flannery to Mass early every morning, and then each retired to the day's work: Sally to care for the children, Flannery to her garage room to write, and Robert to his teaching at a nearby college. In the evening, Robert Fitzgerald remembers, "when the children had been fed and quieted for the night we would put a small pitcher of martinis to soak and call the boarder. Our talks then and at the dinner table were long and lighthearted, and they were our movies, our concerts, and our theatre."[28] O'Connor enjoyed this life for a year and a half and undoubtedly would have continued it if lupus had not stricken her as she traveled home for Christmas in 1950.

It is pointless to speculate on how Flannery O'Connor and Eudora Welty might have developed if they had settled permanently in the North, but we can be certain that by living away from the South for a time they became citizens of a much wider intellectual world which they never abandoned. McCullers's migration two years after her marriage was final, so her participation in that wider world is apparent in the physical location of her adult life. In fact she had many more opportunities than Welty and O'Connor, spending several sojourns at Yaddo and living for extended periods in New York City or in a Brooklyn ménage which included W. H. Auden, Richard Wright, Louis MacNeice, Klaus and Erika Mann, Benjamin Britten, Paul Bowles, and Gypsy Rose Lee. But at a deeper level McCullers's situation may not have been so very different from Welty's or O'Connor's. McCullers knew she could never get away from the South. "No matter what the politics, the degree or non-degree of liberalism in a Southern writer, he is still bound to this peculiar regionalism of language and voices and foliage and memory," she said.[29] It is ironic that she should have used the masculine pronoun for the writer because the attitude toward women was one of the most persistent influences of Southern life that bound her, as it did Eudora Welty and Flannery O'Connor. All three were permanently marked by their upbringing as Southern girls. Their departures from conventional notions of feminine charm and their deviation from proper destinies as wives and mothers would emerge as troubled issues in their fiction. Writing is, after all, an audacious profession in the sense that it is oracular and authoritarian, as Sandra Gilbert and Susan Gubar point out in *The Madwoman in the Attic*.[30] To set oneself up as a crafter of fiction in the great tradition requires a powerful conviction of one's gifts and rights. How could a person brought up to be soft and yielding, warm and self-sacrificing, dare to intrude herself upon the public mind? How could she presume?

The general problem for all women, which has been explained in its classic form by Virginia Woolf and more recently explored by Ellen Moers and by Gilbert and Gubar, is accentuated for Southern women by the traditions I have outlined in chapter 1. Welty, McCullers, and O'Connor did have the support of a positive maternal heritage to establish the concept of female strength, but for them its specific form was unacceptable. They did not want to become what their mothers were, and by going away to the North for advanced education, they had already distinguished themselves as different. But what could they do next? All of them were back in the South after their schooling, and the only established professional place for them was the schoolroom. None of them took it. McCullers laid the issue to rest in a public sense by marrying. Behind the acceptable facade of a young wife in Fayetteville, she could absorb herself in finishing a first novel. Who would know she wasn't baking bread or scrubbing the floor or ironing Reeves's shirts? Eudora Welty tried her hand at journalism and worked for the WPA. Those were interesting, unorthodox jobs, but once she had established herself as a writer she could give them up and devote herself completely to her craft.[31] However, Welty has an unusual confidence and an acceptance of her individual self which McCullers and O'Connor never found. For some reason she was able to be positive about the limited possibilities for feminine life in the South. Even though Carson McCullers moved to New York after the success of *The Heart Is a Lonely Hunter*, she was never able to project such a solution for her characters or to celebrate the kind of escape from gender which her own way of life implied. Flannery O'Connor is the most pessimistic of all three in the possibilities she suggests for educated Southern women like herself. In her fiction she portrays several young women who are intellectuals or teachers. One, in an early story, "The Crop," is a spinster writer in a little Southern town who writes wistful tales of love about rural folk and then is disgusted when she meets the vulgar reality in the street. Miss Willerton's fiction is only a sentimental projection of her own frustrated desire for affection. Joy-Hulga Hopewell of "Good Country People" is O'Connor's best-known unpleasant female intellectual, a large and hulking girl "whose constant outrage had obliterated every expression from her face." Her Ph.D. in philosophy has done her no good at all, for her bad heart and wooden leg doom her to a life with her mother on their farm. There is also the enraged, acne-faced Wellesley student who throws a book at Mrs. Turpin in "Revelation" and then tries to strangle her, and the elementary school principal Mary George in "The Enduring Chill," who wears Girl Scout shoes and is expert at sardonic remarks and insults. These are devastating portraits of resentful sterility, and there, but for the grace of God, goes Flannery O'Connor.[32]

Another way to look at these horrifying portraits is to see them as objectifications of the way conventional society ladies looked at young women like Welty and McCullers, as well as at Flannery O'Connor. A sensitive young woman not physically pretty and determined to be bookish might well have applied this kind of harsh description to herself. All three writers did portray people like themselves from conventional social perspectives, and it is important to realize how potentially devastating such images could be. To defend themselves, young women with literary ambitions needed the example of people like themselves. Like their Southern male contemporaries they found such examples in the best writers they could read. All of them read the Greek tragedians, Shakespeare, the nineteenth-century English novelists, the Russians, some of the French. And each had individual preferences which were important models and sources for her own writing. In Welty's case, mythology has been a lifelong passion. Jane Austen and Chekhov, Faulkner, Virginia Woolf, and E. M. Forster have also been especially important to her.[33] Her choices of books to review for the *New York Times* reveal other literary affinities: E. B. White, S. J. Perelman, Isak Dinesen, Patrick White, Elizabeth Bowen, Ross Macdonald, and Ford Madox Ford.[34] Carson McCullers said she was especially drawn to the Russians, Eugene O'Neill, Joyce, Proust, Nietzsche, and Dinesen. Her fiction also reveals the influence of D. H. Lawrence, Sherwood Anderson, Gertrude Stein, and Willa Cather.[35] Like Welty, Flannery O'Connor was an avid childhood reader of mythology. Writers who were especially important to her were Nathaniel Hawthorne, Faulkner, Nathanael West, Dostoevsky, Samuel Johnson, Teilhard de Chardin, Sophocles, Joyce, Kafka, Flaubert, Balzac, Conrad, and Poe.[36]

But there is a problem of persona involved here which cannot be overemphasized. The experience of reading these writers was predominantly masculine. Everyone can feel the effect of a tragedy, but while one experiences it, one lives in the mind of the hero. If he is Lear or Hamlet rather than Medea or Clytaemnestra (tainted portraits of women at that), one is living the experience as a male. A female reader lives the anguish of a *father* betrayed by *his* daughters or the *son* sick with loathing of *his* mother who posted with such dexterity to incestuous sheets. What happened to Lear's queen or Prospero's wife? How does Cordelia feel when her father disowns her for speaking the truth, and what are Ophelia's soliloquies in her private moments after her father's murder by the young man she loved? As Virginia Woolf put it, "It was strange to think that all the great women of fiction were, until Jane Austen's day, not only seen by the other sex, but seen only in relation to the other sex. And how small a part of a woman's life is that."[37]

American women who are serious readers grow up figuratively padding through James Fenimore Cooper's forests in Natty Bumppo's deerskin moccasins, or trying their sea legs on the decks of the *Pequod*, or sitting naked with Jim on a raft and drifting down the Mississippi while dreamily smoking a corncob pipe. Flannery O'Connor describes a long period of fascination with *The Humerous [sic] Tales of E. A. Poe*: "These were mighty humerous—one about a young man who was too vain to wear his glasses and consequently married his grandmother by accident; another about a fine figure of a man who in his room removed wooden arms, wooden legs, hairpiece, artificial teeth, voice box, etc., etc.; another about the inmates of a lunatic asylum who take over the establishment and run it to suit themselves."[38] Even if she laughed, O'Connor was inhabiting a male world when she read these stories, marrying a grandmother, taking apart a mechanical masculine body, perhaps even discovering with Poe that the greatest rapture came from observing the death of a beautiful woman.

The experience of reading amounts to a strange and potentially dangerous voyeurism. It is all very well to empathize with beings different from oneself; that is the very essence of fiction's value. But if the empathy is unbalanced, one's vision ends up skewed. When most of a person's imaginative experience occurs inside the minds of the opposite sex, every time she returns to the world of everyday life from the dream life of the printed page, she is like a tomboy forced to come in from play, clean up, and put on a dress. Women readers are the truest tomboys of all; every time they enter a fiction created by a man they enact an imperceptible, delicious trespass upon the other gender's territory. They could not achieve this feat so often or so easily if males and females did not share a majority of the same human terrain. How else could novelists like Charlotte Brontë and George Eliot and scores of others have successfully hidden behind male pseudonyms? But because different subjects and fields of action are conventionally supposed to interest the different sexes, the girl who reads about adventurous travels and heroic exploits is engaging in forbidden activities. She must have always felt some hidden guilt for this disobedience. Girls were emphatically *not* supposed to tiptoe through dangerous forests in the company of Indian men, or sleep in the smelly berth of a whaling ship with a tattooed Queequeg, or, worst of all, spend the day lolling naked on a raft with a black man.[39]

The effect of a serious immersion in literature for the mind of a sensitive young woman is ironic because it simultaneously liberates and cripples. She is liberated from her gender and admitted to membership in the wider masculine world, but on terms which condemn the female that her body dooms her to being in normal life. After every flight of fancy in the glorious company of Homer, Plato, Sophocles, Aeschylus, Chaucer, Shakespeare, Dostoevsky, Kafka, Joyce, and Faulkner, she is dumped back into the body she has been taught to despise as weak, the kitchen she has seen in fiction as petty, the company of women she has learned are irrelevant to the world of heroic action. She has formed her imagination through male conventions of misogyny, so that when she returns to herself, she is more deeply imprisoned than ever.

And what if she wants to be a writer? The anxiety of influence described by Harold Bloom as typical for males becomes a serious problem of identity for women writers. Gilbert and Gubar describe their problem in the Bloomian universe where sons fight an Oedipal battle to assert themselves against the overwhelming power of their literary fathers. In this drama the woman writer is "a freakish outsider."

> Not only do these precursors incarnate patriarchal authority . . . , they attempt to enclose her in definitions of her person and her potential which, by reducing her to extreme stereotypes (angel, monster), drastically conflict with her own sense of her self—that is, of her subjectivity, her autonomy, her creativity. On the one hand, therefore, the woman writer's male precursors symbolize authority; on the other hand, despite their authority, they fail to define the ways in which she experiences her own identity as a writer.

Two basic choices are available for the girl who begins to write seriously, as Carson Smith and Flannery O'Connor did in adolescence. She can deny or ignore her sex and write like a man, or she can seek women precursors who will authenticate her dedication to the art and show her the way to confront the great human questions as they appear in the lives of women. If she denies her femininity and accepts the masculine conventions of literary tradition, she will have access to the established arsenal of imagery, setting, and heroic motif which men have used to create the literary persona through combat and victory. But in writing with such traditional materials, she pays the grave price of living a psychological lie. Gilbert and Gubar elaborate:

> For though writers . . . do use masks and disguises in most of their work, though what Keats called "the poetical Character" in some sense has "no self" because it *is* so many selves, the continual use of male models inevitably involves the female artist in a dangerous form of psychological self-denial that goes far beyond the metaphysical selflessness Keats was contemplating. As Barrett Browning's Sand sonnets suggest, such self-denial may precipitate severe identity crises because the male impersonator begins to see herself as freakish—not wholesomely androgynous, but unhealthily hermaphroditic. In addition, such self-denial may become even more than self-destructive when the female author finds herself creating works of fiction that subordinate other women by perpetuating a morality that sanctifies or vilifies all women into submission.[40]

On the other hand, she can seek alternative precedents within or parallel to the main current of masculine tradition, which vindicate the importance of feminine experience. Then she will be imaginatively freed to affirm herself in the world of her fiction, to create characters who can place in the imaginary garden the real toads women have always known. The result is a truer fictional picture of the normal world. Bloom's Oedipal explanation of how the individual literary voice authenticates itself is just as incomplete as King's Freudian theory of the Southern Renaissance. Females have no place in either system except as objects of masculine attention. Gustave Flaubert was bold and even generous in seeking to explore the frustrated longings of a romantic young woman in Normandy, but if a woman had written *Madame Bovary*, Emma's frustrations might have sought other objects than men, other avenues of rebellion than romantic intrigue.[41]

Jane Eyre is a truer picture of a young woman's ambitions to have a wider life than the domestic one offered by a household in the provinces. When Jane arrives at Thornfield to begin her duties as governess, she appears to be the timid sort of woman perfectly adapted for narrow and humble circumstances. Charlotte Brontë reveals, however, that even she is agitated to a painful restlessness by restricted scope. Jane protests:

> It is in vain to say human beings ought to be satisfied with tranquility: they must have action; and they will make it if they cannot find it. Millions are condemned to a stiller doom than mine, and millions are in silent revolt against their lot. Nobody knows how many rebellions besides political rebellions ferment in the masses of life which people earth. Women are supposed to be very calm generally: but women feel just as men feel; they need exercise for their faculties, and a field for their efforts as much as their brothers do; they suffer from too rigid a restraint, too absolute a stagnation, precisely as men would suffer; and it is narrow-minded in their more privileged fellow-creatures to say that they ought to confine themselves to making puddings and knitting stockings, to playing on the piano and embroidering bags. It is thoughtless to condemn them, or laugh at them, if they seek to do more or learn more than custom has pronounced necessary for their sex.[42]

Virginia Woolf objected to this passage because she felt its vehemence upset narrative continuity and expressed too much of the author's personal bitterness,[43] but in fact it is perfectly in keeping with Jane Eyre's passionate character; she regularly explodes in the face of unjust restrictions and is always closely aware of her emotions and their causes. Brontë has made her heroine as clear-minded and honest as Emma Bovary is sentimental and self-deluding, but both of them are incurable romantics. Brontë simply sees the woman's problem in more inclusive, serious terms.

Charlotte Brontë freed the female literary character from male demands for exclusive attention, and women who wrote fiction after she had opened the door could look at Jane Eyre and see how to rebel against the expectations of the male world represented by Mr. Rochester. They too could figuratively set out across the moors alone with a maternal deity to guide their hazardous journey. Jane's reflections on the moor describe a lonely new kind of independence.

> Not a tie holds me to human society at this moment—not a charm or hope calls me where my fellow-creatures are—none that saw me would have a kind thought or a good wish for me. I have no relative but the universal mother, Nature: I will seek her breast and ask repose. . . .
>
> . . . Nature seemed to be benign and good; I thought she loved me, outcast as I was; and I, who from man could anticipate only mistrust, rejection, insult, clung to her with filial fondness. To-night, at least, I would be her guest, as I was her child: my mother would lodge me without money and without price.[44]

Though they did not strike out so completely alone, Eudora Welty, Carson McCullers, and Flannery O'Connor all found necessary support from the women's tradition of writing. Ellen Moers demonstrates that women writers have always depended on their own special literary heritage, but that the issue is not one of imitation or rivalry. "Each of these gifted writers [George Eliot, Elizabeth Barrett Browning, Emily Dickinson, the Brontës] had her distinctive style," she writes; "none imitated the others. But their sense of encountering in another woman's voice what they believed was the sound of their own is, I think, something special to literary women—perhaps their sense of the surrounding silence, or the deaf ears, with which women spoke before there was such an echo as women's literature."[45] All of our three Southern women responded to these kindred voices, not only in their reading but also through crucial relationships in their personal lives.

Welty has been a lifelong admirer of Jane Austen, and the kinship of the two writers is clear in Welty's brand of social comedy, but a writer of her own era played a more crucial role in her literary education. In her *Paris Review* interview she burst into a spontaneous tribute to Virginia Woolf, explaining:

> She was the one who opened the door. When I read *To the Lighthouse*, I felt, Heavens, *what is this?* I was so excited by the experience I couldn't sleep or eat. I've read it many times since, though more often these days I go back to her diary. Any day you open it to will be tragic, and yet all the marvelous things she says about her work, about working, leave you filled with joy that's stronger than your misery for her. Remember—"I'm not very far along, but I think I have my statues against the sky"? Isn't that beautiful?[46]

Some recent commentators have indicated Welty's debt to Woolf, but they have not adequately stressed how essential the precedent of *To the Lighthouse* was to Welty's method of dramatizing family life in *Delta Wedding*.[47] In *A Room of One's Own*, Woolf is actually describing her own accomplishment when she says that "the resources of the English language would be much put to the stretch, and whole flights of words would need to wing their way illegitimately into existence before a woman could say what happens when she goes into a room."[48] Because Virginia Woolf had learned how to say what happens when Mrs. Ramsay goes into a room, Eudora Welty could see how to celebrate Ellen Fairchild's life in the midst of her family.

A more tangible and more personal kind of help came from the older Southern writer Katherine Anne Porter, who saw Welty's early fiction, admired it, and adopted the young Mississippian as her protégée. Welty remembers her own shyness at the beginning.

> Of course, Katherine Anne Porter was wonderfully generous to me from the beginning. At the time I began sending my first stories to *The Southern Review*, she read them and wrote to me from Baton Rouge inviting me to come down to see her. It took me, I suppose, six months or a year to fully get up my nerve. Twice I got as far as Natchez and turned around and came back. But I finally did get there, and Katherine Anne couldn't have been more welcoming. Later on, she wrote the introduction to my first book of stories, and I owe her very much for that. We've been friends all these years.[49]

As we have seen, Carson McCullers's mother was her earliest admirer and lifelong support, but her closest literary friends seem to have been men; particularly Louis Untermeyer early in her career and later Tennessee Williams and Newton Arvin. During her first summer at Yaddo, she did make an infatuated attempt at friendship with Katherine Anne Porter, but it was firmly rejected. She began by following Porter around and making embarrassing declarations of love. One night, however, she went so far that Porter was forced to be blunt. McCullers pounded on the door of Porter's room, pleading, "Please, Katherine Anne, let me come in and talk with you—I do love you so much." Porter refused to open the door and told her to go away. But a little while later when she opened the door to go down to dinner, there was McCullers, lying across the threshold. Porter had had enough. "I merely stepped over her and continued on my way to dinner. And that was the last time she ever bothered me."

McCullers did have a few literary friendships with women such as Janet Flanner and Muriel Rukeyser, but on the whole she remained essentially a

tomboy, disporting herself at Yaddo, for instance, as one of the boys on
their tours of local bars. Male friends at Yaddo later recalled that she was
so much one of them that she saw women in the same terms they did, even
bragging that she could seduce them. She made a number of husbands
jealous.[50]

If she did not ally herself in life with literary women, she clearly depended upon them in her work. She never mentioned Willa Cather in her
references to writers important in her development, but we shall see in
later chapters that Cather's portrayal of an artistic girl's development in
The Song of the Lark was important in McCullers's creation of Mick Kelly
for *The Heart Is a Lonely Hunter.* Her debt to Isak Dinesen is more obvious
because she wrote two admiring reviews of Dinesen's work, describing in
one of them her first dazed absorption in *Out of Africa* on an automobile
trip in 1938.

> We started driving in the early afternoon and I was so dazed by the poetry
> and truth of this great book, that when night came I continued reading *Out of
> Africa* with a flashlight. I kept thinking that this beauty and this truth could
> not go on, but page after page I was more enchanted. At the end of the book,
> I knew that Isak Dinesen had written a great dirge of the Continent of Africa.
> I knew that sublime security that a great, great writer can give to a reader.
> With her simplicity and "unequalled nobility" I realized that this was one of
> the most radiant books of my life.

Later, when McCullers came to write *The Ballad of the Sad Café,* Dinesen's "The Monkey" would suggest important motifs to her, especially the
figure of a six-foot-tall Amazon. Eventually, in 1961, she met Dinesen at a
dinner of the American Academy of Arts and Letters and was surprised to
learn that the Danish writer admired her work and had requested to be
seated beside her. The two women took to each other, and McCullers
arranged a luncheon at her house so that Dinesen could realize her wish to
meet actress Marilyn Monroe. It was a brief encounter for McCullers—
Dinesen died a year later in Denmark—but the two writers had recognized a kinship.[51]

Flannery O'Connor seems to have been less willing to pay attention to
her gender than Welty or McCullers, and her education as a writer reveals
very little attention to the fiction of women. She did read the work of
other women, including Dinesen, George Eliot, Virginia Woolf, Djuna
Barnes, Katherine Mansfield, and her contemporaries in the South, Katherine Anne Porter, Eudora Welty, and Carson McCullers, but the writers whose fiction seems to have been most instructive were male. Those
she names specifically are Hawthorne, Flaubert, Balzac, and Kafka.

Robert Fitzgerald mentions her serious interest in three other writers whose influence is clear in her fiction: Nathanael West, William Faulkner, and Sophocles.[52]

In her personal life, however, the most direct single influence on her development as a writer was a woman. Through the Fitzgeralds she had begun a correspondence with Caroline Gordon very early in her career, and gradually the older woman became her mentor.[53] Although only a few of her letters to Gordon are published in *The Habit of Being*, again and again O'Connor writes to the Fitzgeralds or her anonymous friend "A" about rigorous practical suggestions Gordon has made for revising early versions of stories. And, finally, the most searching commentary on the meaning of her stories was stimulated by her younger friend "A," herself a writer and by O'Connor's frequent admission in letters to her, a very perceptive reader. The major literary comrades in her life, therefore, turn out to be women who supplied an essential sense of intellectual community.

It is hard to imagine how Eudora Welty or Carson McCullers or Flannery O'Connor could have achieved her own voice and developed her particular literary strengths without female allies. The kind of support was different for each woman, but it was directly relevant to her understanding of her vocation and appropriate to her sexual orientation. Virginia Woolf was doubtless a far profounder literary influence on Eudora Welty than Katherine Anne Porter was, for Porter was really primarily an encouraging older friend, as Elizabeth Bowen would also be later. But both Woolf and Porter shared with Welty a positive view of their sex and an apparent ease in writing about a world where feminine concerns were central. Carson McCullers, on the other hand, learned most of her important lessons from male writers but echoed Willa Cather and Gertrude Stein in her portraits of adolescent girls. These were two writers who, like McCullers, were troubled by questions of sexual identity in their own lives and their fictional treatment of the issue helped prepare the way for Mick Kelly and Frankie Addams. Isak Dinesen was the only woman writer to whom McCullers acknowledged a bond, and *The Ballad of the Sad Café* seems to have been in part a challenge to Dinesen's treatment of female independence in "The Monkey." Flannery O'Connor's intellectual life was sustained by correspondence with close women friends more than by anything else except her reading. Some of her correspondents were men, but those who engaged her fullest attention and to whom she wrote most frequently were women. Although she remained the leader in these exchanges and they come after the fact of her writing, she needed some realm where she could discuss ideas, her reading, and the issues and characters in her fiction. Caroline Gordon was more a coach than a model, a critic who helped O'Connor refine the mechanics of her craft. Gordon's sustained professional encouragement was essential in O'Connor's isolated life.

Welty, McCullers, and O'Connor did not know each other personally, though Welty and McCullers met at the Breadloaf writers' conference in 1940 and were at Yaddo together in 1941. Welty has politely expressed regret at not having had a chance to know McCullers then,[54] but they were so very different in character that it is hard to imagine much personal sympathy between them. Given McCullers's frustrated infatuation with Katherine Anne Porter, and her need to be the center of attention, we might even guess that jealousy could have prompted coldness toward Welty. Whatever circumstances prevented these three contemporaries from knowing each other personally, they were certainly aware of each other's work, but from a calculated distance, as if keeping separate were a special necessity. Welty is characteristically generous in her remarks about McCullers's and O'Connor's fiction; McCullers hinted broadly that O'Connor was derivative of her; and O'Connor praised Welty but said that she intensely disliked the work of McCullers.[55] Nevertheless, all three writers are Southern women inevitably marked by their region's paradoxical attitudes toward the lady, conscious of the views of the South expressed by the male writers of the Southern Renaissance, but supported by strong traditions of feminine moral influence and literary accomplishment. As a result their fiction shares certain preoccupations. Taken together, Welty, McCullers, and O'Connor show the mind and the life of the South from a new set of related perspectives. Contrary to Leslie Fiedler's charge twenty years ago that these women were merely "distaff Faulknerians" who corrupted a vigorous masculine impulse,[56] they fill in troublesome blank spaces of Faulkner's Southern world by presenting the interior life of its women, a life he was incapable of understanding. On the whole, Welty celebrates that life in all its variety, while McCullers and O'Connor challenge some of its traditional assumptions. All three raise central questions of human identity and dramatize the terrible costs of restricting it.

Chapter Three

The Enchanted Maternal Garden of *Delta Wedding*

The first version of what would become *Delta Wedding* gave only faint promise of its potential as a pastoral hymn of fertility. Eudora Welty has explained to interviewers how her agent Diarmuid Russell persuaded her to expand an early story. "I sent what I thought was a story in to Diarmuid called 'The Delta Cousins,' and he wrote back and said, 'Eudora, this is chapter two of a novel. Go on with it.' . . . And it never occurred to me that I could write a novel, but he spotted it. . . . So I just went on from there, and 'The Delta Cousins' became *Delta Wedding*."[1] Neither Russell nor Welty herself at that moment could have predicted exactly how the novel would shape itself, but it owes much of its development to the new possibilities suggested by Virginia Woolf's dramatization of family life centered on a mother's creative power.

Welty's first encounter with Woolf had produced a profound shock of recognition. Because of its bearing on *Delta Wedding*, her response is worth quoting again: "She was the one who opened the door. When I read *To the Lighthouse*, I felt, Heavens, *what is this?* I was so excited by the experience I couldn't sleep or eat." Women all over the United States wrote Woolf that they had never before found an author whose writings were so close to their own thoughts, but for Welty the kinship was one of vocation and craft as well as interior life. In a 1958 review of Woolf's posthumous *Granite and Rainbow*, Welty testifies to the qualities of mind which must have stimulated her own literary sensibility.

> That beautiful mind! That was the thing. Lucid, passionate, independent, acute, proudly and incessantly nourished, eccentric for honorable reasons, sensitive for every reason, it has marked us forever. Hers was a sensitivity beside which a Geiger counter is a child's toy made of a couple of tin cans and a rather common piece of string. Allow it its blind spots, for it could detect pure gold. In the presence of poetic fire, it sent out showers of sparks of its own. It was a mind like some marvelous enchanter's instrument that her beloved Elizabethans might have got rumor of and written poems about.

John Crowe Ransom was one of the first to recognize echoes of that marvelous sensitivity in *Delta Wedding*. He believed the resemblance to be fortuitous, but Welty's tributes to Woolf and her own practice in *Delta Wedding* imply a more direct link. [2]

Such influence should, however, not be misunderstood. Welty has frequently stressed the highly personal process involved in composing fiction.

> You don't start by saying, "These ingredients are to go in my novel: A, B, C, 1, 2, 3," and so on. It has to start from an internal feeling of your own and an experience of your own, and I think each reality like that has to find and build its own form. Another person's form doesn't, may not, even apply. I know it doesn't help in the act of writing because you're not thinking of anything but your story. You're not thinking, "How did Joyce do this?" That's fatal.

Nevertheless, she does acknowledge an affinity and a common heritage among writers. Speaking about the kinship of Southern writers, she says,

> I feel that we are all like bathers in the same sea. We all understand and know what we are partaking of. But I think we're each going about it in our own way. So far as I know we haven't had any definite effect on each other's work. There could be many unconscious effects; I read all the time, I love to read, and I live in books a lot. But as far as the act of writing goes, I have never felt the touch of any other imagination on mine as I write. I think that must be true of us all.

Welty goes on to explain that although Faulkner's work did not help her in specific technical ways, it did help her to see her Mississippi world in fuller terms. Thus she suggests that absorption in the work of other writers opens new perspectives, raises questions, and generally invigorates the imaginative life. But the process of absorbing literary experience, like the absorption of what Welty calls "actual happenings," is a subtle one which reshapes such materials as it integrates them into the writer's own imaginative life "because fiction amalgamates with all kinds of other things. When it comes out as fiction, it's been through a whole mill of interior life, you know."[3]

Welty learned many valuable lessons from other writers: the importance of mastering the delightful confusion of the family scene from Jane Austen, the great mystery of the particular and concrete from Chekhov, the relation of houses to human character from Faulkner, but they all went through her interior mill, just as her WPA experiences of Mississippi life did. What came out as fiction was her application of those lessons to the organic forms of her stories and novels. Just as her book reviews grow out of "a fellow feeling for fiction writers" in an attempt to get at what they were trying to do, our appreciation of her achievement should grow from a sympathetic understanding of the interplay between the fiction she loved to read and the stories she wrote.[4]

Ellen Moers assumes that a creative interdependence is critical for women writers. *Literary Women* presents striking evidence of such interrelationships in the nineteenth century, demonstrating the cheerful competition Jane Austen felt with the now-forgotten Mary Brunton over the theme of self-control, describing George Eliot's *Adam Bede* as a kind of lower-middle-class revision of Austen's *Emma*, and defending Emily Dickinson's "borrowings" from Elizabeth Barrett Browning's *Aurora Leigh* as complementary elaborations of themes in the original. Moers's point is, of course, that women writers provide for each other a complex imaginative validation of their experience which is lacking in the masculine literary tradition. While Welty resists such theories, her answer to a male interviewer's question of why there have been "so few really great women writers" is revealing.

> Well, I think there have been not a few great women writers, of course. Jane Austen. I don't see how anyone could have a greater scope than Jane Austen. Consider Virginia Woolf. The Brontës. Well, you know as many as I do: great women writers. I'm not interested in any kind of a feminine repartee. I don't *care* what sex people are when they write. I just want the result to be a good book. All that talk of women's lib doesn't apply *at all* to women writers. We've always been able to do what we've wished.

Clearly, the question aroused ambivalent feelings. First, in response to the questioner's condescension, Welty defends the achievements of women writers; then she backs away, dissociating herself from feminism. Yet all the writers she mentions are distinctively feminine in their treatment of theme, point of view, and setting.[5]

Virginia Woolf's feminism in particular is so central to her entire creative life that it is difficult to imagine Welty's failing to respond to it. As we
explore the elements of *To the Lighthouse* which reappear in *Delta Wedding*,
we shall begin to see how only another woman could have helped Welty
develop the celebration of distinctly feminine fertility and community
which existed merely as germs in "The Delta Cousins." In taking up
Woolf's themes of marriage and the maternal role from *To the Lighthouse*,
Eudora Welty was unconsciously agreeing with that novel's argument for
the central power of womanhood. The technical surprises which greeted
Welty in *To the Lighthouse* were available in similar form elsewhere, for
Woolf herself had been profoundly influenced by Proust and Joyce.[6] But
Woolf's deliberate differences from Joyce suggest why Eudora Welty
found her particularly compelling.

Virginia Woolf deliberately rejected the masculine tradition of a com-
prehensible central consciousness and the author's full access to characters'
minds. We see this as early as *Jacob's Room*, according to Jane Marcus, who
has pointed out a striking contrast in method between that book and
Joyce's *Portrait of the Artist as a Young Man*. Both novels rebel against the
nineteenth-century *Bildungsroman*, but Woolf's departure is far more radical. Joyce takes us into the subjective life of his developing artist and never
abandons Stephen's consciousness of self, which becomes an almost Byronic heroism by the end, despite the ironies which are intended to soften
it. In *Jacob's Room*, however, Woolf sees the whole heroic convention from
the outside—from the excluded female position—so that Jacob's male
mind is almost completely unknown. We come to know him chiefly as an
enigma, and our sense of him is delineated by the shapes around that
mystery. Our introduction to the subject of the novel begins with an older
brother's half-finished sentence, "Well, if Jacob doesn't want to play" and
his mother's question, "Where *is* that tiresome little boy?" We see him in
glimpses as a little boy, but from his mother's perspective, and we continue to catch fragmentary glimpses until we learn very indirectly and
from a great distance that he has been killed in the war. Through most of
the novel, the narrator is unsure, looking in on him from outside the rooms
in which he lives and works, and not daring to conjecture about his inner
life.[7]

Woolf felt just as much excluded from the masculine literary tradition as
she was in fact from the privileged schoolboy and university world where
her brother Thoby (the model for Jacob), her husband Leonard, and her
rival James Joyce absorbed that tradition. By now we know her work and
her life well enough to be certain that she purposefully created a literary
mode which would place women's experience in the center, denying the

masculine egotism she found so reprehensible in Joyce.[8] *Mrs. Dalloway*
serves in part as a counterstatement to *Ulysses*, presenting the female vision
of existence which Joyce failed to provide. Unlike Molly Bloom's male-
oriented soliloquy, Mrs. Dalloway's musings are centered on independent
feminine experience.

Although Woolf intended *To the Lighthouse* as an elegy for her father, that
novel is a far more positive tribute to her mother's beauty, maternal
creativity, and profoundly intuitive intelligence than it is to Leslie Stephen's slightly ridiculous abstract speculations or his masculine heroism.
Two-thirds of the novel's length is occupied by the opening section, which
centers on the figure of Mrs. Ramsay as she is seen from many points of
view, including that of her own subjective consciousness. Described as
both a life-giving fountain and "a rosy-flowered fruit tree laid with leaves
and dancing boughs," she is the creative support for the whole social world
of her extended family.[9] The long first section of the novel climaxes with
her public triumph in the ritual of the dinner party, symbolically celebrating the engagement of Paul Rayley and Minta Doyle which Mrs. Ramsay
has orchestrated. Even the final section, set after Mrs. Ramsay's death,
relies on her memory for its resolution in the successful landing of her
husband and children at the lighthouse and the simultaneous completion
of Lily Briscoe's painting.

In transforming "The Delta Cousins" from a short story about a nine-
year-old girl's sexual initiation into a hymn of feminine fertility, Welty
created a mother figure equal in sensitivity to Woolf's Mrs. Ramsay and
employed a similarly fragmented point of view to evoke the multiple dimensions of experience. As in *To the Lighthouse*, Welty renders the swirl of
family life in flashes, glimpses, fleeting moments, often in the life of children, for whose portrayal she has a special gift. Like Mrs. Ramsay, Ellen
Fairchild is the central figure unifying the family, notably in resolving a
crisis precipitated by her sister-in-law Robbie's angry challenge to family
solidarity. Most important in *Delta Wedding*, however, is the dramatization
of the wider network of family life around the central event of the wedding. Welty's novel unfolds almost entirely through feminine perspectives.
These seem to take their form naturally and unconsciously from the oldest
wedding story our culture has preserved with a feminine perspective—the
myth of Demeter and Kore, archetypal mother and daughter. Point of
view in the novel alternates between Ellen Fairchild and her many
daughters, both natural and surrogate. The story begins with nine-year-
old Laura McRaven's experience in journeying from her city home in Jackson to the plantation of her Fairchild cousins, where she will become a
surrogate daughter to her Aunt Ellen and seek complete acceptance in the

family. The perspective then shifts to Ellen as she comforts her motherless niece and broods over the coming marriage of her daughter Dabney. The interaction between Ellen and her various daughters continues to shift the novel's perspectives among women and girls as they reflect upon the human relationships of courtship, marriage, and family which are dramatized in the ritual events leading to Dabney's wedding. The end of the novel rounds out the opening symmetry, with Laura's final vision.[10]

Where men and women gazed and marveled at Mrs. Ramsay in *To the Lighthouse*, the women of *Delta Wedding* focus their adoring attention on a man, George Fairchild, who Ellen realizes has inherited his dead brother Denis's function as both hero and sacrificial beast for the whole family.[11] Two relative outsiders to the main family unit at Shellmound corroborate Ellen's musings, but in a spirit of defense, wishing to protect him from the pressure of such extravagant demands. Storing up her fiery love for her Uncle George, Laura wishes Shellmound would burn down so she could rescue him, "for she felt they all crowded him so, the cousins, rushed in on him so, they smiled at him too much, inviting him too much, daring him not to be faultless, and she would have liked to clear them away, give him room" (p. 76). George's estranged wife Robbie also fiercely strives to protect him.

> Only she could hold him against that grasp, that separating thrust of
> Fairchild love that would go on and on persuading him, comparing him,
> begging him, crowing over him, slighting him, proving to him, sparing him,
> comforting him, deceiving him, confessing and yielding to him, tormenting
> him . . . those smiling and not really mysterious ways of the Fairchilds. [pp.
> 148–49]

George is the beloved one, the epitome of family virtues, the vitalizer, protector, and hope for the future, but Robbie and Laura and Ellen are right in sensing his vulnerability. Viewed from outside by his demanding relatives, he is heroic, but within himself he is a mere mortal wounded by the horrors he encountered in the war, outside the pastoral haven of Shellmound. He must be sustained by women who understand him as a person, as Ellen and Laura do from a distance and Robbie does intimately and essentially as his wife. Robbie's defiant assertion, as she returns to him after angrily running away, is justified. "What if it was she who had run away? It was he who was lost, without her, a Fairchild man, lost at Shellmound" (p. 149). Ultimately George's dependence on Robbie and his relation to everyone else in the family is positive, cooperative, and complementary. Unlike Woolf's Mr. Ramsay, who demands sympathy from

women and takes it away with him to his lonely heroic outpost of intellectual struggle, George gives as much as he takes. He never intrudes upon
the integrity of others, but only intervenes occasionally to prevent genuine
danger. Dabney understands this as she watches her uncle allow a butterfly to flutter by his face without moving to frighten it, but her mother
knows more fully his respect for the world outside him. "Only George left
the world she knew as pure—in spite of his fierce energies, even heresies,
as he found it; still real, still bad, still fleeting and mysterious and hopelessly alluring to her" (p. 80).[12]

Delta Wedding shares with *To the Lighthouse* an appropriate setting for the
celebration of family life and fertility. Both novels take place in September
under a harvest moon, in a family sanctuary removed from the distractions
of public life. Welty has explained on several occasions that to emphasize
this kind of protected world she chose the year 1923 for her story, a year in
which no floods or wars or other external disturbances could intrude upon
the private community she wanted to explore.[13] Both Mrs. Ramsay and
Ellen Fairchild preside over a garden paradise where the youngest of their
eight children frolic and older children learn about courtship and marriage
which their mothers are engaged in promoting. Mrs. Ramsay subtly ma-
nipulates Paul Rayley's proposal to Minta Doyle and plans to lead other
"victims" to the marriage altar while her nubile daughter Prue basks won-
deringly in the glow surrounding Paul and Minta. Ellen Fairchild directs
the preparations for Dabney's wedding, strives to sympathize with the
unwelcome bridegroom, and provides necessary mediation in reconciling
George and Robbie.

Woolf's scene is a house in the Isle of Skye where the Ramsay family
customarily spend their September holiday, and most of the novel celebrates the festive atmosphere created by Mrs. Ramsay. But time, war, and
disease creep in unexpectedly to destroy most of Mrs. Ramsay's accom-
plishments by the end of the novel. She herself dies, her promising mathe-
matician son Andrew is killed in the war, her daughter Prue dies of pregnancy complications a few months after a brilliant wedding, and the
marriage of Paul Rayley and Minta Doyle quickly turns sour. Our return
to the house ten years later is a sad and chastened event attended by fewer
than half the number in the original boisterous congregation.

While Welty's plantation is surrounded by potential dangers and described with ironies which prevent the reader's complacent acceptance of
appearances, the essential affirmation of harvest in both vegetable and
human terms is never denied. Shellmound is a paradoxical place whose
name and topography imply some of its complex significance. Set in the
most fertile part of Mississippi, the rich river delta whose shape recalls

ancient motifs of female fertility, the plantation takes its name from an Indian mound in one of the cotton fields. Welty describes it through Dabney's eyes as she looks at the place where she first noticed the mysterious and slightly sinister overseer who would be her husband: "And she looked with joy, as if it marked the preeminent place, at the Indian mound topped with trees like a masted green boat on the cottony sea" (pp. 30–31). This fertile protuberance brings together the lovers whose wedding is the novel's consummation, but the mound itself is the remnant of a lost world.

Many critics have noticed that the shell reference in the mound's—and the plantation's—name suggests a certain protected, empty quality in the social world centered there, but history tells us more. Indian mounds like the one in the novel are a distinctive part of the Delta landscape, left behind in ceremonial groupings by the Middle Mississippian Indian civilization of mound builders. The inheritors of those ancient monuments, the Choctaws, call one of these mounds "The Great Mother" and regard it as the birthplace of their race. At the center of the mound, they say, the Great Spirit created the first Choctaws, who crawled through a hole or cave into the light of day. Welty's Shellmound may have been suggested by an actual place, a tiny community not far from Greenwood that was named for a nearby Indian mound with mussel shells on its top. Thus archaeology reveals a mythic tradition of female power in the actual landscape Welty adapted for her novel.[14]

Whether or not Welty knew about the Choctaw traditions associated with the mounds, she defined her Delta landscape in terms of another myth with obvious fertility emphasis. Dabney's suitor Troy, first associated with the mound rising from the fertile bottomland, is a threatening figure who on the social level is not considered a suitable husband and on a symbolic level is a rapacious intruder like the god of the underworld who ravished Demeter's daughter Kore, or Persephone.

Combining associations of fertility with the general sense of the shellmound as a remnant of a past culture, Welty is able to make a rich point about the revitalization of another outmoded way of life—the antebellum Southern tradition associated with Fairchild family legends. For all their charm, the family remain essentially childish because of their habit of retreating from trouble and mythologizing their past to make it pretty and comforting. Robbie, a lower-class outsider like Troy, knows that the world the Fairchilds have invented is unreal. With a hardheaded desire born of poverty, she wants honesty that will allow her "to touch the real, undeceiving world within the fairy Shellmound world to love George" (p. 149). Because her marriage with George is reaffirmed, we know that she and Troy will ultimately revitalize the outmoded "aristocratic" world of Shellmound plantation by their marriages into it.

Welty's interest in dramatizing a maternally sustained family may have been stimulated by Woolf's, but specific development of the general motif, as well as her use of similar narrative techniques and setting, is entirely her own. She had been exploring the possibilities of describing human fertility in mythic terms in the stories published together as *The Wide Net* in 1943, before she wrote *Delta Wedding*. The young hero of the title story undergoes a ritual baptism and meets the king of the snakes to make himself worthy of his pregnant wife, and both "Asphodel" and "Livvie" present Pan-like fertility figures who tingle with erotic energy and dance with feet like hooves around astonished women.[15] *Delta Wedding* continues this exploration, as *The Golden Apples* will do later. Specific echoes of *To the Lighthouse* in Welty's first novel show how imperceptibly the materials of Virginia Woolf's fiction must have sifted down into Welty's already richly developed imaginative life, to be absorbed and transformed in her description of the fertile Mississippi world she had already begun bringing to life in her short stories.

Some of these echoes begin in the realistic world but have reverberations in the mythic world that Welty now explores. Both novels contain scenes of motherly care for children. *To the Lighthouse* opens with Mrs. Ramsay measuring a stocking on her son's leg. "Stand still. Don't be tiresome," says Mrs. Ramsay to James (p. 45). While this event provides a long and central scene for Woolf's novel, there is only a fleeting reference to such fitting of clothes in *Delta Wedding*. It comes in a very different kind of situation but is similarly associated with the role of motherhood. Ellen Fairchild sees a mysterious girl in the bayou woods while she is looking for a lost pin, and the encounter becomes a mystic conjunction of archetypal mother and daughter by the end of the scene. The epiphany begins when Ellen commands the shy stranger to come out from her hiding place behind a tree; as the beautiful girl reveals herself, "a whole mystery of life" opens up for Ellen.

> *"Stand still," said Ellen.*
> *It was a thing she said habitually, often on her knees with pins in her mouth. . . .*
> She felt sometimes like a mother to the world, all that was on her! yet she had never felt a mother to a child this lovely. [p. 70, my emphasis]

Both Mrs. Ramsay and Ellen Fairchild are shown putting children to bed in the timeless maternal act of soothing and comforting. For Woolf, this event is only a minor coda to the climactic triumph of Mrs. Ramsay's dinner party. For Welty, however, Ellen's soothing Bluet to sleep emphasizes the themes of courtship and sexual initiation associated with a lost garnet pin, at the same time that it pays tribute to maternal solace. Ellen tells her small daughter the dream she has had about the pin her husband had given her during courtship.

> "Mama dreamed about a thing she lost long time ago before you were born. It was a little red breastpin, and she wanted to find it. Mama put on her beautiful gown and she went to see. She went to the woods by James's Bayou, and on and on. She came to a great big tree. . . . Hundreds of years old, never chopped down, that great big tree. And under the tree was sure enough that little breastpin. [pp. 64–65]

The dream is prophetic, for after Bluet has drifted into her nap her mother goes out into the woods and encounters the mysterious girl by such a tree. This Kore figure will prove to have an important symbolic connection with the lost pin.

Another clear echo of *To the Lighthouse* is Battle Fairchild's fondness for declaiming romantic poetry. But where Mr. Ramsay's recitations tend to be Byronic self-dramatizations, Battle's quotations from Tennyson and from his own brother Denis's sentimental pastorals are more often comic than heroic (pp. 9, 154–55). For instance, when Robbie interrupts dinner by her surprise return to Shellmound, Battle intones Denis's lines: "You shun me, Chloe, wild and shy, / As some stray fawn that seeks its mother / Through trackless woods." Although Battle may be using the poetry to divert attention from an embarrassing social situation, the poem also links Robbie symbolically to the mysterious wood nymph both Ellen and George have encountered that day. We shall see how that association functions in the rich mythological network which widens the meaning of realistic experiences in the novel.

Two symbolic details in Woolf which Welty uses far more systematically and richly to develop the theme of human fertility are the lost pin and bees. As we turn to an exclusive consideration of *Delta Wedding*, we shall look very closely at Welty's complex development of these motifs. For present purposes, we need only remember that in *To the Lighthouse* Minta Doyle loses a brooch which was an heirloom, and that she loses it on the beach when Paul Rayley proposes marriage to her. The brooch represents both female family tradition and Minta's virginity—jewels she loses by her alliance with a man. Bees are used in Woolf's novel to imply Mrs. Ramsay's queenliness, the hivelike refuge she creates around herself, and her fertility. At one point she is thought by Lily Briscoe to attract people as a hive does bees, and to have from a distance "an august shape; the shape of a dome" (pp. 79–80). Later, in tribute to his wife's triumph at the dinner party, Mr. Ramsay recites a poem which associates her with the fertile imagery of garden and bees. "Come out and climb the garden path,

Luriana Lurilee. / The China rose is all abloom and buzzing with the yellow bee" (p. 166). Similar associations cluster about Ellen Fairchild's lost garnet pin and carefully developed references to bees. When Welty uses these motifs, she weaves them as strong bright threads in a rich tapestry of ritual and myth celebrating the cycle of human fertility in harmony with the landscape.

More than thirty years ago, John Edward Hardy made a convincing case for the pastoral nature of *Delta Wedding*. We have seen how the novel shares with *To the Lighthouse* a harvest setting removed from the turmoil of urban life, and such places are much like the archetypal pastoral retreat. But Welty's novel stands more in the affirmative comic center of the pastoral convention which came down to us from the Renaissance. Part of the reason may be, as Hardy claims, that "the tradition of the Southern novel has been all but exclusively pastoral from the start," with its emphasis on a traditionally graceful bucolic life removed from the squalor of the industrial North. But Hardy goes on to argue that never before in Southern letters had there been "such fully *conscious* exploring of the implications of the mode as Welty's." It is hard to know how conscious this exploration really was, but Hardy is astute in referring readers to Renaissance sources for instructive parallels to the pastoral qualities of *Delta Wedding*—"its wit, its merging of realism and magic, its delicacy, its formal and elegiac ironies, its universal mythiness."[16] In Renaissance works such as Sidney's *Arcadia* and Shakespeare's great comedies and romances, we find the characteristic Renaissance use of classical fertility myth to represent the renewing and cleansing powers of the natural world. As David Young explains in *The Heart's Forest*, Shakespeare's pastoral plays dramatize a sojourn in an idealized natural setting which "usually entails some psychological adjustment in the characters, most frequently their fulfillment, even purification, through love."[17] Quite naturally, the usual tone of the pastoral is comic, and plot moves toward fulfillment of romantic love in the celebration of wedding. *A Midsummer Night's Dream*, *As You Like It*, and *The Tempest* all present the characteristic pastoral flight from corrupt court to enchanted natural retreat. There lovers endure confusion as an initiation but are finally united in triumphant ritual. Despite pastoral transformations, however, sojourners in the timeless world of ritual renewal must return to civilization to take up their lives in mundane reality, where time, pain, and death hold sway.

Whatever Welty's conscious awareness of Renaissance pastoralism may have been, these same patterns are at work in the charmed and protected world of Shellmound. Already we have noticed the dreamy impracticality of life among the Fairchilds which Robbie dislikes and resists. Hardy points out other important evidence of Welty's pastoral purposes in the description of Mary Lamar Mackey's interminable piano playing which transforms the house and its occupants into a forest realm. At a particularly excruciating moment of Robbie's surprise return to Shellmound, Mary Lamar begins to play, and we are told that "like the dropping of rain or the calling of a bird the notes came from another room, effortless and endless, isolated from them, yet near, and sweet like the guessed existence of mystery. It made the house like a nameless forest, wherein many little lives lived privately, each to its lyric pursuit and its shy protection" (p. 156).

The whole novel performs a similar transformation for its readers because it places some of the most painful dilemmas of intimate life in a setting which affirms the possibility of affection, cooperation, and renewal. *Delta Wedding* thus serves as a timeless garden where readers experience the pastoral sojourn. With nine-year-old Laura McRaven, who is chiefly conscious of her age and the loss of her mother, we enter the Delta, bearing a burdensome awareness of time and death. Through participation in the feminine rituals of hearth, meadow, wood, labyrinth, beehive, and sacred river, we will be initiated into the eternal cycles of fertility.

This progression is unusual in American literature. As R. W. B. Lewis, Leo Marx, and Leslie Fiedler have shown, the American pastoral motif places an innocent white man in an idyllic retreat with a dusky companion who introduces him into the secrets of the simple, natural life. Cooper's Deerslayer novels, Melville's *Moby-Dick*, and Mark Twain's *Huckleberry Finn* first established the pattern in our literary life which dominated the genre of the Western and continues to give shape to more recent serious fiction like Saul Bellow's *Henderson the Rain King* and Ken Kesey's *One Flew Over the Cuckoo's Nest*.[18] All these works and their countless offspring in popular culture deny the importance of women, express a longing for escape from the responsibilities of civilization, and pretend that the prototypical American hero is one who has thrown off the corruption of old European culture by rediscovering Eden in the New World and settling into permanent innocent bliss.

But this masculine dream was hopeless from its inception. The pastoral escape is always temporary and must be, for humans have been communal creatures for thousands of years. The European settlers, not all male by any means, brought the destructive machine into the New World garden when they arrived. The ringing of axes and the explosion of muskets spelled the doom of the garden, which had been primarily a figment of the European literary imagination in the first place. Leo Marx explains that our writers have been dimly conscious of this paradox, for symbols of industrial civilization have haunted the American pastoral from Hawthorne and Thoreau to the writers of our own time. However, few of these writers have seriously explored the relation of industrialism to the heroic impulses which they celebrate, impulses which in historical fact were exploitative. Annette Kolodny has documented the contradiction between the early settlers' identification of the landscape with the feminine and their aggressive seizure of the land for cultivation. In their own symbolic terms, the settlers committed a kind of rape which the American literary imagination has been reluctant to acknowledge.[19]

While most American fiction has pretended blindness to the ethics of Manifest Destiny, we have seen how Welty's fellow Mississippian William Faulkner confronted the defilement of the American garden and the mistreatment of its "native burghers," as Shakespeare called them. W. J. Cash and Lillian Smith could have seen a connection between Isaac McCaslin's conscience in "The Bear" and the gyneolatry they found in Southern culture. As we saw in chapter 1, the public worship of women intensified Southern men's private guilt over miscegenation and their disastrous over-cultivation of the land which they saw as feminine. This betrayal resulted in a strengthening of women's moral power over their men. Combined with the influence of "chivalry" and the historical necessity for women's self-reliance during the Civil War, that kind of strength created a hidden matriarchy behind the patriarchal Southern facade. This is the reality Eudora Welty portrays in *Delta Wedding*, but she does so in a positive way, by celebrating feminine power in harmony with the landscape and fully cooperative with men.[20] The world of Shellmound Plantation thus stands as an alternative to Faulkner's Mississippi by emphasizing the maternal center of family life within the pastoral mode.

To create this positive vision of traditional Mississippi life, Welty reaches back to our culture's deepest mythic sources to restore the pastoral's proper emphasis on fertility and renewal. In particular she draws from the myths of Demeter and Dionysos, deities whose complementary functions Sir James Frazer recognized by setting them side by side in *The Golden Bough*. Welty knew *The Golden Bough* as well as traditional versions of Greek and Roman, Norse, and Irish myths,[21] and her wide use of myth for fictional purposes is well known. In *Delta Wedding*, however, she exploited mythic sources which she could not have known were very closely interwoven in prehistoric cultures whose central religious preoccupation was the feminine fecundity of the landscape. Thus it seems that almost by instinct she fixed upon ancient symbolic patterns which once were central to a world view dominated by maternal powers in an idealized garden setting. Only in recent years have archaeologists and mythographers found evidence linking Demeter and Dionysos to Neolithic religion and revealing corresponding functions and powers which Frazer implied and which Welty makes central to the pastoral world of *Delta Wedding*.

The oldest recorded myth of feminine fertility and renewal is the Homeric Hymn to Demeter, which Welty knew in the romanticized nineteenth-century versions of her childhood books. It describes the abduction of Demeter's daughter Kore (Persephone) from a flowery meadow by Hades (Pluton/Plutos), god of the underworld. Demeter's grief, the aid of her sister goddess Hecate of the underworld, the punishment of all creation for the rape by the Great Mother's withholding of fertility, then finally its restoration on the return of Persephone—these events define "the most pervasive of all Greek divine tales," according to mythographer G. S. Kirk. The most powerful rituals of Greek religion—the Eleusinian Mysteries—were established by Demeter in the Homeric Hymn. Most scholars believe that the hymn serves to explain or justify a religious practice already in existence and of pre-Greek origins. Although the issue is still controversial, analysis of Mycenaean clay tablets in Linear B dating back to the same period as the remains at Eleusis makes Dionysos's pre-Greek origins and close associations with Demeter increasingly certain.[22]

In the worship of Dionysos, as well as in the Homeric Hymns, meadowlike dancing grounds were sacred places where circle-dances promoted fertility and associated maidens with growing plants. Deborah Dickmann Boedeker has shown that these sites are protected by mother goddesses, as in the Homeric Hymn "To Earth the Mother of All." The hymn sings of the great nourisher of all life and of her gift of "fruitful land"—ἄρουρα— a word often used metaphorically to denote woman as bearing seed and fruit. Those blessed by Mother Earth have children who are like the fruits of the soil. In particular, the hymn says that "their daughters in flower-laden bands play and skip merrily over the soft flowers of the field." This scene is much like the blissful meadow where Persephone and her maiden companions gathered flowers when Hades suddenly appeared; Boedeker demonstrates that such places were typical sites for rape in Greek myth and cult.[23]

These mythic backgrounds turn out to be very important for an understanding of Flannery O'Connor's farm stories, as well as for Eudora Welty's much more obviously related treatment of landscape and human fertility. For now, however, we should simply recognize the erotic feminine quality of the landscape in these traditions and remember its connection with the complementary deities Demeter and Dionysos, to see how Welty revives their symbolic force in *Delta Wedding*.

At the very beginning of the novel, the landscape is described as having a dreamy, fertile quality.

> The land was perfectly flat and level but it shimmered like the wing of a lighted dragonfly. It seemed strummed, as though it were an instrument and something had touched it. . . .
> In the Delta the sunsets were reddest light. The sun went down lopsided and wide as a rose on a stem in the west, and the west was a milk-white edge, like the foam of the sea. The sky, the field, the little track, and the bayou, over and over—all that had been bright or dark was now one color. From the warm window sill the endless fields glowed like a hearth in firelight. . . . [pp. 4–5]

Ellen Moers points to this vision of the Delta as the one clearly female landscape in Eudora Welty's fiction, similar in a general sense to other open, sweeping terrains in women's writing which she finds to be places of self-assertion. One of these is the moors of *Jane Eyre*, where, as we have seen, the heroine experiences a lonely independence under the guidance of a maternal deity. Moers identifies such terrains with the contours of women's bodies and suggests that ravines and springs or rivers are particularly erotic landmarks. It does not take a very large imaginative leap to move from Moers's open landscapes back to the meadow where Persephone played with her girlish companions and the open pastures where Maenads worshiped their god.[24] Moers's special contribution is her demonstration that women writers make a distinctive use of feminine topography, and I would argue that Eudora Welty presents her glowing, hearthlike Delta as an especially rich Southern locus for feminine assertion.

Traditionally the Southern lady asserted herself by demanding the protective indulgence of her men, and Welty includes a glimpse of that attitude in *Delta Wedding*. But much more seriously the novel supports the active movements of women through cotton fields and bayous rich with symbolic meaning. Aunt Tempe is the aging belle in the novel who makes the spoiled, essentially frivolous claims for her sex. "It was laziness on men's part, the difficulties that came up in this world. A paradise, in which men, sweating under their hats like field hands, chopped out difficulties like the green grass and made room for the ladies to flower out and flourish like cotton, floated vaguely in Tempe's mind, and she gave her head a little toss" (pp. 187–88). Tempe's Southern world is a Delta Eden where she and other ladies grow like the cotton under men's sweating husbandry.

Much closer to the independent feminine assertiveness described by Ellen Moers is Dabney's joyous early-morning ride on her new filly, the day before her wedding. Dabney tiptoes out before any of the family is awake, "into the early eastern light which already felt warm and lapping against her face and arms." The freshly awakened land seems to welcome the girl and her little horse.

> Flocks of birds flew up from the fields, the little filly went delightedly through the wet paths, breasting and breaking the dewy nets of spider webs. Opening morning-glories were turned like eyes on her pretty feet. The occasional fences smelled sweet, their darkened wood swollen with night dew like sap, and following her progress the bayou rustled within, ticked and cried. The sky was softly blue all over, the last rim of sunrise cloud melting into it like the foam on fresh milk. [p. 120]

As she rides across the fields to visit the beautiful old house where she and Troy will live after their marriage, she inwardly rebels against the traditional Southern value of sacrifice for "honor," vowing, "I will never give up anything."

On her way back home she makes a different kind of assertion, daring to look at the "creepy and scary" whirlpool in the thick bayou woods, scene of family legends about ghosts and drownings. Here once in childhood, she had seen her wild young uncles Denis and George emerge naked from swimming and interrupt a knife fight between two black boys. But on this day before her wedding, Dabney gazes into the whirlpool in a vertigo of sexual fascination. The whirlpool is an erotic feminine place into which she takes her last look as a virgin.

> She parted the thonged vines of the wild grapes, *thick as legs*, and looked in. There it was. She gazed feasting her fear on the dark, vaguely stirring water.
>
>   There were more eyes than hers here—frog eyes—snake eyes? She listened to the silence and then heard it stir, churn, churning in the early morning. She saw how the snakes were turning and moving in the water, passing across each other just below the surface, and now and then a head horridly sticking up. The vines and the cypress roots twisted and grew together on the shore and in the water more thickly than any roots should grow, gray and red, and some roots too *moved and floated like hair*. [p. 123, my emphasis][25]

The connection between water and sexuality is reinforced by Welty's description of Dabney after her honeymoon, lounging with her husband at a family picnic. "In catching sight of love she had seen both banks of a river and the river rushing between—she saw everything but the way down.

Even now, lying in Troy's bared arm like a drowned girl, she was timid of the element itself" (p. 245). The Yazoo River has similar symbolic associations for nine-year-old Laura.

The bayou woods around the whirlpool are a mysterious precinct where Ellen will meet the nameless girl in an encounter that widens out to connect the older and younger women as Demeter and Kore with the feminine meadow of the myth. Just before she meets the beautiful stranger, Ellen walks along enjoying the shady architecture of the noble old cypresses but thinking anxiously of the cotton fields outside and of the overseer who is to marry her daughter. Ellen "felt as if the cotton fields so solid to the sight had opened up and swallowed her daughter."

These associations are more fully developed in an earlier scene where Dabney, her nine-year-old sister India, and her cousin Laura encounter Troy as they ride horseback across Mound Field. Dabney thinks of this field as "the pre-eminent place" where she first noticed Troy a year before, and her association of him with dark and explosive forces helps us realize that this place is symbolically the preeminent meadow with its *omphalos*, or entrance to the underworld, where the earth yawned and Hades emerged to snatch Persephone from her innocent, flowery play. Now, just a few days before her wedding, Dabney sees Troy as a distant figure riding across her path on his black horse, his arm raised in greeting like a gun against the sky. She shuts her eyes and sees "a blinding light, or else it was a dark cloud—that intensity under her flickering lids." "She thought of him proudly (he was right back of the mound now, she knew), a dark thundercloud, his slowness rumbling and his laugh flickering through in bright flashes" (pp. 31–32). Welty knew that storm and earthquake, attributes of Zeus and Poseidon, could be associated with their brother Hades. Indeed, Hades was often called Zeus.[26]

If Troy Flavin's positive qualities can be stimulated, he, like Hades/Pluton, will become a source of new riches from the feminine earth. When Persephone returned from her underworld marriage, her mother welcomed her like a Maenad and the land burst forth in fruit. Something similar is possible with Troy, as Welty suggests when she has him appear with a womblike sack full of his mother's quilts which symbolize both the traditional feminine art of the mountain people from whom Troy descends and the fertility of the landscape which he and Dabney will imitate. As Troy displays the quilts and brags about his mother's skill, he declares his choice of one called Delectable Mountains to cover the marriage bed; "that's the one I aim for Dabney and me to sleep under most generally, warm *and* pretty." The sexual connotations of the bedroom landscape are not lost on Aunt Tempe, especially when Troy says Dabney should wait to thank his mother until she has tried the quilts. "That's what will count with Mammy. She might come if we have a baby, sure enough." By now, even the maiden aunts are beginning to quiver (p. 113).

Before Troy's embarrassingly candid hopes can be realized, however, the bride must be blessed by the keepers of matriarchal family traditions, and threats to the wedding must be removed by fertility rituals including a symbolic trip to the underworld which echoes the Eleusinian Mysteries. In order to trace the passage of these rituals, we must be familiar with the other major actors in the rites and their symbolic presence in *Delta Wedding*.

We have just seen how Welty associates Troy with the Hades or Pluton of the Persephone myth. While everyone knows his important role, few are aware of his connections with Dionysos. In fact, the abduction of Persephone in the Homeric Hymn occurs on the Nysan Plain, named after the sacred mountain of Dionysos's birth and perhaps even echoed in the second syllable of his name.[27] We have already seen how close Dionysos is to Demeter in ancient religious traditions, and he is associated with a character in Welty's novel who is in some ways parallel to Troy.

As John Allen has pointed out, one important Fairchild name is a traditional contraction of "Dionysos,"[28] and a moment's glance at references the adoring women of the family make to his wildness and his Maenad wife and daughter should reveal his mythic stature. Though he is dead, "it was Denis and always would be Denis that they gave the family honor to. . . . Denis was the one that looked like a Greek God, Denis who squandered away his life loving people too much, was too kind to his family, *was torn to pieces* by other people's misfortune, married beneath him, *threw himself away in drink*, got himself killed in the war" (my emphasis). If this is not enough to alert us, Tempe says, "These fields and woods are still full of Denis, full of Denis. If I were to set foot out there by myself, . . . I'd meet the spirit of Denis Fairchild first thing." Dabney responds to this comment about her dead uncle by looking over at his retarded daughter Maureen, who, "eyeing her, stuck out her tongue through her smiling and fruit-filled mouth" (pp. 116–17). Such a description is appropriate to the realistic level of action in the novel, but it also clearly links Maureen to the fertile Bacchic abandon associated with her father.

Denis's function has been taken over by his brother George, similarly adored by all the women in the family as both savior and sacrificial beast. In a moment of typically reckless bravery two weeks before the action of the novel begins, he has performed the part of St. George by defeating a "dragon" which threatened to kill Denis's heir—and, by implication, to violate some sacred family spirit. That dragon is also the intruding urban machine in the pastoral garden—the train which brings Laura from the city to attend the wedding but also kills the mysterious nymph Ellen met in the bayou woods, as it nearly killed George and Maureen on the trestle. George's saintly heroism and near self-sacrifice are ultimately secondary to the underlying Dionysian qualities which Allen has shown define his almost magical charm. His and Robbie's amorous play in the Yazoo River during a family picnic is one instance when these Bacchic qualities are displayed. George carries her dripping out of the river and flings her onto a bed of flowers and vines, where they lie smiling and twined together in the moonlight. As the family looks on, one of the children sprinkles them with handfuls of grass and pomegranate flowers (a plant sacred to both Hades and Dionysos) (p. 25). Later in the novel, George arrives to be reunited with his wife after their quarrel and separation, with shoulders bare "as a Greek god's, his hair on his forehead, as if he were intoxicated, unconscious of the leaf caught there, looking joyous" (p. 166).

On a symbolic level George is the appropriate consort for the central Demeter figure of Ellen Fairchild, whose name by coincidence or design recalls Helen, a Minoan tree-goddess closely associated with Dionysos in the Linear B tablets from Mycenaean Pylos and also related to Persephone. These relationships return us to the Eleusinian Mysteries, where Dionysos sometimes seems to be a consort of Mother Demeter, even identified by some scholars as Hades or Pluton himself. Similarly, Demeter and Persephone have been seen as dual aspects of the great goddess, with Hecate representing the third of her attributes.[29]

By now the mythic associations of *Delta Wedding* are undoubtedly beginning to seem very tangled. We must keep in mind the Protean nature of these old stories and also the fact that they only serve as suggestive references to establish a symbolic frame of meaning for the novel. Welty was not systematically adapting myths as James Joyce did in *Ulysses*, but she was, perhaps only half-consciously, reaching back through allusions to universal meanings which the rituals of her story embody. To understand the way these work themselves out in the overall movement of *Delta Wedding*, we must assume that there is a mythic dimension shadowing realistic events and occasionally intervening in them. In this mythic realm Ellen represents a Demeter who has many daughters (some who are only daughter-surrogates, such as her nieces Laura and Maureen, her sister-in-law Robbie, and the mysterious nymph she meets in the woods) and whose proper symbolic consort is George. As Michael Kreyling has pointed out, there are many important moments of sympathetic harmony between Ellen and George, without any suggestion of disloyalty to their mates.[30] At these moments, Ellen and George function as presiding deities over the family wedding preparations, representing the benign fertility of female and male.

George, however, is very closely parallel to Troy Flavin in realistic matrimonial terms. In this regard, George's separation from Robbie threatens to destroy Dabney's chance of happiness with Troy, as Ellen understands very well. George and Robbie had married earlier and on a realistic level similarly represent a potentially unfortunate union of an "aristocratic" Fairchild with a member of the lower class. A quarrel over George's foolhardy attempt to protect Maureen from the train has brought their marriage close to disaster. As promoter of wedding fertility, Ellen must somehow arrange their reconciliation if her own daughter Dabney is to have a chance with Troy. A series of preparatory rituals leads up to the climactic confrontation between Ellen and Robbie, who has returned to find her husband but is full of bitter resentment toward the Fairchild clan. Ellen faces Robbie's anger and restores her to George, thus removing the threat to Dabney's marriage and, in a larger sense, the danger to family unity. Then all that remains is a blessing of the bride and groom's house and an initiation to prepare Laura as a flower girl so that the wedding can proceed auspiciously.

The first ritual of preparation comes in effect at the hearth, the evening of Laura's arrival at Shellmound. Ellen takes her niece into the big plantation kitchen to help her bake a coconut cake whose recipe is a feminine family secret. While she works the ingredients together, Ellen worries about Dabney's happiness, but the act of combining sugar, butter, eggs, and flour in the proper order becomes a kind of sympathetic magic as she associates the cake with the memory of George's carrying Robbie dripping up from the Yazoo and flinging her on the bed of flowers in the moonlight. The cake will be an embodiment of the happiness George and Robbie symbolize as precursors for Dabney and Troy, but Ellen cannot be certain the recipe will work.

> As Ellen put in the nutmeg and the grated lemon rind she diligently assumed George's happiness, seeing it in the Fairchild aspects of exuberance and satiety; if it was unabashed, it was the best part true. But—adding the milk, the egg whites, the flour, carefully and alternately as Mashula's recipe said— she could be diligent and still not wholly sure—never wholly. [p. 26]

Later in the novel, a complementary magic cake will be needed to fulfill Ellen's hopes. That cake will be a black aphrodisiac patticake made by the Negro matriarch Partheny, and it will be tasted by Troy, Robbie, and the servant girl Pinchy who is "coming through" puberty to womanhood.

Dabney's visit to her maiden aunts Jim Allen and Primrose at the Grove, the original plantation house down on the river, is the next important ritual in the novel. Peggy Prenshaw has explained how these aunts serve as virginal priestesses of family tradition, passing down stories of matriarch Mary Shannon Fairchild to the children of the family and preserving feminine arts of cooking and sewing. They guard the sacred texts—Mashula Hines's cookbook and Mary Shannon's diary "full of things to make and the ways to set out cuttings and the proper times, along with all her troubles and provocations" as a pioneer wife in the tangled Mississippi wilderness of one hundred years past. The old house has an eternal coolness in summer; "like the air of a dense little velvet-green wood it touched your forehead with stillness." Outside, the shadowy Yazoo flows along a tangled bank shaded by cypresses, and the side yard is knee-deep in mint and flowers. Inside the house, two portraits of Mary Shannon look down at the "foolish, breakable little things" in the parlor. As Dabney leaves to return home, the aunts insist that she accept a precious heirloom from this immaculate museum as a wedding present: the little china night light that has comforted generations of Fairchilds in the dark. The little lamp holds mystery and family tradition which Welty associates in one of her essays with fiction itself.[31] In *Delta Wedding* this fiction is the family legends that tell of the heroic taming of the wilderness to create the plantation and then the gallantry and tragedy of the Civil War.

We have already seen that Ellen Fairchild's meeting with the strange girl on James's Bayou has far greater significance than a casual encounter. Ellen feels awed at the epiphany which seems to transform ordinary reality into an eternal religious moment. The meeting takes place on a bank in the dense bayou woods where the last remnants of an Indian tribe had burned their pottery just before their own extinction. To Ellen "it seemed an ancient place and for a moment the girl was not a trespasser but someone who lived in the woods, a dark creature not hiding, but waiting to be seen, careless on the pottery bank" (p. 70). Ellen tells the girl that she had been looking for the garnet pin she had lost, but as Ellen begins to represent "a mother to all the world" in the deepening mystery of the encounter, the lovely girl assumes the role of the eternal daughter, whose sexuality is symbolized by the rose-shaped garnet pin Battle had given Ellen during their courtship. In the mythic traditions of Demeter, the Kore figure is the maiden manifestation of the great goddess, and Hecate is the aged crone. Thus it is not really strange that the mysterious young woman can share the attributes of the mother when she asserts her freedom from Ellen's control. As the girl speaks, "a half-smile, sweet and incredibly maternal, passed over her face. It made what she said seem teasing and sad, final and familiar, like the advice a mother is bound to give her girls" (p. 71).

Later in the day we learn that this nameless Kore has somehow substituted for Ellen's daughters in bearing the consequences of the danger of rape and tragedy. In the evening Ellen confides to her brother-in-law about meeting the strange girl, and she is amazed to learn that George had met her too. George explains calmly, "I took her over to the old Argyle gin and slept with her, Ellen." Hurt and melancholy, sure now that George is miserable without Robbie, Ellen also realizes that George has saved the family from some obscure threat.

> She had feared for the whole family, somehow, at a time like this (being their mother, and the atmosphere heavy with the wedding and festivities hanging over their heads) when this girl, that was at first so ambiguous, and so lovely even to her all dull and tired—when she touched at their life, ran through their woods. She had not had a chance to face this fear before, for at the time she had had to cope with the runaway girl herself, who was only the age of her daughter Dabney, so she had believed. But at last she was standing quietly in the long twilight with George, bitterly glad (now it was certain: he was not happy) that he had been the one who had caught the girl, as if she had been thrown at them; for now was it not over? [p. 80]

After Dabney's wedding is successfully concluded, we learn with Ellen that "it" had not yet been over. The photographer who has come down from Memphis to take the wedding pictures reports, between flashes from his camera, that his train had hit and killed a girl. The photographer has captured her body on film, as he is now capturing the bridal party. For Ellen this is "a vision of fate; surely it was the young girl of the bayou woods that was the victim this man had seen" (p. 218). By sleeping with her, George had made her the Persephone who disappears into the world of death. If Shellmound were not a place where myth overlaps with ordinary experience, this sacrificial substitute could not have banished danger from Dabney's life.

The day after Ellen's meeting with the bayou maiden, Dabney's older sister Shelley, accompanied by India and Laura, conducts a symbolic trip into the underworld which restores another Kore figure to the world of light and sets the stage for the solution of George's problem and the most serious threat to Dabney's wedding. Shelley's ostensible mission is to do some shopping in town and visit old Partheny, who was midwife to Ellen during her first child's birth and who raised two generations of Fairchilds before she retired from duty. Partheny is a formidable old black woman of magic powers, and we should note that her name comes from the Greek word for virgin and suggests independent female fertility (parthenogenesis). Partheny functions as a Hecate figure dominating the female labyrinth. When we enter Brunswick-town, the black residential neighborhood, we seem to descend from the sunny road into a witches' cave, "into the abrupt shade of chinaberry trees and fig trees." The place is "dead quiet except for the long unsettled cries of hens" and the whirr of pigeons. It is populated only by old women during the day and filled with the smells of scalding water, feathers, iron pots, and darkness. "A devious, invisible vine of talk seemed to grow from shady porch to shady porch, though all the old women were hidden. The alleys went like tunnels under the chinaberry branches, and the pony cart rocked over their black roots" (p. 128).

Partheny reveals herself to her girlish visitors by stepping out from behind the screen of thick butter-bean vines that protects her little house from curious eyes. She is "taller than a man, flat, and narrow, the color of midnight-blue ink" (p. 128). At the end of their visit, with a look of malignity, pride, and authority, she gives Shelley a strange cake to take to George with orders to "tell him mind he eat it tonight at midnight, by himse'f, and go to bed. Got a little white dove blood in it, dove heart, blood of a snake—things. . . . his love won't have no res' till her come back to him" (p. 131).

Next the girls visit the graveyard and are introduced to the world of the dead by Charon-like Dr. Murdoch, who has assisted at all the family births and deaths. Like Brunswick-town, the cemetery is shielded from ordinary life by vegetation. Here quiet and fragrant gloom is created by a dense high wall of honeysuckle vines around the cemetery and big cedars and rosebushes inside among the graves. Laura is pierced by grief when she sees the new grave of her mother and remembers her lonely father back in Jackson. "She tried to see her father coming home from the office, . . . If she could not think of that, she was doomed; and she was doomed, for the memory was only a flicker, gone now" (p. 134). Life and death intermingle in this pastoral plantation world, as Laura suddenly realizes here among the remains of the dead, and she fears loss of her individual self in this timeless realm.

The final episode of the underworld journey is the visit to the Fairchild store, a treasure-house of family bounty whose gloom is filled with fertile smells and suggests the riches of Pluton.

> The air was a kind of radiant haze, which disappeared into a dim blue among hanging boots above—a fragrant store dust that looked like gold dust in the light from the screen door. Cracker dust and flour dust and brown-sugar

particles seemed to spangle the air the minute you stepped inside. . . . All
was warm and fragrant here. The cats smelled like ginger when you rubbed
their blond foreheads and clasped their fat yellow sides. Every counter smelled
different, from the ladylike smell of the dry-goods counter with its fussy
revolving ball of string, to the manlike smell of coffee where it was ground in
the back. There were areas of banana smell, medicine smell, rope and rubber
and nail smell, bread smell, peppermint-oil smell, smells of feed, shot, cheese,
tobacco, and chicory, and the smells of the old cane chairs creaking where
the old fellows slept. [p. 137]

Laura searches here for a present to give her Uncle George and declares,
"Nothing you have is good enough!" Little Pan-like Ranny cries, "Nine,
ten, a big fat hen!" and suddenly there is Robbie. Never mind that Robbie
is weeping and angry. She has been found, and she is the only gift good
enough for George. She is a missing Kore, whose restoration to her Dionysian husband will ensure a propitious union for Troy and Dabney. In
fact, just after the Fairchilds have left the store, Troy appears there and
gently persuades Robbie to go to Shellmound to find George. Troy will
even stop her along the way and give her a bite of Partheny's magic patticake that has been given him by India and that he has already tasted.
The charm begins to work, if only on a level of dramatic irony. As Troy
and Dabney move on across the cotton fields toward Shellmound, Troy
gives the patticake to Pinchy, who has been acting distracted, even crazed,
through the days of her "coming through." We must assume that Partheny's charm takes its effect on her too, because that evening there is a
chorus of cries from the servants, "Hallelujah! Hallelujah! Pinchy's come
through!"

Robbie's return to Shellmound is a dangerous event with its own ritual
overtones. She arrives angry, hot, and exhausted from her long midday
walk across the fields, and George is not even there to meet her. Instead of
finding any welcome, she stumbles into the family at dinner, and she lets a
bird into the house when she comes in. That is an omen of death, as all the
Fairchilds realize, jumping up from the table to chase it and leaving Ellen
to confront the aggrieved Robbie. The bird is a female brown thrush, like
Robbie a wild and shy creature, and her frantic beating against walls and
windows parallels Robbie's desperate struggles against entrapment in the
Fairchild clan. Both represent grave threats; if Robbie's anger cannot be
tamed, George's happiness will be destroyed, and the hope it embodies for
Dabney and Troy will be blasted. Ellen faces Robbie's accusations of Fairchild snobbishness towards her, tries to quiet her grief over her separation
from George, and then, when George appears in the door looking joyous
to see his wife again, Ellen charges him with having made Robbie suffer.

At that moment shouts from upstairs herald the bird's capture, and Ellen realizes that danger has been barely averted. "The Yellow Dog had not run down George and Maureen; Robbie had not stayed away too long; Battle had not driven Troy out of the Delta; no one realized Aunt Shannon was out of her mind; even Laura had not cried yet for her mother. For a little while it was a charmed life" (p. 166). Then Ellen faints in relief.

During the ensuing turmoil of wedding preparations and the very public reconciliation of George and Robbie, Laura and her cousin Roy slip away to visit Marmion. What follows is a dual ritual blessing the old place and symbolically initiating Roy and Laura into puberty. Marmion is a beautiful house, "an undulant tower with white wings at each side, like a hypnotized swamp butterfly," but it was blighted by tragedy just after it was built and thus has stood empty for more than thirty years. The evil spell is removed in a fertility ritual performed by another black matriarch, crotchety old Aunt Studney, who always carries a huge, mysterious sack believed by the Fairchild children to be the place babies come from. Laura and Roy come upon Aunt Studney going into the deserted house with her sack. The old woman stands in the middle of the tower room, hovering over her sack like a bird over an egg, while Roy runs round and round, up the spiral staircase of the tower, and Laura plays notes on a little "fairy" piano. All at once Aunt Studney makes "a cry high and threatening like the first note of a song at a ceremony, a wedding or a funeral, and like the bark of a dog too, somehow" (p. 176). Suddenly the place is alive with bees.

Carol Moore has argued that these bees mean bad luck, and that "one hasn't to look far to find these associations between bees and the pains of life, even death itself." Yet that interpretation is clearly at odds with the positive tone of description in this episode and with the fertile reference to a bumblebee who "with dragging polleny legs went smotheringly over the abelia bells" in Ellen's garden the day after the wedding (p. 225). Both butterfly and bee were sacred animals of the Neolithic mother goddess, representing life, fertility, and rebirth. In the classical period the bee is a symbol of the feminine potency of nature and is associated with Demeter and Persephone.[32] Positive attitudes towards bees, supported by these symbolic traditions, are everywhere in our culture. Even without knowing them, however, we can easily understand Welty's connection of bees with feminine fertility. Bees have always been known to have a highly organized community ruled by a powerful queen. They serve the pollenating office so necessary to the reproduction of flowers, and they make a food that has always been considered a pure sign of nature's bounty.

The tower room at Marmion, where bees seem to swarm from Aunt

Studney's womblike sack, is twice described in highly significant terms. On her solitary morning ride, Dabney gazes at her future house and imagines "the chandelier, chaliced, golden in light, like the stamen in the lily down-hanging" (p. 122). The flower image is picked up again in the scene where Aunt Studney performs her ritual. "Out of the tower's round light at the top, down by a chain that looked the size of a spider's thread, hung the chandelier with its flower-shaped head covered with clusters of soft and burned-down candles" (p. 175). Once we realize that the room itself is a kind of flower, we understand that Eudora Welty intended Aunt Studney's ritual to be a kind of pollenation that prepares for a new flowering of life in the old house.

Roy's excited spiral ascent of the tower has clearly sexual overtones. At the climactic moment when Aunt Studney makes her strange cry, Roy crows from the top of the tower, "Troy! Troy! Look where I am! . . . I see the whole creation. Look, look at me, Papa!" As if to mark his phallic achievement, a bee stings Roy at the nape of his neck. Then as he and Laura are leaving Marmion they share a discovery which unites them temporarily as young initiates in Aunt Studney's magic. "Catching the high sun in the deep grass, like a penny in the well, was a jewel. It might have been there a hundred years or a day. They looked at each other and with one accord dropped down together on the grass. Laura picked it up, for Roy, unaccountably, held back, and she washed it with spit" (p. 177).

Laura keeps this pin that looks like a rose, the very one her Aunt Ellen had been searching for when she met the beautiful girl in the bayou woods. Shaped like the flower traditionally identified with feminine beauty, the pin represents feminine sexuality even more obviously than the brooch Minta Doyle loses in *To the Lighthouse* when she agrees to marry Paul Rayley. It had been Battle Fairchild's courtship gift to the virginal Ellen, now appropriately rediscovered by her niece who is on the brink of puberty. Laura is not to have it long, however. During the boat ride back to Shellmound, Roy suddenly throws his cousin into the Yazoo River.

> As though Aunt Studney's sack had opened after all, like a whale's mouth, Laura opening her eyes head down saw its insides all around her—dark water and fearful fishes. A face flanked by receding arms looked at her under water—Roy's, a face strangely indignant and withdrawing. Then Roy's legs drove about her—she saw Roy's tied-up toe, knew his foot, and seized hold. [p. 178]

The boy pulls his cousin up by the hair, gets her back in the boat, and then explains that he "thought girls floated." "You sure don't know much," says Laura. Neither of them knows much about the rituals from which they have just emerged. Symbolically, however, they have been confronted by the mysteries of human fertility. Together the eight-year-old boy and the nine-year-old girl have attended at a pollenation ceremony, Roy supplying boyish phallic energy and Laura sounding the magic note on the little piano while Aunt Studney releases the bees. Together they have discovered the jeweled feminine talisman in the grass, and then Laura has been baptized in the River of Death which is also the womb of life reminding her of Aunt Studney's sack. In the process the garnet pin is lost again, this time in the fertile waters of the Yazoo. Laura's baptism is more than an introduction to this mysteriously erotic element. It cleanses the taint of her mother's recent death so that she can participate in Dabney's wedding without threatening its hopeful tone.

The wedding day dawns auspiciously after the rehearsal party the night before, where George and Robbie's dancing and kissing reunion has been the main event. All the bridal bouquets and shepherds' crooks and cakes and candies arrive fresh from Memphis on the train. Cars are washed out in the yard, cut flowers are collected from Ellen's garden, and the kitchen bustles with baking and the preparation of whole tubs of chicken salad. When the ceremonial hour approaches, both Negro matriarchs make their appearances, Aunt Studney enigmatically in the kitchen, and Partheny clothed in queenly purple outside Dabney's room, in time to array the bride. "She went straight and speaking to nobody to Dabney's closed door and flung it open. 'Git yourself here to me, child. Who dressin' you? Git out, Nothin',' and Roxie, Shelley, and Aunt Primrose all came backing out. The door slammed" (p. 210).

Little space is devoted to the wedding itself because, after all, weddings are almost anticlimactic culminations of the drama of preparation. We all know the basic ritual, so that Welty only needs to say, "Mr. Rondo married Dabney and Troy." What is important to notice is the visual symbolism of the bridal tableau, for it completes the pastoral implications that have hovered about the event from the beginning, as well as reminding us of the parallels with Hades's abduction of Persephone.[33] The bridesmaids all carry shepherds' crooks crowned with flowers, and the color of their dresses fades from American Beauty red at the two sides farthest from the bride to pale pink nearest her and pure white for Dabney herself. Into this dainty pastoral scene Troy, like the dangerous fiery god of the underworld, "came in from the side door, indeed like somebody walking in from the fields to marry Dabney. His hair flamed." The harvest moon rises on the dance after the wedding, and the bride and groom drift away into the mysterious night.

Between their departure and return to Shellmound, Welty describes the family's recovery from the festivities in terms that emphasize fertility and childbirth. The morning after the wedding Ellen rises ahead of the rest of her family to tend her thirsty and battered garden. Her attachment to her flowers recalls Mrs. Ramsay's similar concerns but also clearly links child-birth and family to the cultivation of her roses, petunias, dahlias, camel-lias, hyacinths, and abelias with their polleny bumblebees and butterflies and birds. "What would happen to everything if she were not here to watch it, she thought, not for the first time when a child was coming. Of all the things she would leave undone she hated leaving the garden un-tended—sometimes as much as leaving Bluet, or Battle" (p. 226).

Just after the wedding, Ellen had inadvertently gestured towards a fer-tile future for Dabney and Troy by recalling the birth of her own first child, Shelley. It had seemed almost parthenogenetic because Dr. Mur-doch had fallen victim to his new anaesthesia machine, and Partheny de-livered the baby. In a final emphasis on the theme of birth, Laura remem-bers a stocking doll her own mother had made her one summer day, a spontaneous gift from mother to daughter associated with the Delta (named "Marmion") and representing perhaps the secret of childbirth.[34]

Delta Wedding ends with a family picnic three days after the wedding, in which the whole extended family is reunited on the grounds of Marmion with the newly married couple, just back from their honeymoon in the exotic nether world of New Orleans. Persephone has been restored to her mother, and a new vitality stirs in the family. The Delta landscape is as magical this final night as it was in the opening pages of Laura's arriving vision. Here it forms the background for Ellen's musings on the eternal cycles of fertility and their relation to her own womanhood.

> The night insects all over the Delta were noisy; a kind of audible twinkling, like a lowly starlight, pervaded the night with a gregarious radiance.
>
> Ellen at Battle's side rode looking ahead, they were comfortable and silent, both, with their great weight, breathing a little heavily in a rhythm that brought them sometimes together. The repeating fields, the repeating cycles of season and her own life—there was something in the monotony itself that was beautiful, rewarding—perhaps to what was womanly within her. . . .
>
> They rolled on and on. It was endless. The wheels rolled, but nothing changed. Only the heartbeat played its little drum, skipped a beat, played again. [p. 240]

In this enchanted maternal world the individual is only a momentary pulse beat in the changeless rhythm.

Ellen has invited her niece to stay on at Shellmound as an adopted daughter, and at first Laura has agreed with delight. She has longed to be part of her Fairchild cousins' rich life. But we have seen her frightened realization in the cemetery that absorption in Shellmound would be a kind of doom, and she feels that "in the end she would go—go from all this, go back to her father" in Jackson. Her response must be ours as readers. Like Laura we must leave the pastoral garden and return to the modern urban world of work, time, and pain. At the picnic India shares a secret with her cousin: "I'm going to have another little brother before long, and his name shall be Denis Fairchild." Denis will be reborn, and with Laura we see that it has all happened before. The cycles of renewal so vividly performed in the pastoral world will continue to sustain hope when we return to ordinary human experience.

Chapter Four

Venturesome Daughters

L aura has the final word in *Delta Wedding*, claiming to know the destiny of a shooting star as it falls and opening her arms to the whole mystery of experience represented by the radiant night. This wide gesture marks her difference from everyone else at the picnic. When she rejects traditional plantation life to return to her father's world in Jackson, she makes the choice that many of the South's "New Women" would make. Jackson, Memphis, Birmingham, and Atlanta were then, as now, the centers of New South industry, open to modern technology and also to intellectual and cultural change from all over the world. Laura wants the contemporary milieu of such cities rather than the dreamy rural existence with its heart in the past. Her older cousin Shelley is similarly preparing to reject the old ways of her mother's life. Even Dabney refuses to behave as a traditional Southern lady, though she will spend her life at Shellmound. These young women are only a few of Eudora Welty's granddaughters of the Old South who have stepped out to assert their independence.

Welty is most explicit about Dabney's revolt in *Delta Wedding*, though she does clearly indicate that Shelley's life will be even more unconventional. On her way to visit her spinster aunts at the Grove, Dabney is half-aware of her need to break away.

Sometimes, Dabney was not so sure she was a Fairchild—sometimes she did not care, that was it. . . . Something, happiness—with Troy, but not necessarily, even the happiness of a fine day—seemed to leap away from identity as if it were an old skin, and that she was one of the Fairchilds was of no more need to her than the locust shells now hanging to the trees everywhere were to the singing locusts. [p. 33]

Traditional Fairchild life is a shell she has outgrown, and like the locusts who have left theirs on the trees, Dabney will break out to live in a new form nearby. She expects a similar change to come over Troy after their wedding. "He had not revealed very much to her yet. He would—that dark shouting rider would throw back the skin of this very time, of this moment. . . . There would be a whole other world, with other cotton, even" (p. 33).

This excited sense of her independent future causes Dabney to fidget during her visit with Jim Allen and Primrose, and to burst out with impertinent mischief when her aunts ask prim questions. At one point, as they all sit politely talking in the parlor, Dabney has a sudden urge to break all the little antiques around her. Then when Jim Allen asks who her bridesmaids are, she answers, "Those fast girls I run around with. The ones that dance all night barefooted" (p. 43). On leaving, she makes a final naughty effort to shock her aunts, by saying loudly, "I hope I have a baby right away" (p. 48). When she arrives back at Shellmound, Dabney unconsciously abandons the heritage embodied in the china night light which her aunts have tried to pass on to her.[1] Dismounting, she sees Troy's silhouette in a lighted window and runs impetuously towards the house. The little night light falls and smashes on the ground. Only days later, at the rehearsal dinner, does Dabney stop to regret what she has done. Shelley understands that "it seemed so unavoidable to Dabney, that was why she cried, as if she had felt it was part of her being married that this cherished little bit of other people's lives should be shattered now" (p. 193).

Regret will not alter Dabney's vow to live her own way, rejecting the antebellum myths of glory which generations of aunts have preserved at the Grove. In the thoughts Welty gives Dabney on her solitary morning ride to Marmion, she insistently counters Southern heroic male ideas, the kind Faulkner memorialized in his fiction when he dramatized his own great-grandfather's death at the hands of a former business partner. Dabney's grandfather suffered a somewhat similar fate.

Marmion had been empty since the same year it was completed, 1890—when its owner and builder, her grandfather James Fairchild, was killed in the duel he fought with Old Ronald McBane, and his wife Laura Allen died broken-hearted very soon, leaving two poor Civil War-widowed sisters to bring up the eight children. . . . Honor, honor, honor, the aunts drummed into their ears, . . . To give up your life because you thought that much of your *cotton*—where was love, even, in that? *Other* people's cotton. Fine glory! Dabney would not have done it. [p. 120]

Once Dabney marries Troy, his more homespun practical integrity will replace the feudal code which governed "aristocratic" Fairchild behavior.[2]

Dabney shares a special kinship with her Uncle George because, as we have seen, both their marriages are problematic alliances with lower-class people of the sort Faulkner dramatized in his Snopes novels. The rise of the poor whites in Southern life may have seemed to some a tragic destruction of the aristocratic order by vulgar opportunists. In Welty's comic vision, however, people like Robbie and Troy in *Delta Wedding*, Bonnie Dee Peacock in *The Ponder Heart*, and Fay Chisom in *The Optimist's Daughter* bring with them a candid vitality that is sorely needed.[3] Robbie's bluntness offends great-aunts Mac and Shannon, as well as snobbish Tempe, but Ellen Fairchild appreciates Robbie's directness and knows she satisfies George as no one else could. At the end of *Delta Wedding*, George speaks of returning from his city life in Memphis to live at the Grove. He and Troy plan to introduce new farming methods and crops to the plantation, modernizing its activities and moving away from old-fashioned reliance on cotton. This stirring of fresh energy is matched by Robbie's determination to confront the portraits of matriarch Mary Shannon and replace her as the central female authority in the old house. Thus the novel ends with the Grove as well as Marmion about to be opened up, refurbished, and inhabited by vital young people with fresh ideas.

Meanwhile, Shelley Fairchild is off to Europe with Aunt Tempe, leaving the Delta far behind—at least temporarily. There have been numerous previous hints that she is not going to settle into domesticity, even to the extent that impatient Robbie and Dabney do.[4] Shelley has been a tomboy, but at the same time she finds herself frightened of walking the railroad trestle with her brothers and sisters the day the Yellow Dog nearly kills George and Maureen. Emotionally cautious and serious, Shelley holds herself aloof, watching and analyzing the actors in the family drama. A passage from her diary reveals her perceptive understanding of Dabney, Troy, George, Robbie, and her father and mother. Remembering the episode of the train almost running down George and Maureen fills her with terror, because she alone of all the family understands how deeply George and Robbie wounded each other that day.

While most Fairchilds cheerfully ignore trouble, Shelley takes it se-

riously. One night in particular, she blunders into an understanding of
violence and pain which most of her family never sees. Because Troy is
late for the rehearsal dinner, Shelley is sent to fetch him. She bursts into
his office to find him sitting in a starched white suit facing a tense group of
field hands who have been fighting. Three of the men are wounded, and
the fourth menaces Troy with an ice pick. Shelley has always known that
Troy's job as overseer was to put trouble down when it erupted among the
Negro plantation workers, but she has only the typically vague feminine
sense of what this means. His ability to control masculine violence is close
to George and Battle's mysterious knowledge of the rage which bubbles
under the graceful surface of Southern life. It is an often bloody reality,
most closely associated with Negroes, from which the men protect the
matriarchal plantation world. Shelley stands frozen in its midst and
watches Troy calmly shoot the man who had been ready to throw the pick
at him. We learn that the fight Troy has stopped had a sexual cause—
Pinchy. "Pinchy cause *trouble* comin' through," says one of the blacks to
another as they carry the wounded Root M'Hook out of the door. Shelley
must jump over blood on the doorsill in order to get out of the office and
back to the safety of the big house.

She has been introduced to the dark, bloody side of life which Dabney
will never know, even as Troy's wife. Surprisingly, Shelley's main reaction
is not fear. She stays icily calm through the fight, and then, as she runs
home along the bayou, she feels anger welling up.

> Suppose the behavior of all *men* were actually no more than this—imitation of
> other men. But it had previously occurred to her that Troy was trying to
> imitate her father. (Suppose her *father* imitated . . . oh, not he!) Then all men
> could not know any too well what they were doing. Everybody always said
> George was a second Denis.
>
> She felt again, but differently, that men were no better than little chil-
> dren. . . . Women, she was glad to think, did know a *little* better—though
> everything they knew they would have to keep to themselves . . . oh, forever!
> [p. 196]

Shelley's rejection of the masculine code of honor has different sources,
different terms, than Dabney's, but she deplores its violence just the same.
As John Edward Hardy remarks, both sisters realize that white men's
"tolerance for the blood of Negroes is an essential part of their maleness."[5]
Although she sides with the feminine values of peace and life as Dabney
does, however, Shelley realizes at bedtime the night of this unpleasant
revelation that the existence of violence and horror cannot be ignored.
"There was a whirr and a clawing at the window screen back of the light.

A big beetle, a horned one, was trying to get in. All at once Shelley was sickeningly afraid of life, life itself, afraid *for* life. . . . She turned out the light, fell on her bed, and the beating and scratching ceased" (p. 197).

After the wedding, Shelley dances with George and ponders her future. The cavorting movement of her uncle's body transmits a sense of the excitement awaiting her, though she realizes "she might not be happy either, wholly, and she would live in waiting, sometimes in terror." Dabney's marriage has a finality that separates the sisters' fates. Shelley's thoughts flee from contemplation of Dabney's life with Troy, "to an open place— not from one room to another room with its door, but to an opening wood, with weather—with change, beauty" (p. 220). Whereas Dabney's world will be one of domestic enclosures, Shelley's will be outside in wilder terrains. Indeed, Shelley's contemplative nature, love of books, and habit of writing may well turn her eventually into someone like Eudora Welty herself.

Young cousin Laura will treasure the understanding of tradition which she gained at Shellmound, but she will never really be part of the old-fashioned bucolic world there. She is a creature of the modern world who is precociously aware of the need to balance traditional community with independence. When the children are playing "Go in and out the Window" in Ellen's garden, Laura thinks, "It was funny how sometimes you wanted to be in a circle and then you wanted out of it in a rush" (p. 73). Her status as a family visitor to Shellmound allows her to do both, the novel following her progress into the circle for acceptance and participation in the wedding ceremony, and then out of it again as she prepares to go back to her father in Jackson.

Delta Wedding has been the primary focus of our attention to Eudora Welty because it is more centrally concerned with feminine identity than any of her other major fiction. While it does suggest a new spirit of assertiveness in the lives of Southern women, however, most of its emphasis is on the traditional domestic sphere of women's lives. Welty's next book, *The Golden Apples*, takes a much closer look at rebellion against that limited scene of action through the character of Virgie Rainey. Even more sexually emancipated than Faulkner's Caddy Compson or her daughter Quentin, Virgie is almost perversely independent. Ruth Vande Kieft identified the key images of plaid and the hummingbird for understanding Virgie's character years ago in her admirable study of Welty's fiction.[6] Virgie's mother proudly acknowledges her daughter's love of "struggling against a real hard plaid" when she sews. This habit reveals Virgie's pleasure in turning rigid conventional patterns into organic shapes that will fit the curves of her body. The other telling image is that of the hummingbird, that exotic, quicksilver little creature who hovers in one place only long enough to sip the sweetness from bright flowers. The tiny bird is associated with a number of characters in the stories, as Vande Kieft explains, but its darting pursuit of sensuousness is particularly close to Virgie's restless behavior.

Virgie's name refers to her self-reliance rather than to chastity. She is a virgin in her freedom from male control, for her sexual adventures never compromise her. Like Dionysian King MacLain and his son Ran, Virgie radiates an erotic force almost synonymous with life itself. She begins to understand this at her mother's funeral when she senses that she and Ran are uniquely passionate people in the roomful of mourners. A similar sense of alliance comes when old King makes a hideous face at her over the buffet table and then suddenly makes her feel refreshed by cracking a little bone to extract its marrow. Father and son are as keenly hungry for the marrow of life as Virgie is. King and Virgie particularly refuse to be tied by convention, but because Virgie is female, her rebellion is more radical. Like Caddy Compson, she asserts her natural right to ignore the double standard and express her sexuality outside of marriage.

Welty does not react to such frank eroticism with the horror Faulkner expresses through Quentin Compson's anguish or Jason's contempt. Indeed, throughout her fiction she champions women's free choice of lovers and their essential sexual wholeness. This inviolability is most clearly seen in her presentation of rape. Ellen Fairchild accepts her brother-in-law's dalliance with the bayou girl, and we have seen that the encounter seems to work ultimately as a charm against danger. In "At the Landing" Jenny Lockhart is raped first by Billy Floyd and later repeatedly by the fishermen at the landing when she goes out in search of the elusive Floyd. The story implies that she is finding the fulfillment she lacked while living with her genteel grandfather. Virgie Rainey's piano teacher, Miss Eckhart, in *The Golden Apples* refuses to be humiliated by a black man's attack on her at night when she was walking alone. The townspeople would have liked her to move away in shame rather than simply go on with her life as if nothing had happened, but she seems to see her problem as nothing more than a temporary indisposition. King MacLain's predatory habits are known all over Morgana, but Welty presents them comically, as in the case of Mattie Will Sojourner, whose husband is outwitted and left behind while King prances off through the woods with his wife. Most critics excuse these antics as analogous to Zeus's seduction of mortal maidens, and one of Welty's chapter titles, "A Shower of Gold," makes this association clear. Nevertheless, on a realistic level King is an incorrigible philanderer who deserts his gentle wife Snowdie. In most of these instances, rape appears to be a natural, if sometimes inconvenient, sexual encounter from which women, like slightly annoyed hens, pick themselves up, shake their feathers, and go on about their business. The roosters strut away to further conquests.

As upholders of conventional morality, respectable town women in Welty's fiction would like to believe the myth of ladylike purity, but they do not strongly condemn irregular behavior. Nevertheless, Virgie's flagrant disregard for propriety is harder for them to ignore than King MacLain's because she does not spend most of her time out of town as he does. On one particular occasion, Virgie parades her defiance in their genteel faces. She has not sought any confrontation, but she is thrown into it by the accident of being flushed with her half-naked lover from the deserted MacLain house by fire. Virgie and her young man run out the front door of the house into a virtual wall of astonished feminine rectitude—a troop of ladies making their stately progress down the street after their regular Rook party. The sailor boy, wearing only his pants, is chided by a chorus of ladies, "Why, Kewpie Moffitt!" and runs away in shame down the street. But shame has no place in Virgie's life. "Look at that!" one lady cries, "I see you, Virgie Rainey!" Virgie simply stalks down the sidewalk calmly clicking her high heels "as if nothing had happened in the past or behind her, as if she were free, whatever else she might be" (p. 325). The ladies watch in a sudden hush, clutching their parasols. They must content themselves with gossip and the notion that Virgie is simply an eccentric. Thus they do not like to allow her knowledge of domestic arts during the preparation for her mother's funeral.

> Virgie went back once more to the kitchen, but again the women stopped what they were doing and looked at her as though something—not only today—should prevent her from knowing at all how to cook—the thing they knew. She went to the stove, took a fork, and turned over a piece or two of the chicken, to see Missie Spights look at her with eyes wide in a kind of wonder and belligerence.[7]

Virgie insists by this action that she is as normal a woman as the others, despite her independence of marriage.

Sexual autonomy as a central necessity of Virgie's life is paralleled by her similar freedom from any serious professional commitment. Miss Eckhart had patiently nurtured the wild girl's musical gifts in hopes that she would someday become a great performer, but Virgie had persistently resisted the pressure in small acts of rebellion, finally refusing to be constrained by her teacher's beloved metronome. When Virgie discontinued her music lessons in high school and began steady work playing the piano in the town movie house, she lost her special gift. Perhaps only Miss Eckhart's kind of obsessive dedication would have allowed Virgie to develop her talent. Cassie Morrison stands as an instructive contrast to Virgie because she pursues a serious musical career only to end up a spinster music teacher like Miss Eckhart.

Virgie's refusal to commit herself leaves only one bond in her life—her loyalty to her mother. After a brief absence from Morgana in her late teens, Virgie settles down to life with her mother, working steadily but only mechanically for a lumber company which ironically is destroying the woods that symbolize the natural energies motivating her. She continues to satisfy her physical needs outside of marriage with various men, one of whom often leaves a tribute of freshly shot quail on her doorstep. Her mother accepts her wayward daughter's habits, only fretting every afternoon that she will not get home in time to milk the cows. "It's a wonder, though," Mrs. Rainey marvels when her daughter comes home each day on time. "A blessed wonder to see the child mind" (p. 430). Virgie would not show such consideration to anyone but her mother.

When Katie Rainey dies, Virgie must come to terms with the loss of the only person who had a just claim upon her life. The daughter performs a ritual the evening of the death which releases her from the bonds of obligation to her mother but simultaneously reaffirms her essential connection to wider natural powers.

> She stood on the willow bank. It was bright as mid-afternoon in the openness of the water, quiet and peaceful. She took off her clothes and let herself into the river.
>
> She saw her waist disappear into reflectionless water; it was like walking into sky, some impurity of skies. All was one warmth, air, water, and her own body. All seemed one weight, one matter—until as she put down her head and closed her eyes and the light slipped under her lids, she felt this matter a translucent one, the river, herself, the sky all vessels which the sun filled. She began to swim in the river, forcing it gently, as she would wish for gentleness to her body. Her breasts around which she felt the water curving were as sensitive at that moment as the tips of wings must feel to birds, or antennae to insects. *She felt the sand, grains intricate as little cogged wheels, minute shells of old seas, and the many dark ribbons of grass and mud touch her and leave her, like suggestions and withdrawals of some ancient bondage that might have been dear, now dismembering and losing itself.* She moved but like a cloud in skies, aware but only of the nebulous edges of her feeling and the vanishing opacity of her will, the carelessness for the water of the river through which her body had already passed as well as for what was ahead. [pp. 439–40, my emphasis]

This peaceful and delicious baptism frees her from her mother's life but merges her own being with the harmony of nature, dissolving her stubborn will in the flow of the timeless river. "She was very beautiful," Welty has said, "she was kin to the earth and the sky and all that."[8] Now she is prepared for the funeral she must endure the next day.

When the funeral is over and she has gone to bed, Virgie is disturbed by an apparition which reveals how the maternal qualities of nature are related to the restless yearnings she once expressed in music. She has known that the incoherent pain of her mother's cows calling to be milked is similar to the need she relieved by playing the piano. Through the long years of life with her mother, she has taken some comfort in using her talented fingers for milking these kindred female beasts. The night after her mother's funeral, Virgie is roused from bed by a pounding on the porch floor outside. Trembling, she goes to the door in her nightgown and finds an old country woman with a night-blooming cereus to give her. The strange old crone has appeared out of the night to present an erotic feminine flower as a tribute to Virgie's former beauty and her music. The flower acts as an image to connect Virgie's music to the feminine yearnings she senses in the cows. "Virgie looked at the naked, luminous, complicated flower, large and pale as a face on the dark porch. For a moment she felt more afraid than she had coming to the door" (p. 453).

Virgie's fear persists after the old woman has disappeared into the darkness, but even as she throws the troubling flower down into the weeds, she has a vision of her daughterly connection with the river and the maternal moon.

> She knew that now at the river, where she had been before on moonlit nights in autumn, drunken and sleepless, mist lay on the water and filled the trees, and from the eyes to the moon would be a cone, a long silent horn, of white light. It was a connection visible as the hair is in air, between the self and the moon, to make the self feel the child, a daughter far, far back. [p. 454]

This vision, made possible by the gift of the night flower, helps us to fully understand Virgie's evening swim the day before as her reintegration into a harmonious, supporting feminine nature.[9]

The final scene of *The Golden Apples* attempts a reconciliation of opposites, but it is not conclusive. A gentle rain falls on the MacLain cemetery and the surrounding world, very similar to the snow falling everywhere at the end of James Joyce's "The Dead," as Albert Devlin has remarked.[10] Welty's rain seems to be related to a new modesty which will allow Virgie to live the rest of her life in a kind of harmony with the opposing forces represented by the intolerable demands of Miss Eckhart on the one hand and the natural world on the other. Virgie has always been driven by natural forces similar to those motivating King MacLain, and thus she has thought she hated the grim German spinster who so longed to transmit her musical vocation to her gifted pupil. Now in the rain Virgie understands the significance of Miss Eckhart's picture of Perseus and Medusa.

> Miss Eckhart, whom Virgie had not, after all, hated—had come near to loving, for she had taken Miss Eckhart's hate, and then her love, extracted them, the thorn and then the overflow—had hung the picture on the wall for herself. She had absorbed the hero and the victim and then, stoutly, could sit down to the piano with all Beethoven ahead of her. With her hate, with her love, and with the small gnawing feelings that ate them, she offered Virgie her Beethoven. She offered, offered, offered—and when Virgie was young, in the strange wisdom of youth that is accepting of more than is given, she had accepted *the* Beethoven, as with the dragon's blood. That was the gift she had touched with her fingers that had drifted and left her. [p. 460]

At the end of *The Golden Apples* Virgie has confronted and finally understood her past. She is a self-styled exile, freed by her mother's death, sharing her temporary shelter from the rain with an old black beggar woman in this final scene. These two feminine outcasts hear a message which affirms their relation to wild and fabled creatures. "They heard through falling rain the running of the horse and bear, the stroke of the leopard, the dragon's crusty slither, and the glimmer and the trumpet of the swan" (p. 461).

The Golden Apples offers no firm evidence about what Virgie's life will become after her mother's death, but it will probably continue to be uncommitted and searching. In one final close portrait of independent feminine life, Welty examines the fate of a woman from another small Mississippi town who has committed herself to her art and thus does not suffer Virgie's restlessness. That woman is Laurel Hand in *The Optimist's Daughter*, and she shares much with her creator. Recently Welty has commented on the close relationship between the two books. "One may have led to the other. Virgie and Laurel were such different people, backgrounds and everything, but they were doing the same thing" in coming to terms with their memories at the end of their stories.[11]

The Optimist's Daughter reiterates many familiar themes from *Delta Wedding* and *The Golden Apples*, especially in its emphasis on family gatherings for important rituals such as weddings and funerals, in the motif of the brash and determined lower-class women who capture beloved males of

prominent families, and in the emphasis on the abandoning of old traditions in favor of new trends represented by suburban housing tracts and
interstate highways. Most important for our purposes among all these familiar materials is the troubled relationship between mother and daughter
whose resolution is essential for the main character's knowledge of herself,
as it was in *The Golden Apples.* Virgie Rainey could not finally face the past
and silence its claims until her bondage to her mother had been dissolved,
and similarly Laurel Hand is forced by her father's death and the antics of
his abrasive new wife Fay Chisom to reevaluate the bitter disappointment
of her dying mother Becky. Only then does she face the grief of her own
buried past and free herself to return to her independent life as a fashion
designer in Chicago, leaving the old family house and possessions behind
with Fay in Mount Salus, Mississippi.

In some ways *The Optimist's Daughter* seems to have served for Eudora
Welty a purpose similar to the one John Griffin Jones described for Laurel's final recovery and release of the breadboard that contains her "whole
solid past." Welty agreed with Jones's comment that when Laurel leaves
the breadboard with Fay, "she is making a commitment through memory
to her future, she is able to live on without being drowned by memory."[12]
Just as Virgie Rainey put her mother's spirit to rest on the evening of her
swim and Miss Eckhart's memory to rest that afternoon in the rain, Laurel
Hand makes peace with her mother's ghost in *The Optimist's Daughter.*

What precipitates Laurel's encounter with her mother's accusing spirit
is the shock of her stepmother's vulgar scene at her father's funeral. Ironically, Fay makes a spectacular protest against death that reveals a daughterly bond with fat old Mrs. Chisom, who has arrived unexpectedly from
Texas in a trailer with the whole unruly Chisom clan for the funeral. Fay
had earlier lied about her own family, claiming that they were all dead and
that she would never have abandoned her aging parents as Laurel did, for
what Fay calls selfish reasons of ambition. Yet that is exactly what Fay had
done in leaving Texas to make her fortune as a typist in Mississippi. She
defied her mother to make a new life for herself, but, *in extremis* at the
funeral of her elderly husband, she acts as her mother would. She stalks
into the parlor full of mourners where Judge McKelva lies on display in a
pink satin-lined coffin. Glistening in black satin and high heels herself,
Fay runs toward the coffin but is caught up short by her mother's voice.

> "She's wasting no time, she's fixing to break aloose right now," said Mrs.
> Chisom. "Didn't even stop to speak to me."
> Fay cried out, and looked around.
> Sis stood up, enormous, and said, "Here I am, Wanda Fay. Cry on
> me.". . .
> "Get back!—Who told *them* to come?" cried Fay.[13]

Fay turns her back on her mother and cries to the dead judge, "O, hon, get up, get out of there. . . ."

> "Can't you hear me, hon?" called Fay.
> "She's cracking," said Mrs. Chisom. "Just like me. Poor little Wanda Fay."
> "Oh, Judge, how could you be so unfair to me?" Fay cried, ... "Oh, Judge, how could you go off and leave me this way? Why did you want to treat me so unfair?"

Genteel old family friends try to calm Fay, but she breaks wildly away and throws herself at the coffin, "driving her lips without aim against the face under hers." One of the judge's contemporaries, an imposing old matriarch, drags Fay screaming out of the room, while Mrs. Chisom's voice comes through the confusion, "Like mother, like daughter. Though when I had to give up her dad, they couldn't hold me half so easy. I tore up the whole house, I did" (p. 103).

Although the vital bond between Fay and her poor-white family is affirmed by this behavior, Fay does not intend to lose her independence by allowing the Texas Chisoms to turn her fine old McKelva house into a boardinghouse and move in with her, as they suggest. Instead, she tells them she wants to return with them to Texas for a reunion with her brother DeWitt. Thus turned aside from migration, all the Chisoms head back west after the funeral. Laurel is left alone in the old family house with her memories for the last time.

That night she confronts the unresolved anguish of her past in the tiny sewing room where she has sought refuge from a chimney swift trapped in the house. Some critics suggest that this sign of ill-fortune, like the brown thrush in *Delta Wedding*, is analogous to the lower-class wife of the family's beloved man.[14] Another possibility is that the bird represents the dangerous forces of memory unleashed in Laurel's mind by the funeral day's events. In any case, Laurel finds many mementos of her parents' lives in the little room, and the past floods back. Chiefly she remembers her mother's life in the West Virginia mountains—"up home" where Becky had taken her many childhood summers to visit her grandmother. Welty has said that all this West Virginia material is autobiographical, so that we might guess that writing the novel allowed her to recover and evaluate some of her own past through Laurel Hand. She explained to John Griffin Jones:

> To me memory is terribly important, a source and a force, too. If you've ever tried to go back and recall *all* of something—you may not be old enough yet— but you do realize that there're things back there you had no idea were still there. The more you try to remember, the more comes up. . . . Writing does

the same thing, it brings your past to the surface. I don't often put really straight autobiographical things in my work, but when I wrote *The Optimist's Daughter*, all that part about West Virginia was true.[15]

Laurel thinks back to cozy scenes with her mother in the sewing room which must be close to Eudora Welty's own experience. "Firelight and warmth—that was what her memory gave her." She thinks of where her baby bed used to stand and pictures her mother sitting at the old treadle sewing machine.

> When her mother—or, at her rare, appointed times, the sewing woman—sat here in her chair pedalling and whirring, Laurel sat on this floor and put together the fallen scraps of cloth into stars, flowers, birds, people, or whatever she liked to call them, lining them up, spacing them out, making them into patterns, families, on the sweet-smelling matting, with the shine of firelight, or the summer light, moving over mother and child and what they both were making. [p. 159]

From this idyllic picture of mother and daughter, Laurel moves back to images of summer "up home" in one of those wide, sweeping vistas Ellen Moers finds to be typical landscapes of feminine assertion.

> Bird dogs went streaking through the upslanted pasture through the sweet long grass that swept them as high as their noses. While it was still day on top of the mountain, the light still warm on the cheek, the valley was dyed blue under them. While one of "the boys" was coming up, his white shirt would shine for a long time almost without moving in her sight, like Venus in the sky of Mount Salus, while grandmother, mother, and little girl sat, outlasting the light, waiting for him to climb home. [p. 165]

Welty explained to Jan Nordby Gretlund that this was a scene from her own early childhood. "The way my uncles looked coming home at night through the far-off fields, just white shirts showing down the mountain. . . . I still recall this, and I just put it all in there."[16]

Laurel's memory fixes upon her grandmother's pigeons, who taught her a terrible truth about human dependency. As a small girl she had seen the birds, "sticking their beaks down each other's throats, gagging each other, eating out of each other's craws, swallowing down all over again what had been swallowed before: they were taking turns." Even as a child, Laurel understood the relevance of this scene for human relationships. "Parents and children take turns back and forth, changing places, protecting and protesting each other: so it seemed to the child." Thus as a grieving middle-aged adult, Laurel is led to realize the necessary pain of loss when this reciprocal dependency is dissolved by death.[17] Laurel's own mother had cried uncontrollably when she learned of her mother's death up in the West Virginia mountains. When Becky herself came to die, she began bitterly accusing her husband of not being able to sustain her. The pigeons might have taken turns protecting and protesting each other, but against the onslaught of death their human analogues were helpless. "Why do you persist in letting them hurt me?" Laurel's mother would demand during her five years of pain and blindness. Suddenly Laurel realizes that her own husband Phil might have similarly protested. This understanding comes to her because she is able to evaluate her memories of the relations between her grandmother, her mother, and herself. She finds crumbling old letters from her grandmother to her mother and sees a similarity between her mother's rebellion and independence from the grandmother's world and her own choice of an independent life in Chicago, far from the family home in Mississippi: "Widowed, her health failing, lonely and sometimes bedridden, Grandma wrote these letters to her young, venturesome, defiant, happily married daughter as to an exile, without ever allowing herself to put it into so many words" (p. 180).

The final message in the letters is the key to Laurel's epiphany. "I will try to send Laurel a cup of sugar for her birthday. Though if I can find a way to do it, I would like to send her one of my pigeons. It would eat from her hand, if she would let it." The grandmother understands her granddaughter's fastidiousness about human commitments and wishes to involve her in the grotesque give-and-take of close human involvement illustrated by the pigeons' feeding off each other.[18] Laurel understands the point in a flash, which brings back with terrible urgency the desperate need of her husband for his unlived life.

> A flood of feeling descended on Laurel. She let the papers slide from her hand and the books from her knees, and put her head down on the open lid of the desk and wept in grief for love and for the dead. She lay there with all that was adamant in her yielding to this night, yielding at last. Now all she had found had found her. The deepest spring in her heart had uncovered itself, and it began to flow again.
> *If Phil could have lived—*
> But Phil was lost. Nothing of their life together remained except in her own memory; love was sealed away into its perfection and had remained there.
> *If Phil had lived—* [p. 181]

After all the years of independent widowhood, the perfection of this memory is shattered. "Now, by her own hands, the past had been raised up, and *he* looked at her, Phil himself—here waiting, all the time, Lazarus. He looked at her out of eyes wild with the craving for his unlived life, with mouth open like a funnel's." Through her mother's grief, Laurel has reached her own.

> "Laurel! Laurel! Laurel!" Phil's voice cried.
> She wept for what happened to life.
> "I wanted it!" Phil cried. His voice rose with the wind in the night and
> went around the house and around the house. It became a roar. "I wanted it!"
> [p. 181]

Laurel faces again the raw anguish of her most intimate grief and must accept that it can never be assuaged.

The next morning, however, she has absorbed this truth, and she prepares to return to her life in Chicago. Through the agency of the breadboard, she finally frees herself of her past, leaving it behind with Fay, who has absolutely no comprehension of its meaning. The finely crafted board is a repository of memory because Phil had made it as a special gift for Laurel's mother and Becky had used it for kneading her excellent bread. Two kinds of loving craft, masculine carpentry and feminine baking, are united in the object which has stood years of affectionate family service. Insensitive Fay, who seems to have no domestic skills, has defaced the board by her primitive method of cracking nuts on it with a hammer. When Fay disputes Laurel's right to take the breadboard away with her from Mount Salus, the clash of their attitudes toward the past reveals a crucial difference in their abilities to live in the present.

Both Fay and Laurel may have defied their mothers' expectations by venturing forth to lives far from the family home, but Laurel never denied her mother's values or the nourishing traditions of the past. Fay, in contrast, never admitted the existence of her family until the whole brood of Chisoms turned up unexpectedly for Judge McKelva's funeral. Her reaction to seeing her mother and sister is less than hospitable, and her trip back to Texas with them is more a method of ensuring their departure than an expression of affection. Once she is back in Mount Salus again after her three-day visit, she seems to have completely forgotten her family. "The past isn't a thing to me," she declares to Laurel. "I belong to the future, didn't you know that?"

Welty explained to John Griffin Jones that such an attitude afflicts its bearers. "If they had memory it would've taught them something about the present. They have nothing to draw on. They don't understand their own experience."[19] In the novel Laurel sees that Fay "was without any powers of passion or imagination in herself and had no way to see it or reach it in the other person. Other people, inside their lives, might as well be invisible to her" (p. 206).

Laurel's time in Mount Salus has brought her memories back with a painful acuity which helps her to understand not only her dead parents and husband, but even her grasping, vindictive stepmother. She realizes, as Fay denies the value of the past, that memory "will come back in its wounds from across the world, like Phil, calling us by our names and demanding its rightful tears." The surrender of grief brings understanding and peace. Thus Laurel can forgive Fay, lay the breadboard "down on the table *where it belonged*" (my emphasis), and relinquish her claim to the objects which belonged to her past. Her confrontation with Fay has taught her that memory "lived not in initial possession but in the freed hands, pardoned and freed, and in the heart that can empty but fill again, in the patterns restored by dreams" (pp. 207–208).[20] Laurel's old friends urge her to give up her job in Chicago and return to live out her life with them in the old familiar setting, taking her mother's place in their bridge game, but she knows that she does not belong in Mount Salus. She has long ago established a solid independent life for herself in the North by building on the patterns of value her parents transmitted to her in childhood. Perhaps these are symbolized by the one object she takes away with her—a little stone boat carved "up home" by her father when he was courting her mother. From the very stone of Becky's beloved place, he carved a symbol of movement which their daughter takes away to another life built on the living foundation of memory.

Chapter Five

Tomboys and Revolting Femininity

Memory plays very little part in the lives of Carson McCullers's heroines, and they live in a world practically devoid of traditional Southern femininity. They are contemporaries of Virgie Rainey and Laurel Hand, yet they inhabit a flat present bereft of myth, history, or even family traditions. Surrounded by the tawdry everyday life of modern Southern towns, they seem to exist in a void, alienated from the few models of femininity available to them. The only warmth provided by women comes from Negro cooks. Mick Kelly's mother rarely appears in *The Heart Is a Lonely Hunter*, and then only to issue impatient or dispirited orders about Mick's baby-sitting chores or the management of the family's boardinghouse. She is a scarcely believable stick figure by comparison with the vivid presence of Portia. The cook's vigorous and compassionate views of the world provide the only adult guidance for Mick and her little brothers, yet Portia is more like a practical older sister or aunt for Mick than a mother. The real maternal figure in the novel is the androgynous cafe keeper Biff Brannon, but Mick shies away from his solicitations. In *The Ballad of the Sad Café* Miss Amelia Evans has been raised motherless and has lost even her father long before the action of the novella begins. Frankie Addams of *The Member of the Wedding* knows her mother only as a timid and sad-looking picture shut up under the hand-kerchiefs in her father's bureau drawer. Berenice the cook is the wise black mammy figure who has raised the motherless child, but her race prohibits Frankie from following her example as a woman. Without mothers, these feminine protagonists define themselves most comfortably in masculine terms. The crisis for each of them comes as social pressures force them to abandon masculine independence and accept a feminine identity in-creasingly fraught with anxiety as McCullers progresses in her exploration of the problem from novel to novel.

Anne Goodwyn Jones has described the relation between the absence of mother figures and ambivalence about feminine identity in Southern women's writing from 1859 to 1936. Surely this problem is an expression of profound discomfort with the traditions of Southern womanhood. One of the best tactics for ignoring conventions is to omit their exemplars, in this case the mothers who represent what the daughters are trying to es-cape. In *Reinventing Womanhood*, Carolyn Heilbrun explains that the rejec-tion of the mother and identification with the father is a typical pattern for assertive, successful women; the distinctive heritage of white Southern women which we have explored in chapters 1 and 2 makes this an es-pecially tangled process for them. McCullers's own situation is an extreme example of both the strength of matriarchal tendencies in Southern life and the difficult problem of self-definition for the Southern girl who wants to become a writer. As we have already seen, her mother dominated her childhood and hovered solicitously nearby through most of her life. Yet, as her brother suggested, perhaps the force of their mother's personality was too powerful for the daughter to contemplate; Carson McCullers remained a Southern woman whose imagination was frozen in collision with soci-ety's expectations. In Mick and Frankie she presents ambitious, artistic girls who are disoriented and terrified when they are forced to identify themselves as female at puberty. Because she performed the radical experi-ment of creating the grotesque amazon Amelia Evans, between *The Heart Is a Lonely Hunter* and *The Member of the Wedding*, the images which define this crisis for Frankie Addams are the images of sexual freaks in an am-bience of androgynous longings, homosexuality, and transvestitism.[1]

Such imagery is directly related to the tradition of the tomboy so dear to the hearts of English and American fathers from late Victorian times. In childhood, a lively girl could romp with boys, wear their clothes, and cut her hair short. She had complete physical freedom and often served as a lively companion for her father, a temporary stand-in for a son. As Bertram Wyatt-Brown explains, this tradition seems to have been es-pecially prevalent in the American South. In frontier days, girls were raised without much sexual differentiation from males until puberty. Later in the antebellum period a similar childhood liberty was common, contrasting sharply with the absolute restrictions the patriarchy placed on adult women in marriage. We remember Mary Chesnut's bitter description of herself and her fellow Southern women as slaves, but before marriage many young ladies "could ride as well as their brothers, and not a few of them could handle firearms with great accuracy and skill," according to a nineteenth-century commentator.[2]

All that changed when the time came for courtship. Kate Chopin immortalized the Southern tomboy type and her problem of sexual adjustment in her short story "Charlie." One of seven daughters of a handsome widower, Charlotte is her father's favorite. With her boy's nickname, short hair, and wild temperament, she is a charming oddity galloping about the plantation in "trouserlets" on a black horse. Her physical courage and her ability to ride and shoot and fish coincide with another talent: she is a natural poet. Thus Chopin has made a conjunction between the tomboy's physical assertiveness and literary talent, a connection Carson McCullers would make in the character of Frankie Addams and one very close to the relation of musical ambition and tomboyishness in Mick Kelly.

Chopin reveals the tumult caused by dawning sexuality for such girls when she describes Charlie's sudden desire to become a young lady because of love. Anne Goodwyn Jones shows that the girl's bond with her father has unmistakably erotic connotations, but the attraction which changes her behavior is her infatuation with young Firman Walton. In the female seminary where Charlie has been sent to be civilized after a series of unruly escapades, she determines "to transform herself from a hoyden to a fascinating young lady, if persistence and hard work could do it."[3] The result is a ridiculous caricature of femininity, as Charlie singes her hair with curling irons, soaks her rough hands in creams, doggedly practices dancing, and covers herself with frills and jewelry. In one area, however, she succeeds in arousing the applause of all her classmates. The poetry which she produces effortlessly and has not valued as an accomplishment suddenly wins an important prize in the school, and Charlie is finally accepted as a person of consequence. This success occurs, however, almost in spite of her efforts to become "a fascinating young lady."

When her love for Walton is disappointed by his engagement to her conventionally pretty sister Julia, Charlie abandons the ladylike charade in a rage of disappointment and returns to her trouserlets and her active plantation life. By now her father has been seriously hurt and needs her help in managing his affairs. Their shy young neighbor Gus Bradley declares his long affection for Charlie, and the story ends implying their eventual marriage. Jones is right to find this ending weak,[4] and I would suggest that it is troubled by Chopin's awareness that she is running counter to "propriety" when she restores Charlie's boyish independence. Before writing "Charlie" she had suffered a storm of criticism for *The Awakening* which effectively discouraged her from seeking to publish further work. Edna Pontellier was considered shocking in her abandonment of domestic duty for personal freedom, but Charlie's return to her tomboy ways also violated conventional notions of femininity. Chopin does not seem able to look very deeply into the social and psychological consequences for someone like Charlie who cannot act the part of the submissive lady. In fact, the girl who persists in her boyish freedom through adolescence becomes odder and odder, as social indulgence changes to disapproval. Dresses must be worn; manner must be restrained and graceful. As a girl the tomboy is charming, but as an adult she is grotesque.

Ambitions are the psychological equivalents for the physical assertiveness of the tomboy, and again the requirements of submissiveness and restraint for the Southern lady have traditionally discouraged the pursuit of professional, artistic, or political goals. In modern life these pressures exert themselves subtly, woven as they are throughout the texture of adolescent experience. But they produce a fear that to be female and to dare to achieve is to venture into dangerous territory, to violate one's gender, to become a kind of freak. The girl who insists on following her ambitions almost inevitably pays the price of shame and guilt as an adult; she must live with a troubled sense of herself as a woman because she has abandoned the familiar boundaries of her gender. Women writers since the early nineteenth century have documented the problem, and Virginia Woolf spent an important part of her creative life describing the waste and distortion of character resulting from the narrowly restricted lives forced upon gifted women because of their sex. Woolf gained her own independence more easily than her predecessors, but for her as for ambitious women of later generations, there are still "many ghosts to fight, many prejudices to overcome."[5] This has been particularly true in the South, and McCullers began to discover the horrifying dimensions of the problem as she progressively explored feminine independence in the portraits of Mick Kelly, Amelia Evans, and Frankie Addams.

Virginia Woolf's ghosts are the phantoms of guilt which cripple the imagination, focusing the most sensitive women writers' attention on negative self-images and preventing professional women from confident assertion of their gender. Barbara Clarke Mossberg has shown how the writing of both Emily Dickinson and Gertrude Stein is obsessed by the need to come to terms with the hatred for almost everything conventionally female which they have absorbed from dominant social attitudes. As people who rejected the devalued and restricted intellectual life of their sex, each was nevertheless bound by the inescapable fact of living in a female body and being judged as a woman by those around her. Similar ambivalence troubles contemporary women poets, as Sandra Gilbert points out. Poets like Diane Wakoski, Adrienne Rich, and Sylvia Plath see themselves in a strange confusion of contradictory images: an arrow, a blackbird, an androgyne, a watercolor that washes off, a bone scepter, "a naked man fleeing across the roofs," a guerrilla fighter, a tree, a pig. Sylvia Plath may write, "I / Have a self to recover, a queen," but she never really succeeds, and neither do the others. This failure of imagination to supply positive self-images applies not only to the confessional poetic self but also to the public image of the successful woman. Carolyn Heilbrun argues that "women writers (and women politicians, academics, psychoanalysts) have been unable to imagine for other women, fictional or real, the self they have in fact achieved." As psychoanalysts they have not developed theories which embody their own female strengths; as writers they have not created female characters as independent as themselves; as academics they have not encouraged women students to aspire to what they as women have achieved. They have had to adopt the perspective of their masculine colleagues and function professionally as males.[6]

Understanding these problems of self-definition, we should have no trouble interpreting the psychic paralysis of Sylvia Plath's gifted young writer in *The Bell Jar,* whose talent is rewarded not by serious literary regard but by a summer of luncheons and fashion shows on the staff of *Mademoiselle.* Esther Greenwood's real interests are drowned in a sea of cosmetics, flowers, perfumes, fashionable hats, and piles of flouncy dresses. This conflict between serious ambition and the pressure of conventional femininity is exactly the problem that confronts Mick Kelly and Frankie Addams in Carson McCullers's fiction. McCullers's portrayal of their dilemma is especially valuable because she concentrates on puberty, the time when demands for "femininity" first press in upon a girl, and she allows her protagonists to be more sharply aware of their choices than Plath allows Esther Greenwood to be. Esther is paralyzed because she cannot even look at the contrary impulses within herself. She tries to escape them by blotting herself out, in a sense accepting the verdict implied by *Mademoiselle's* refusal to acknowledge her identity as a serious writer. Mick and Frankie have the immense advantage of tomboy self-reliance and a habit of scrappy assertiveness. Their passage into womanhood may be acutely painful, but at least childhood experience helps them to confront their confusion head-on. Through Mick and Frankie, McCullers provides an unusually perceptive treatment of the problem which warps so many gifted women's lives, but between them she makes the grotesque experiment of picturing a tomboy who refuses to acknowledge it.

Another woman writer had very likely helped to show her the way by suggesting means for objectifying the self-reliance and assertiveness of a tomboy with artistic ambitions. Several of the images Willa Cather used in *The Song of the Lark* to reveal Thea Kronberg's restless energies reappear in *The Heart Is a Lonely Hunter*. The picture of Thea pulling her baby brother Thor all over her Colorado town in an express wagon is an effective way of objectifying the frustrating domestic responsibilities imposed on this adventuresome girl. Rather than stay home passively baby-sitting, Thea roams and explores, dragging her burden behind her, just as Mick Kelly will do with her brother Ralph in McCullers's novel. Thea has a secret life of books and artistic dreams in her attic room, apart from the mundane activities of her family. This is another effective motif which McCullers seems to echo in describing Mick's "inside room" of imagination where she tries to write music and dreams of becoming a great composer. Finally, both girls physically express their vague new energies by roaming the streets at night. Cather describes Thea in terms which reveal the correspondence between physical restlessness and psychological confusion: "Many a night she left Dr. Archie's office with a desire to run and run about those quiet streets until she wore out her shoes, or wore out the streets themselves; when her chest ached and it seemed as if her heart were spreading all over the desert."[7] Mick similarly wanders along dark sidewalks, defying the fears which she knows keep most girls indoors. But, unlike Thea, she loses this freedom when she accepts her sexual status as a woman. She becomes afraid of the dark.

At the beginning of *The Heart Is a Lonely Hunter*, Mick Kelly is presented with a deliberate emphasis on her masculine appearance and her unfeminine ambitions. She is described through the mind of Biff Brannon, who feels an uneasy tenderness for her boyishness. "He thought of the way Mick narrowed her eyes and pushed back her hair with the palm of her hand. He thought of her hoarse, boyish voice and of her habit of hitching up her khaki shorts and swaggering like a cowboy in the picture show."[8] Rejecting her older sisters' obsession with movie stars and continual primping, Mick dreams of becoming famous by the age of seventeen. She imagines herself as a great inventor of tiny radios and portable flying machines, but her most consistent ambitions are focused on music. She tries to build a violin out of a broken ukulele, practices the piano in the school gym every day, and attempts to compose music in her secret notebook. At night she explores the rich neighborhoods of town, hiding in the shrubbery outside the windows of houses where the radios are tuned to classical music stations. In her adolescent fantasies, Mick imagines a brilliant future for herself: "Later on—when she was twenty—she would be a great world famous composer. She would have a whole symphony orchestra and conduct all of her music herself. She would stand up on the platform in front of the big crowds of people. To conduct the orchestra she would wear either a real man's evening suit or else a red dress spangled with rhinestones" (p. 205). The images she projects for her future self waver from masculine to feminine, from evening suit to rhinestone-spangled dress, because there is no tradition of female composers upon which she can model her daydreams.

In fact, Mick's sense of romantic heroism is entirely masculine. In the key scene tying her musical sensitivity to her troubled emotions she listens to Beethoven's *Eroica* symphony in the shrubbery outside one of the houses. Originally written in Napoleon's honor, that symphony is heroically overblown, like Mick's emotions. She feels that the first movement "was her—the real plain her," with all her plans and feelings. The last movement is "glad and like the greatest people in the world running and springing up in a hard, free way" in a masculine kind of assertion. Her response to the music is ecstasy and terrible pain. To alleviate this pain she resorts to a typically female kind of masochism, turning her frustration back upon herself.[9] As she had done earlier in the story when driven frantic by an inner voice crying, "I want—I want—I want," she pounds her thighs with her fists. Her response to the *Eroica* is shockingly violent. "The rocks under the bush were sharp. She grabbed a handful of them and began scraping them up and down on the same spot until her hand was bloody. Then she fell back to the ground and lay looking up at the night. With the fiery hurt in her leg she felt better" (p. 101).

Mick's reaction to the *Eroica* is clearly no voluptuous sublimation or misplaced pleasure but a frantic effort to release intense emotions which she must feel are forbidden. The circumstances of her musical life are fraught with guilt and the corresponding need for secrecy. Her musical pleasure is illicit, stolen in the darkness from wealthy people by a kind of voyeurism. Mick's own world has no time for her impractical addiction to the arts. Thus there is no constructive outlet for the emotion stimulated by the music, an emotion identified with her ambitions and sense of her own importance. So she turns all the energy upon herself, wounding her flesh to blot out her emotions with physical pain.

Mick's turbulent feelings do not always find masochistic expression, as we have seen in her habit of wandering all over town at night. When the normal world is asleep and she is safe in darkness, she has a masculine physical freedom, but it exposes her to the danger which has always served as an effective curb on girls' activities. "Girls were scared a man would come out from somewhere and put his teapot in them like they were married. Most girls were nuts. If a person the size of Joe Louis or Mountain Man Dean would jump out at her and want to fight she would run. But if it was somebody within twenty pounds her weight she would give him a good sock and go right on" (p. 84). Clearly Mick understands the danger, but with a boyishly sturdy confidence she refuses to be intimidated.

Despite her independence Mick lives with profound anxiety. Like the young Jane Eyre, she expresses her fears in childish paintings of disasters, the most telling of them called "Sea Gull with Back Broken in Storm." She is haunted early in the novel by a nightmare which opposes her fantasies of success and prefigures her destiny. She dreams she is swimming through enormous crowds of people, pushing and shoving them out of her way. Sometimes she is on the ground, trampled by the crowds until her insides ooze out on the pavement (pp. 33–37). Mick's sleeping mind, at least, knows that the world will not allow her to succeed in realizing her dreams of independence and art.

McCullers makes us see that the smothering of Mick's ambitions coincides with her acceptance of womanhood. When the novel opens she is a twelve-year-old tomboy. At thirteen she starts high school and is thrown into the teenage world of cliques and the mysterious, clumsy courtship rites which are initiations into adult sexuality. Confused by the social rules, she feels herself an outsider. Boldly she decides to hold a prom party to end her isolation, and her preparations for the party take on the unmistakable significance of a ritual cleansing. For the first time in the novel, she shucks her khaki shorts, T-shirt, and sneakers, and takes a long bath to wash the grime and indeed all vestiges of childhood away. She emerges for the party as from a cocoon, metamorphosed into the conventional female in an adult dress, a hairstyle with spit curls, high heels, and makeup. "She didn't feel like herself at all" (pp. 90–91). And in fact she looks ridiculous—the clothes borrowed from her older sisters are too big, the imitation diamond tiara perches oddly in her close-cropped hair, and she is unsteady in high heels. She is a caricature of a woman, just as Charlie was when she tried to transform herself and as Frankie Addams will be under similar circumstances in *The Member of the Wedding*.

The air at Mick's party fairly crackles with sexual tension as boys and girls in unfamiliar plumage try to act their adult roles as dancing partners. When the party is broken up by a crowd of younger neighborhood ragamuffins, all the guests explode outdoors, finding relief in wild games of chase. The crowd erupts in a dash toward a ditch where the city is digging up the street. Jumping into the ditch, Mick learns with a rude shock how she is crippled by feminine clothes. The high-heel shoes make her slip, and her breath is knocked out as her stomach slams into a pipe. Her evening dress is torn, her rhinestone tiara lost. The physical details of the accident suggest a physical punishment for inappropriate behavior. Mick returns home bruised and humiliated, evidently having learned her lesson. That night she decides that she is too old to wear shorts: "No more after this night. Not any more" (p. 99). With her renunciation of these clothes, she renounces childhood and its boyish freedom.

Within a year of the symbolic party, Mick is trapped in a narrow adult world which reduces her to little more than a machine. She has her first sexual experience with the boy next door and then leaves adolescence behind, quitting school to take a job and help support her family. Neither Mick's friend Harry Minowitz nor she fully understands the magnetism or the mechanics that bring their bodies together on a picnic they have taken by themselves in the country. While it is happening, Mick stares into the sun, clenches her fists, and counts to distract herself from her fear (pp. 234–35). Once the experiment is over, both she and Harry are ashamed, and Mick tells him plainly that she didn't like it. Lovemaking "was like her head was broke off from her body and thrown away," robbing her of rational control. After this experience, a "queer afraidness came to her. It was like the ceiling was slowly pressing down toward her face" (pp. 266–67). Suddenly she is afraid of the dark and of solitude. Once she learns she is not pregnant, however, and has decided to go to work to help her family survive, the fear subsides. In its place comes a kind of paralysis. Her job at the dime store shuts out her private world of music and stifles her fantasies. The long days of work leave her feeling exhausted, caged, and cheated, but she can find no clear cause for her frustration. At fourteen she is a grown woman whose life seems to have reached a dead end. There we leave her.

Not long after the dramatic success of this first novel, Carson McCullers began another one with a similar girl as her main character. The story which would eventually become *The Member of the Wedding* began with twelve-year-old tomboy Frankie Addams suddenly beset by terrifying but nameless anxieties which make her life seem freakish. This book took McCullers more than five years to write and caused her considerable pain, at least in part because the problems of sexual ambivalence which are central to Frankie's confusion were shared by McCullers in her tangled relation with her husband Reeves.[10] After struggling for two years with what she then called "The Bride and Her Brother," McCullers paused to write a new tale which explored Frankie Addams's anxiety in a bold new way. For it she created her two greatest freaks—a huge, mannish Amazon and her twisted, dwarfish lover—in a nightmare vision of the tomboy grown up, without any concessions to social demands for sexual conformity.

Miss Amelia Evans is really a monstrous creature, and yet McCullers admiringly describes her many talents, her muscular strength, and her control of the squalid village world of *The Ballad of the Sad Café*. Miss Amelia's freakishness is crucial to the meaning of this grotesque fable, and it derives from a sexual horror expressed repeatedly in the fiction of Carson McCullers's most productive years. McCullers claimed that "Love, and especially love of a person who is incapable of returning or receiving it, is at the heart of my selection of grotesque figures to write about— people whose physical incapacity is a symbol of their spiritual incapacity to love or receive love—their spiritual isolation."[11] Miss Amelia's physique is indeed symbolic of her spirit, but her peculiarities are more specific than mere "spiritual incapacity." They clearly reveal the story's function as a gothic parable enforcing sexual conformity.

Louis D. Rubin perceptively suggests that McCullers destroys Mick Kelly and Frankie Addams as characters when she tries to force them beyond the pain of adolescent sexual awakening and into an acceptance of womanhood. She could not really imagine such acceptance because she never found it herself. Friends often commented on her childlike manner, and her adult photos reveal the same kind of fierce boyishness she described in both Mick and Frankie. She deliberately dressed in men's clothes, flaunting her androgyny at Yaddo during the summer of 1941 when she was writing *The Ballad of the Sad Café*. At this same time her marriage was disintegrating, and Virginia Spencer Carr's biography makes the conclusion almost inescapable that Carson was largely responsible because of her sexual rejection of Reeves McCullers. That summer she declared to Newton Arvin, "I was born a man."[12] It is this identification with the masculine which stimulated her imagination to explore the dangerous psychological territory of *The Ballad of the Sad Café*.

One critic calls McCullers's flat, childlike narrative tone "a kind of buffer to fend off what would otherwise be unbearable,"[13] but I would instead describe it as a strategy for placing the action far enough away from ordinary life to allow forbidden impulses free scope . . . at least for a while. The form of *The Ballad of the Sad Café* allows McCullers to indulge the desire to appropriate male power and thus escape the position of a woman. There can be no other explanation for Miss Amelia's strapping physique, her skill at masculine trades, or her rejection of everything female, most apparent in her indignant refusal to play the physical part of a woman in

her ten-day marriage to Marvin Macy. Her later relationship with Cousin
Lymon is never threatening because he is not a real man who sees her as
female. Behind the dream of independence represented by Miss Amelia's
"masculinity," however, lies the fear of male vengeance which triumphs in
the story's conclusion, as Marvin Macy and Cousin Lymon join forces to
destroy the usurper. The formerly invincible Amazon is left shrunken and
imprisoned in the slowly collapsing shell of her once prosperous cafe.

The folktale atmosphere of *The Ballad of the Sad Café* may owe something
to Isak Dinesen's *Seven Gothic Tales* (1934), whose strange ambience Carson
McCullers never ceased to praise after first reading them in 1938. Dinesen's work remained very close to her, and it is quite understandable that
three years later, while she struggled to resolve Frankie Addams's anxiety
about growing too tall, she might have remembered Dinesen's portrait of
six-foot Athena Hopballehus in "The Monkey." Probably this process was
not conscious; her imagination simply revived the motif of the Amazon in
order to explore for herself some of the problems of sexual identity and
female independence which Dinesen treats in her exotic fable. Robert S.
Phillips was the first to comment on the similarities between *The Ballad of
the Sad Café* and "The Monkey,"[14] but I think he overstates the extent of
those similarities. The only clear parallels are the motifs of the Amazon
and her bitter hand-to-hand combat with a hated male suitor. These
motifs are developed in very different ways by the two writers, and the
stories move through entirely different atmospheres to almost opposite
conclusions about the sources of female autonomy. Since McCullers's novella is a kind of challenge to the arguments implied by Dinesen's story, it is
useful to remind ourselves of the significance of the Amazon maiden in
"The Monkey."

The fairy-tale world of "The Monkey" is centered in the female dominion of Cloister Seven, a retreat for wealthy unmarried ladies and widows
of noble birth. It is ruled by a virgin Prioress with mysterious powers who
resembles a sybil, the Chinese goddess Kuan-Yin, and the Wendish goddess of love. To all of the Cloister's inhabitants it is "a fundamental article
of faith that women's loveliness and charm, which they themselves represented in their own sphere and according to their gifts, must constitute the
highest inspiration and prize of life."[15]

Athena Hopballehus embodies this ideal femininity in heroic form. She
is a motherless only child who has been raised by her father in a nearby
castle, surrounded by "an atmosphere of incense burnt to woman's loveliness" (p. 130). The father admits, however, that "She has been to me *both*
son and daughter, and I have in my mind seen her wearing the old coats of
armor of Hopballehus" (p. 136, my emphasis). The problem implied in
this reference to androgynous childhood training is never explored in the

story, but perhaps it is meant to suggest an excess of independence. At eighteen Athena is six feet tall, powerful and broad-shouldered, with flaming red hair and the eyes of a young lioness or eagle. Athena is what her name suggests, a human type of the warrior goddess, whom Dinesen also associates with the virgin huntress Diana and "a giant's daughter who unwittingly breaks men when she plays with them" (p. 129). When a proposal of marriage is made by a handsome young cavalry officer named Boris, the Prioress's nephew and Athena's childhood playmate, Athena's fierce autonomy sparks an indignant refusal.

Although forceful womanhood dominates the world of "The Monkey," the story's central problem is not Athena's fate but rather the decadence of the Prioress's nephew Boris. This overcultivated young man is the central consciousness of the narrative, and the plot follows his reluctant entrance into normal manhood through the manipulations of his aunt. The old ladies of Cloister Seven, having heard rumors of Boris's implication in a homosexual scandal, give him an ambiguous welcome when he arrives from the capital city. They think of him as "a young priest of black magic, still within hope of conversion" (p. 113). A sort of conversion is indeed accomplished by the end of the story, but only because the Prioress uses deception and magic to force the resisting bride and groom together. Threatening Boris by revealing her knowledge of the scandal, she induces him to drink a love potion and force himself upon Athena. The maiden responds with her fist and knocks out two of his teeth. Dinesen tells us that all the young women Boris had previously rejected "would have felt the pride of their sex satisfied in the contemplation of his mortal pursuit of this maiden who now strove less to escape than to kill him" (p. 153). A fierce battle ensues, and she is about to strangle him when he transforms the nature of the conflict by forcing his mouth against hers. Instantly her whole body registers the terrible effect of his kiss. "As if he had run a rapier straight through her, the blood sank from her face, her body stiffened in his arms," her strength dissolved away, and she collapsed. Both Boris's and Athena's faces express "a deadly disgust" with the kiss (pp. 154–55).

In her ability to overcome even this revulsion, the Prioress emerges as the very incarnation of the Wendish goddess of love, half-monkey and half-human. Because Boris and Athena witness the Prioress's grotesque exchange of shapes with her monkey on the morning after the seduction attempt, they are united as initiates to the mystery of her power. They submit to her insistence that the sexes cannot remain separate; Boris must pay homage to a female power; and the proud young Athena must renounce her heroic virginity in an alliance with him.

No union of male and female, however reluctant, occurs in *The Ballad of the Sad Café*. In contrast to Athena's essentially female power, Miss Amelia's remarkable strength depends on her masculinity, in a world devoid of feminine qualities. All the characters who have speaking parts are males, except for Miss Amelia, who never betrays even a hint of conventionally feminine behavior.

Like Dinesen's Athena, Miss Amelia is a motherless only child raised by an adoring father, but McCullers gives her Amazon a more exaggerated physique and a mysterious authority. At the height of her adult pride, Miss Amelia is the central personality of her town. An imposing figure, she is "a dark, tall woman with bones and muscles like a man," hairy thighs, and short-cropped hair brushed back from her forehead like Mick Kelly's and Frankie Addams's. In the building she inherited from her father, she operates a profitable general store which gradually becomes the town's only cafe. She produces the best liquor in the county from her secret still in a nearby swamp; sells chitterlings, sausage, and golden sorghum molasses; owns farms in the vicinity; and is adept at all manual skills such as carpentry, masonry, and butchering. The most impressive of all her powers, however, and the one which with the magical properties of her whiskey best reveals her nearly supernatural dimensions, is her ability to heal the sick. Like a sorceress or witch, she brews her own secret remedies from roots and herbs. "In the face of the most dangerous and extraordinary treatment she did not hesitate, and no disease was so terrible but what she would undertake to cure it."

There is one notable exception to Miss Amelia's healing powers: "If a patient came with a female complaint she could do nothing. Indeed at the mere mention of the words her face would slowly darken with shame, and she would stand there craning her neck against the collar of her shirt, or rubbing her swamp boots together, for all the world like a great, shamed, dumb-tongued child."[16] Her embarrassed confusion is a natural consequence of her total identification with masculinity and her childlike sexual innocence. Even in adulthood, Miss Amelia preserves the tomboy attitudes we encountered in Mick Kelly. For both of these characters, the first physical encounters with men are unpleasant surprises. We remember Mick's distaste for her one experience of lovemaking with Harry Minowitz, and how it brought the necessary renunciation of childhood freedom with womanhood.

Miss Amelia, however, refuses to accept the diminished status of woman. When she rather absentmindedly marries Marvin Macy, the whole town is relieved, expecting marriage to soften her character and physique, "and to change her at last into a calculable woman." Instead, after the bridegroom follows her upstairs to bed on their wedding night, Miss Amelia stamps downstairs in a rage, wearing breeches and a khaki jacket. Until dawn she reads the *Farmer's Almanac*, smokes her father's pipe, and practices on her new typewriter. During the ensuing ten days of the abortive marriage, she sleeps downstairs and continues to ignore her husband unless he comes within striking range, when she socks him with her fist. Macy disappears from town in disgrace, leaving Amelia victorious in her Amazon virginity (pp. 30–33).

For ten uneventful years Miss Amelia goes about her solitary life, aloof, stingy, maintaining her strange control of the town. Then one night the little hunchbacked Cousin Lymon mysteriously appears on her doorstep, wins her heart, and causes momentous changes both in her life and the life of the town for six years before the sinister return of Marvin Macy. The question is why Miss Amelia should have rejected a vigorous normal man, only to fall in love with a twisted midget. Joseph Millichap sees traditional folktale elements in the characters of Marvin Macy and Cousin Lymon: Macy is a sort of demon lover, and Cousin Lymon is reminiscent of the figures of mysterious stranger and elf. But Millichap comes closer to answering our question when he says that Cousin Lymon "is a man loved without sex, a child acquired without pain, and a companion which her [Amelia's] limited personality finds more acceptable than a husband or a child."[17] Marvin Macy had been sufficiently ennobled by his love for Miss Amelia so that he might have been a tolerable mate for her, but by accepting her feminine part in the marriage Amelia would have had to renounce the masculine sources of her strength. Such a capitulation to the female mysteries which she has avoided all her life would be unthinkable. Her enraged reaction to Macy's forlorn attempts at lovemaking clearly expresses the insult they represent to her pride. Cousin Lymon, on the other hand, represents no threat to her power. He is a sickly, deformed mannequin whom she could crush with one blow of her fist, and, from all we can see, he makes no sexual demands. His warped, childlike form clearly indicates his masculine impotence, just as Amelia's grotesquely masculine appearance expresses her inability to function as a woman. With Lymon she feels safe in revealing affection, for she can baby and pet him without any threat of sexuality.

At the heart of Miss Amelia's relationship with Cousin Lymon, there is actually an inversion of traditional roles of male and female. Miss Amelia is physically dominant and provides a living for the household as a husband would. Cousin Lymon is the pampered mate who struts about in finery, is finicky about food and accommodations, and gads about town socializing and gossiping. He functions as a hostess would in the cafe, while Miss Amelia stands aloof and silent in the background. In their intimate conversations before the parlor fire, Miss Amelia sits with her "long legs stretched out before the hearth" contemplating philosophical problems and reminiscing about her father, while Cousin Lymon sits wrapped in a blanket or green shawl on a low chair and chatters endlessly about petty details.

Despite his physical weakness and his vanity, Cousin Lymon seems to embody the spirit of spring and renewal. He has drifted mysteriously into town in April, in a year when the crops promise well and conditions at the local mill are relatively prosperous. Once accepted as Miss Amelia's intimate, he becomes a catalyst for the release of her genial impulses. Her devotion to him brightens her face and gradually engenders a hospitality she had never expressed before. Before the hunchback's arrival, she sold her moonshine by the bottle, handing it out through her back door in the dark. Never was anyone allowed to open or drink this liquor inside the building. But once Cousin Lymon is installed in her house, she begins selling it inside, providing glasses and plates of crackers for consumption on the premises. Gradually the store is transformed into a cafe, with tables where Miss Amelia sells liquor by the drink and serves fried catfish suppers for fifteen cents a plate. Miss Amelia grows more sociable and less inclined to cheat her business associates. Even her special powers are enhanced for healing and for brewing her marvelous liquor. All these positive developments of her character expand themselves in the communal warmth which her cafe comes to provide for the town.

Though Cousin Lymon brings fruitful changes in the lives of Miss Amelia and her town, his own physical state suggests a fatal limitation to prosperity. He remains "weakly and deformed" despite Amelia's pampering and the exercise of her fullest healing abilities. He is also personally malicious, even though he has generally served as an agent for gaiety and warmth. Thus he is naturally drawn to the cruel strength of Marvin Macy, a force which complements his own unpleasant traits. When Macy suddenly returns to town after years in the state penitentiary, Cousin Lymon is immediately infatuated.

Macy embodies all the qualities of "normal" masculinity, but McCullers has cast them in an evil, destructive light throughout the story. Macy may be tall, brawny, and good-looking, but he is also violent and viciously lustful. He is the devil male who mutilates animals for fun and has ruined the tenderest young girls in the region. Amelia refers to Macy's cloven hoof, and the Satanic is also suggested by his red shirt and the fact that he never sweats. Throughout the story he is allied with winter. Even though he had been temporarily reformed by his love for Miss Amelia, their wedding took place on a winter day rather than in the traditionally propitious seasons of spring or summer. His vengeful return to town sixteen years later comes in autumn and brings sinister portents of unseasonable weather, ruining the normally festive ritual of hog-butchering: "there was everywhere the smell of slowly spoiling meat, and an atmosphere of dreary waste" (p. 52). Macy lays claim to the unprecedented snowfall in January which gives the town "a drawn, bleak look" (p. 57). The climactic battle between Miss Amelia and Marvin Macy occurs exactly one month later, on Groundhog Day. Its issue is foreordained by Cousin Lymon's report that the groundhog has seen its shadow and therefore that more winter lies ahead.

Understanding at once that Macy's return to town is a challenge, Miss Amelia begins preparations for a fight, taunting Macy by wearing her red dress as a flagrant reminder of his failure to make her act the part of a woman during their marriage.[18] While she wears the dress, she pokes her biceps constantly, practices lifting heavy objects, and works out with a punching bag in her yard. In the climactic battle between the two antagonists, the question to be decided is not, as in Dinesen, whether a powerful young woman can be subdued so that a union of the sexes can occur. For McCullers, the contest will decide whether a woman can deny her sex and dominate men with a strength analogous to their own.

> Now the test had come, and in these moments of terrible effort, it was Miss Amelia who was the stronger. Marvin Macy was greased and slippery, tricky to grasp, but she was stronger. Gradually she bent him over backward, and inch by inch she forced him to the floor. . . . At last she had him down, and straddled; her big strong hands were on his throat. [p. 67]

Suddenly, at this moment of Miss Amelia's triumph, Cousin Lymon leaps across the room from his perch on the bar to aid his adored male friend. He lands on Amelia's back and changes the balance of force to Macy's advantage. Miss Amelia is destroyed.

The sexual dynamics of *The Ballad of the Sad Café* are an inversion of traditional heterosexual patterns. Contrasts with Dinesen's "The Monkey" help reveal the masculine sources of Miss Amelia's autonomous strength and point up McCullers's complete rejection of heterosexual union. Rather than accepting her femininity by consummating her marriage to the aggressively masculine Marvin Macy, Miss Amelia focuses her affections on the little hunchback who seems to function simultaneously as child, pet, and rather feminine companion. But Cousin Lymon is much less devoted to Miss Amelia than she is to him, and this gives him an emotional advantage over her which proves ultimately disastrous. It seems inevitable that the foppish dwarf should fall helplessly in love with Marvin Macy, thus completing the destructive triangular relationship which McCullers used to develop her theory that "almost everyone wants to be the lover" and that "in a deep secret way, the state of being loved is intolerable to many." But this theory and McCullers's statement that *Ballad* was intended to show the inferiority of passionate individual love to *agape* fail to account for the individual peculiarities of her characters and the sexual dimensions of their problems in love.[19]

The real force of *The Ballad of the Sad Café* lies in its depiction of a masculine Amazon whose transgression of conventional sexual boundaries brings catastrophic male retribution. Unlike Dinesen, who portrayed an uneasy compromise between proud female autonomy and reluctant masculine homage, McCullers sought to deny the feminine entirely and allow a woman to function successfully as a man. She could not sustain her vision, because she knew it was impossible.

The consequences of her experiment in this novella play a part in determining the final form of *The Member of the Wedding*, which inexorably moves Frankie toward an acceptance of conventional femininity. After writing *The Ballad of the Sad Café* in only a few months, when McCullers returned to her long struggle with the materials of *The Member of the Wedding*, she knew that Frankie would have to submit as Miss Amelia had not. The conclusions she reached in her nightmarish folktale must have contributed profoundly to the undercurrent of fear McCullers creates in *The Member of the Wedding* through the image of the freak show which haunts Frankie's mind and indeed the whole novel.

With the character of Frankie Addams we return to the type of the ambitious tomboy on the brink of puberty, baffled by incomprehensible changes in her life. This time the heroine's ambitions are literary rather than musical; Frankie Addams writes plays and dreams of becoming a great poet. Her ambitions are not blighted as Mick's are, but it could be argued that Frankie's attitude toward writing has changed significantly by the end of the novel. However, the focus of McCullers's attention in this book is not on the protagonist's dreams of fame but rather on the psychological trauma she suffers when required to accept her femininity. By the end of the novel she has passed from childhood into adolescence with an acceptance of the facts of adult sex. In the process of attaining her new status, she follows the same general pattern as Mick Kelly. We meet her as a twelve-year-old tomboy with a boy's name and haircut, who wears shorts and a B.V.D. undershirt. She is an expert knife-thrower and has the toughest bare feet in town. Toward the middle of the story, she transforms herself by changing her name to F. Jasmine and putting on a pink organdy dress, lipstick, and Sweet Serenade perfume. She has made herself into a romantic caricature of a female, much as Mick Kelly did for her prom party. As she parades around town in her finery, F. Jasmine meets a soldier who takes her for much older than she is, and with him she has her first adult sexual encounter. This dismaying experience forces her to admit to what men and women do together. Her last illusions are shattered when her brother and his bride refuse to let her go along on their honeymoon. At the end of the book we find her completely changed into a giddy teen-ager, having accepted her femininity and her real name, Frances.

Before this transformation can occur, however, Frankie suffers agonies of loneliness, feelings of entrapment, and fears of freakishness which hover around her in the shapes of the prodigies she has seen at the fair. There are several kinds of freaks which Frankie and her little cousin John Henry West visit at the Chattahoochee Exposition. She is afraid of all of them, but Ellen Moers is right to single out the hermaphrodite as the most important, for it is the quintessential symbol of Frankie's danger. Images of sexual ambivalence are carefully cultivated throughout the novel in the Negro transvestite Lily Mae Jenkins, the Utopias invented by Frankie and John Henry where one could change sex at will or be half male and half female, and John Henry's interest in dolls and dressing in women's clothes. Always such hermaphroditic or androgynous references are placed in a negative frame, for the novel's entire movement is towards Frankie's ultimate submission to the inexorable demand that she accept her sex as female. Just after telling Frankie about Lily Mae Jenkins, wise old Berenice urges her to start looking for beaus and acting feminine. "Now you belong to change from being so rough and greedy and big. You ought to fix yourself up nice in your dresses. And speak sweetly and act sly."[20] Berenice also refuses to countenance sexual transformation in the Utopian dreams she and Frankie and John Henry spin on summer after-noons. Children may play at exchanging sex roles, but adults may not, unless they are to be regarded as grotesques fit only for sideshow displays.

This truth begins to force itself upon Frankie Addams in the "green and crazy summer" of her twelfth year. "Frankie had become an unjoined per-son who hung around in doorways, and she was afraid." McCullers em-phasizes the element of fear so rhythmically that the novel's opening pages swim in a fevered, hallucinatory atmosphere. The central setting is the sad and ugly kitchen, like the room of a crazy house, its walls covered with John Henry's freakish drawings. Here a vague terror squeezes Frankie's heart. And here she, Berenice, and John Henry constitute a strange family or private world cut off from any other. The real doorway where Frankie lingers in baffled fright is the passage between childhood and the clearly defined sexual world of grown-ups which she must enter, for almost all of the specific sources of her anxiety turn out to be sexual. The older girls who have shut her out of their club are preoccupied with boys and gossip about adult sex which Frankie angrily dismisses as "nasty lies" (pp. 1–11).

Yet even she has participated in a secret and unknown sin with a neighborhood boy in his garage, and she is sickened with guilt. Her father has decided she is too old to sleep with him, but she is afraid in her bed by herself. Her most vividly realized fear derives from the changes in her body which she epitomizes in her height. At her present rate of growth she calculates that she will end up over nine feet tall—a freak.

Frankie's fear of freaks surely indicates some subconscious understanding of the qualities within herself which make her peculiar in the eyes of the normal world. McCullers uses the motif of unfinished music to underline and intensify Frankie's dilemma, suggesting the proper resolution to her confused view of herself. In Part 1, Frankie hears a grieving blues tune on "the sad horn of some colored boy" at night. The disembodied sound expresses her own feelings, for she herself is a piece of unfinished music. Just as the tune approaches its conclusion, the horn suddenly stops playing. The music's incompleteness drives Frankie wild, trapping inside her the unbearable emotions it has drawn to a focus (pp. 41–42). Like Mick Kelly, Frankie tries to find release through masochism, beating her head with her fist, as she will do again several times in the story. When she changes her name to the romantic F. Jasmine in Part 2 and waltzes around town in a dress, telling everyone she meets that her brother and his bride will take her away with them on their wedding trip, the unfinished music is resolved in her mind. Her stories about the wedding sound inside her "as the last chord of a guitar murmurs a long time after the strings are struck." Unfortunately, her fantasies of the wedding are doomed to disappointment. We know this long before the event because McCullers returns to the motif of unfinished music, this time in the sound made by a piano tuner at work, which embodies F. Jasmine's romantic dream. "Then in a *dreaming way* a chain of chords climbed slowly upward *like a flight of castle stairs:* but just at the end, when the eighth chord should have sounded and the scale made complete, there was a stop" (p. 81, my emphasis).

The only event that resolves the unfinished music as well as the frantic, disjointed activities of F. Jasmine, John Henry, and Berenice is the transcendent moment when a group of older girls file slowly through the backyard in clean, fresh dresses and are turned golden by the slanting rays of the evening sun. These girls are a sublime vision of Frankie–F. Jasmine's destiny, a vision of ideal feminine grace before which the group in the kitchen stands transfixed in hushed awe. The piano tuner is silent. F. Jasmine's growing body and the outside world demand that she complete herself in the terms of this vision, but she will not submit until her fantasies of escape are smashed.

The meaning of the unfinished music is closely linked to Frankie's spiritual kinship with the blacks of her little Southern town. Both are made clear in the person of Honey Brown, Berenice's young, light-skinned foster brother. Too intelligent and restless to live comfortably in the circumscribed world of Sugarville, the black section of town, he periodically explodes: "Honey played the horn, and he had been first in his studies at the colored high school. He ordered a French book from Atlanta and learned himself some French. At the same time he would suddenly run hog-wild all over Sugarville and tear around for several days, until his friends would bring him home more dead than living" (p. 122). The old black fortune-teller Big Mama explains that God withdrew His hand before Honey was completed, leaving him eternally unsatisfied. It must have been Honey's sad blues horn that Frankie heard in the night, the horn that stopped playing just short of the music's resolution. Big Mama's explanation of Honey's plight describes his frustration clearly enough, but the real cause of Honey's problems is the fact that he, like Frankie, does not fit the categories imposed on him by his Southern town.

Frankie shares a sense of entrapment with Honey and Berenice, but hers is not finally as severe, even though it is more vividly realized in the novel. At first she longs to escape from her hot, stultified town to the cold, snowy peace of Alaska. At the end of Part 1, however, she fixes on the wedding in Winter Hill as the means of escape. The old question of who she is and what she will become ceases to torment her when she decides to be a member of the wedding and go out into the world with her brother and his bride. This absurd fantasy is a denial of the adult sexuality which Frankie cannot bear to acknowledge, but her attraction to it is obvious in her infatuation with the engaged couple. McCullers associates the returning motif of unfinished music with the imagery of prison to show that F. Jasmine's romantic dream will not bring escape. The evening before the wedding, when the piano tuner repeats again and again his unfinished chords, "the bars of sunlight crossed the back yard like the bars of a bright strange jail" (p. 75). In the crazily disoriented recent months, Frankie had feared the eyes of the prisoners in the town jail because she sensed that they, like the freaks at the fair, recognized her as one of them. Even as F. Jasmine, she is closer to them than she knows. Berenice explains that all human beings are imprisoned in their separate bodies and separate minds, blacks even more extremely than others.

We all of us somehow caught. We born this way or that way and we don't know why. But we caught anyhow. I born Berenice. You born Frankie. John

Henry born John Henry. And maybe we wants to widen and bust free. But no matter what we do we still caught. . . . But they done drawn completely extra bounds around all colored people. They done squeezed us off in one corner by ourself. . . . Sometimes a boy like Honey feel like he just can't breathe no more. He feel like he got to break something or break himself. [pp. 113–14]

F. Jasmine feels like breaking things too, but her frustration usually expresses itself rather harmlessly in perverse moods. She is ultimately able to accept the limitations of her sex, which of course are far less cramped than the restrictions of segregation in the 1940s. But McCullers is making a traditional association between the oppression of women and that of blacks, an association most obvious in Harriet Beecher Stowe's *Uncle Tom's Cabin* in the nineteenth century, but also very clear in the relationship of the recent feminist movement to the Civil Rights Movement of the 1960s.[21]

Frankie is caught in a blossoming female body which she must recognize and accept. She must also face the fact that grown men and women make love, and that her body makes her desirable to men. As a younger child she had unwittingly walked in on the lovemaking of a man and his wife who were boarders in her house. Uncomprehending, she thought the man was having a fit. Even at twelve she does not understand the nature of his convulsions, just as she refuses to listen to the "nasty lies" of the older girls and tries not to think of her own wicked experience in the neighbor boy's garage. This innocence makes her dangerously vulnerable when as F. Jasmine she wanders through the town looking older and wiser than her years. The toughness that had served her well as a tomboy betrays her now, so that the soldier she meets in the Blue Moon Cafe assumes she is willing to be seduced. F. Jasmine is paralyzed with horror as the soldier embraces her in his cheap hotel room. She feels she is in the Crazy House at the fair or in the insane asylum at Milledgeville. At the last minute she knocks him out with a pitcher and makes her getaway down the fire escape. Not until late the next night, after the disaster of the wedding, does her mind accept the meaning of this encounter and its relation to her veiled sexual memories and anxieties. By then her brother and his bride have rejected her and she has suffered the humiliation of being pulled screaming from the steering wheel of their car. Back home, she has made a futile attempt to run away and has been recovered by her father in the Blue Moon Cafe, where she had felt she was drowning.

The Member of the Wedding ends in a new world, with Frances reborn as a giddy adolescent. The environment of her childhood has been dismantled completely—John Henry has died horribly of meningitis, Berenice has resigned herself to marriage and quit her job, and Frances is preparing to move to a new house with her father. The final scene takes place in the kitchen, now remodeled so that it is unrecognizable as the freakish prison of the terrible summer. Frances is making dainty sandwiches to serve her new soulmate, an artistic girl two years her senior. No longer a frightened alien, she is united with her friend through a mutual infatuation with poetry and art.

Significantly, the time of the greatest changes in her life coincided with the fair's annual visit to town. As her childhood world collapsed and John Henry lay screaming and dying in a dark room, Frances blithely visited the fair with her friend Mary Littlejohn, this time avoiding the Freak Pavilion which had so fascinated her and John Henry the year before. She no longer feels any association with the freaks, for she is secure in her new feminine identity. Paradoxically, however, there is another kind of freak whose existence she never really confronts. Instead of the exotic monsters at the fair, the new and much grimmer freak is the dying John Henry, his little body hideously twisted and his eyeballs "walled up in a corner stuck and blind" (p. 152). McCullers makes the connection between John Henry and the freaks at the fair by describing them together in one important paragraph very near the end of the novel. But Frances is too happily absorbed in her new friendship and her passion for Tennyson and Michelangelo to give much thought to the sufferings of the little cousin who had been her patient companion during the crazy summer. Nor does she have time to consider the plight of Honey Brown, whose last explosion of frustration landed him in prison about the time of the fair. McCullers has rather ruthlessly removed the "deviants" from Frances's life so that safe conformity can triumph.

The price for this relief from the tensions of strangeness has been high, perhaps too high. Frances is less attractive at the end of the novel than she was as frightened tomboy Frankie. She has become a silly girl who no longer produces her own juvenile works of art—the shows and plays she used to write—but instead gushes sentimental nonsense about the Great Masters. The hard edge of her mind is gone, and all that is left is froth. The struggle against conformity which had identified her with Honey Brown had been a struggle to assert artistic sensibility and intelligence in a world which refused to accept those qualities in a woman or a black man. Honey had expressed his needs by learning French and playing the trumpet, but his music remained unfinished, and he ended up in prison for trying to "bust free" of the narrow limits around his life. Frances avoids such drastic disappointment by giving up and hiding beneath the protective coloration of giddy young womanhood. But if Frances's intelligence is not destroyed, we might speculate that, like Sylvia Plath or Adrienne Rich, she will someday feel the old conflict again and awaken to a fearful "sense of drift, of being pulled along on a current which called itself my destiny, but in which I seemed to be losing touch with whoever I had been, with the girl who had experienced her own will and energy almost ecstatically at times."[22] Without McCullers's two portraits of the artistic twelve-year-old girl and her telling images of sexual freakishness, we could never understand so clearly why "a thinking woman sleeps with monsters" or how those monsters function in the minds of talented girls emerging from childhood.

Chapter Six

Good Country People

lannery O'Connor's fictional world shares a historical flatness with Carson McCullers's, though the urgency of her religious message lends it a peculiarly intense immediacy. Her countryside may not seem to reverberate with the sense of "the past in the present" which Thomas Daniel Young expects of traditional Southern fiction, but her characters are like McCullers's in being vitally connected to the physical world of the South. It is impossible to transplant Mick Kelly or Frankie Addams to Minnesota or California without destroying the context of weather, foliage, language, and culture which defines them. Flannery O'Connor's Southern settings are even more essential to the meaning of her work than McCullers's are. Her stories could occur nowhere else, because of the central role played by her uniquely Georgian landscapes and her cast of country grotesques who are absolutely marked by the language, manners, and fundamentalist Christianity of their region. O'Connor said once that being identified as a Georgia author "is a rather specious dignity, on the same order as, for the pig, being a Talmadge ham."[1] But in the same speech she went on to explain how, at a profound level of imaginative life, the South had nourished her understanding with serious truths unavailable in other parts of the country lacking the Southern experience of tragic defeat. This sense, coupled with her sacramental view of the natural world as bristling with spiritual meaning, produced landscapes which on one level are irrefutably Southern but on another are universal. We have seen similar richness of significance in the Mississippi settings through which Eudora Welty deliberately exploited the feminine qualities of the Southern land as a fruitful context for human action. Though Flannery O'Connor may not have considered that any special relationship existed between women and the landscape, complex associations appear in her fiction, especially in the farm stories, which reveal a troubled attitude toward the whole issue of her sex. An inadvertent link with Carson McCullers's work will provide a clue to the problem for us, so that we can go on to define it more particularly and finally explore its relation to landscape imagery.

Flannery O'Connor, like Eudora Welty and Carson McCullers, was a Southerner whose intellectual interests were contemporary and international, not at all limited by the provincialism of her upbringing. But she was paradoxical in her politics, her view of intellectuals, and her modernity. To a friend she confessed that she couldn't see why Granville Hicks was interested in her since he was a Northern socialist and she was a Southern conservative, yet she voted for Adlai Stevenson in 1952 while her mother voted for Eisenhower, and she voted for Kennedy in 1960 because of his political views as well as his Catholicism. "Actually *I* am the conservative in this family," she wrote a friend in 1962. "Strictly a Kennedy conservative. I like the way that man is running the country." Although her letters are filled with serious discussion of philosophy, theology, and literature, she often protested against being called an intellectual, writing once to Hicks, for instance, "I'm not an intellectual and have a horror of making an idiot of myself with abstract statements and theories." Some of the cruelest satiric portraits in her stories are those of intellectuals and social reformers, from the first Rayber in "The Barber" to Asbury Fox in "The Enduring Chill" and Joy-Hulga Hopewell in "Good Country People" and another Rayber in *The Violent Bear It Away.* She comes especially close to home when she writes to her friend "A" about a distant goal: "If I were to live long enough and develop as an artist to the proper extent, I would like to write a comic novel about a woman—and what is more comic and terrible than the angular intellectual proud woman approaching God inch by inch with ground teeth?"[2] She is thinking about Simone Weil, but she could almost be describing herself.

As her personal library attests, Flannery O'Connor read and thought seriously about the Southern past. Here, as with politics and her intellectual interests, however, her thinking seemed to embrace contradictory impulses. She felt affinities between her own writing and that of the Agrarians, admiring the work of Caroline Gordon, Allen Tate, and Robert Penn

Warren. When she finally got around to reading *I'll Take My Stand* in the last year of her life, she reported to "A," "It's a very interesting document. It's futile of course like 'woodman, spare that tree,' but still, the only time real minds have got together to talk about the South." That sense of the inevitable erosion of Southern life appears in some of the presentations she gave at colleges during her public speaking tours. In one talk she referred to the anguish of many Southern writers who realize that "every day we are getting more and more like the rest of the country, that we are being forced out not only of our many sins, but of our few virtues." Nevertheless, she said she was sick of hearing about the Civil War and was glad the South lost. She admired C. Vann Woodward's *The Burden of Southern History*, but confessed that "Southern history usually gives me a pain."[3]

Personally she refused to play the part of the Southern lady, not only in her early years, as we saw in chapter 2, but also as an adult. At home she preferred to wear old jeans and loose shirts with their tails hanging out, though she observed public proprieties with dresses and high heels when entertaining guests, going to town, or traveling. Her speech was characteristically blunt, delivered with a nasal tone, and often peppered with expressions of the poor whites she brings to life in her stories.[4] The tone of her letters suggests what her conversation must have been like—serious, direct, devoid of polite hypocrisies, funny, but lighted throughout by a calm and solemn courtesy.

As a writer she chafed against local expectations that she would produce another *Gone with the Wind*. She was interested in portraying the immediate life around her and impatient with popular nostalgia for the world that Scarlett O'Hara had supposedly lost. Her fiction occasionally alludes to antebellum sentimentality, as in the grandmother's disastrous fable about the plantation in "A Good Man Is Hard to Find," for instance, or the pretensions of Julian's mother in "Everything That Rises Must Converge." Most devastating of all is the portrait of General George Poker Sash, a profane and lecherous old relic who dies in his wheelchair at his daughter's graduation from college, just as all the glorious lies about his past have been burned out of his mind by his accusing memory.

In an address she gave at her own college in Milledgeville, O'Connor made a distinction between serious and superficial loyalty to the South which does much to explain apparent contradictions.

> The Southern writer has certainly been provided with a variety of riches,
> but if his vision goes no farther than these materials, then he would have been
> as well off without them. His region is something he has to *use* in order to
> illustrate what is beyond it, and when it becomes too sacred for him to use,

then it has become a liability and not an asset. If you are a Southern writer, the danger that you will remain just that, is very great and to the serious writer, it is also rather terrifying.[5]

Her impatience with conventional Southern pride grew from a clear understanding of the false piety it included and the resulting moral and historical blindness. She admired Southern writers like Faulkner and Warren and historians like Woodward, whose visions were genuine, and indeed, she became one of them.

Because O'Connor knew that her use of her Southern materials baffled and shocked most of her readers, she took special pains to explain her vision of essential Christian truths beyond the violent and grotesque pictures she painted. Most of us are therefore well-acquainted with her intention to portray an apocalyptic grace that smashes through the pride of her reluctant prophets, her sour intellectuals, her grasping widows, and her self-congratulatory Pharisees to reveal their helplessness and their need for faith. But many readers still have trouble explaining how her fiction works, either because they cannot accept her Christian vision or because the violence of her stories seems disproportionate to its intended function.[6] Whatever side we take in this controversy, we must eventually explain our admiration for the fiction in terms that reconcile religious and secular responses and also grant its obvious literary merit. For the stories which structurally support O'Connor's intended religious purpose with consistent action and imagery—stories such as "The Artificial Nigger," "The Displaced Person," "A Good Man Is Hard to Find," "Revelation," and "Everything That Rises Must Converge"—the problem of interpretation is simply the traditional problem of belief we have with all the great writers of the past whose world view we may not share. However we may explain it, we will always read Homer, Sophocles, Aeschylus, Euripides, Dante, and Milton with awe and joy. Similarly we can at least metaphorically if not literally accept Mr. Head's lesson in humility and Ruby Turpin's vision of the vast horde of souls rumbling into heaven. As long as we do homage to the ultimate mystery here, we have surely read these stories right.

But there are others which are structurally flawed or unsuccessful, as O'Connor herself freely admitted. She said "A Stroke of Good Fortune" was too flimsy for the message it was supposed to bear, she did not like "The Comforts of Home," and she was very dissatisfied with "The Lame Shall Enter First." We have to examine such stories very carefully to determine whether their shape reveals other concerns than the ones she was aware of. "I certainly have no idea how I have written about some of the things I have, as they are things I am not conscious of having thought about one way or the other," she wrote "A," the friend who always seemed to probe closest to the heart of her thinking. And in another letter she told "A": "Perhaps you are able to see things in these stories that I can't see because if I did see I would be too frightened to write them."[7] One group of stories repeats almost obsessive patterns which must express some of the frightening subjects she could not bear to notice. These fictions are set on small farms like the one where O'Connor lived outside of Milledgeville, every one presided over by a beleaguered widow with one or two children who are either twelve years old or in their thirties. The farm stories are some of her most vivid and absorbing works, and all of them are concerned with the issues of feminine identity and authority. One in particular has a surprising kinship with Carson McCullers's *The Member of the Wedding*, revealing much about the troubling issues of the other mother-dominated stories.

O'Connor had an almost constitutional aversion to Carson McCullers. Unlike Eudora Welty, whose work she respected and whom she liked very much when they met, McCullers was a writer whose work grew more and more distasteful to her. It is quite certain that the two Georgians would not have liked each other if they had known each other personally, because McCullers was jealous of O'Connor's success, as she was of Truman Capote's, feeling that both the younger writers had been poaching on her territory. For her part, O'Connor would have been repelled by McCullers's egotism and would probably have recognized her as one of the self-indulgent "artists" whom she had disliked at Yaddo. When McCullers's last book came out in 1961, O'Connor wrote one of the most indignant comments she ever committed to paper about another writer.

> Last week Houghton Mifflin sent me a book called *Clock Without Hands* by Carson McCullers. This long-awaited-by-the-faithful book will come out in September. I believe it is the worst book I have ever read. It is incredible. If you want to read it, I will send it to you. It must signal the complete disintegration of this woman's talent. I have forgotten how the other three were, but they were at least respectable from the writing standpoint.[8]

Even though O'Connor could no longer remember McCullers's early work by this time, McCullers may have noticed a real though unconscious debt when she smugly told her cousin that her own fiction had been a school from which O'Connor had "learned her lesson well."[9] If this was true, the debt was a small one, of a similar nature to McCullers's much more involved reliance on Isak Dinesen's "The Monkey." Only a small complex of elements in "A Temple of the Holy Ghost" recalls Frankie Addams's situation early in *The Member of the Wedding*, but in both cases one writer's fiction seems to have suggested themes and metaphors which another would unconsciously revive to explore in her own way. What is unusual in O'Connor's case is that such suggestions should have come from a writer she disliked. McCullers must have dramatized a problem important to O'Connor at some deep level of her imagination.

The most specific echo of McCullers's novella in "A Temple of the Holy Ghost" is the symbol of the hermaphrodite, the particular monster at the freak show which was most appropriate to tomboy Frankie's crisis of sexual identity. The strange thing is that although O'Connor used this symbol as a catalyst in a story about a twelve-year-old girl who is similarly confused about sex, "A Temple of the Holy Ghost" never connects the hermaphrodite with the child's need to accept herself as a female human being. O'Connor's story seems for most of its length to be about courtship, but it turns into something very different at the end and thus raises interesting problems of interpretation. Keeping *The Member of the Wedding* in mind will allow us to evaluate their significance.

The main character of "A Temple of the Holy Ghost" is a sour twelve-year-old girl whose widowed mother runs a small farm. The child is never named, but her ugliness and her intelligence make her an unforgettable character. She is fat and clumsy, with a mouth full of braces that glare like tin, but she is a very serious child with relentlessly acute perceptions of the people around her and a precocious moral awareness. Like Sally Virginia Cope in "A Circle in the Fire," Joy-Hulga Hopewell in "Good Country People," and numerous minor characters in other stories, she is a hilarious caricature of her creator, but Martha Stephens is probably correct in seeing her as a more fully rounded self-portrait than any of the others.[10] Most of these fat, intelligent young women only slenderly know themselves and have few emotions besides rage and contempt. This unnamed girl, however, understands her faults and has a sense of humor, real intellectual curiosity, serious ambitions, and an intense religious faith like Flannery O'Connor's.

A crisis of identity for this girl is set off when she and her mother receive a visit from fourteen-year-old twin cousins who do nothing but giggle, pose before mirrors in lipstick and high heels, and gossip about boys. Their giddy adolescence sets the twelve-year-old's character in sharp relief. At the beginning of the story they call each other Temple One and Temple Two in hilarious mockery of an old nun in their convent school who had advised them to protect themselves on dates by reminding boys that they were Temples of the Holy Ghost. The courtship theme which dominates the first half of the plot is underlined by references to the relationship between the spinster schoolteacher Miss Kirby, who boards at the farm, and her suitor Mr. Cheatham, and by the dates with two neighboring farm boys which the child and her mother arrange for the visiting cousins. In her portrayal of the twelve-year-old girl's fascinated disgust with her boy-crazy cousins and their dates, O'Connor parallels Frankie Addams's resentment of the older girls who are busy initiating themselves into the mysteries of courtship. More specifically, however, she echoes several elements of Frankie's situation which occur around the mention of the freaks at the traveling fair.

McCullers's introduction of the freak show "morphidite and miracle of science" in *The Member of the Wedding* is closely followed by Frankie's irrational rage at her cousin John Henry. Berenice asks, "Now what makes you act like that? You are too mean to live" (p. 19). Frankie accepts the charge and thinks of herself as "dirty and greedy and mean and sad." Soon afterward, McCullers describes her fantasy of heroic fulfillment in going off to war as a Marine, flying airplanes, and winning gold medals for bravery (p. 21). Such a daydream expresses the natural desire of a lively child to escape from the demeaning confusion of her normal life and prove herself dramatically in the adult world . . . except, of course, that such adventures are reserved for males.

All four of these events reappear in "A Temple of the Holy Ghost." When her cousins ask the child how she knows about the "men" who will be their dates, she answers silently in a strange interior monologue about war experience. "I know them all right. We fought in the world war together. They were under me and I saved them five times from Japanese suicide divers and Wendell said I am going to marry that kid and the other said oh no you ain't I am and I said neither one of you is because I will court marshall you all before you can bat an eye."[11]

Like Frankie, the child wants the male adventure of war, but for her the female fantasy of power over men is interwoven with martial excitement. She can save them in battle and remain an inaccessible object of desire whom they must obey. Not long after indulging in this fantasy, the child sourly refuses to eat supper with her cousins. And when her old black cook asks, "Howcome you be so ugly sometime?" (p. 242), we are reminded of Berenice's chiding of Frankie. Later, when she goes to bed, the child muses about her ambitions to be a doctor or an engineer or a martyr, clearly realizing that in fact she is lazy and a liar and "deliberately ugly to almost everyone" (p. 243). Then her cousins return from their dates and, when the lights are out, the child goads them into telling her about the hermaphrodite they saw at the fair. She sits in the darkness at the foot of their bed, fascinated by a revelation she cannot understand.

> The child felt every muscle strained as if she were hearing the answer to a riddle that was more puzzling than the riddle itself. "You mean it had two heads?" she said. "No," Susan said, "it was a man and a woman both. It pulled up its dress and showed us. It had on a blue dress."
> The child wanted to ask how it could be a man and woman both without two heads but she did not. [p. 245]

At this point, O'Connor's hermaphrodite represents a sexual prodigy which the boy-crazy cousins find disturbing, but which the sexually innocent child cannot even comprehend. She is so ignorant of the facts of reproduction that she claims rabbits have babies by spitting them out of their mouths. No sexual enlightenment is provided for the child, despite all the previous emphasis on courtship and her fascination with the mystery of the hermaphrodite.

Rather than confront the issue of adolescent sexual confusion as Mc-Cullers does, O'Connor immediately shifts the story to a theological plane which previous references to the Temple of the Holy Ghost and the child's religious musings have anticipated. The child returns to her bed and tries to make sense of what her cousins have told her. She falls asleep with a dreamlike vision of the freak as an evangelist at a tent meeting, witnessing to God's purpose. "God done this to me and I praise him," the hermaphrodite testifies; "I am a Temple of the Holy Ghost." The country people in the audience slap their hands softly in rhythm, chanting, "Amen, amen" (p. 246). Fuller understanding of this vision comes the next day in an epiphany during a benediction service at the convent chapel where the girl and her mother have gone to return the cousins to school. As the priest raises the monstrance, the child thinks again of the freak who understands that his/her strange form is divinely ordained. She imagines the freak saying, "This is the way He wanted me to be" (p. 248), and we are to understand that the child accepts her own sour independence in those terms. O'Connor herself explained that the story demonstrates "an acceptance of what God wills for us, an acceptance of our individual circumstances," and that this acceptance constitutes purity.[12] But purity for the child also includes sexual innocence; for her the hermaphrodite ceases to have a sexual nature as she/he is transformed by her imagination into a symbol of religious mystery.

A Joycean pun supports the rightness of her vision, for the revelation comes at the moment when the priest raises the monstrance. According to the *American Heritage Dictionary* (1969), whose etymologies and appendix of Indo-European Roots have made it the model of contemporary lexicography in English, the word "monstrance" itself derives from the Latin *monstrum:* "Middle English, from Old French, from Medieval Latin *monstrantia*, from Latin *monstrare*, to show, from *monstrum*, MONSTER." Etymology is not an exact science, and Flannery O'Connor was not the sort of writer to ransack linguistic dictionaries for scholarly accuracy. On the other hand, she would not have been beyond using a serious pun for the rich purpose this one serves in "A Temple of the Holy Ghost." As the receptacle for the Host, which is the body of Christ, the monstrance symbolizes God's human receptacle, shaping and showing forth the Word made flesh, much as the body of the ordinary person serves as a Temple of the Holy Ghost. Thus the hermaphrodite's monstrous physical form can be interpreted as a sanctified vessel for the Host (Latin *hostia*—sacrifice or victim). By accepting his/her condition, the freak becomes a martyr for Christ. [13]

O'Connor deliberately parallels the county fair with its freak show to the circus arena in Rome where Christian martyrs were eaten by lions, decapitated, and burned for their faith. This important connection is made in the child's mind when she lies in bed before her cousins return from their dates. She has been wondering about what she will be when she grows up, considering medicine and engineering but discarding those possibilities in favor of the nobler vocation of sainthood. Realizing that she "was a born liar and slothful and she sassed her mother and was deliberately ugly to almost everybody" as well as being eaten up with the sin of Pride, she feels unworthy of sainthood but thinks "she could be a martyr if they killed her quick" (p. 243). Thus the stage is set even before she learns of the freak's existence for her ultimate identification with him/her as an instrument of God's purpose, a Temple of the Holy Ghost whose oddness is a kind of martyrdom.

To induce our recognition of this unusual point, O'Connor places a physical seal of approval upon the child's implicit identification with the hermaphrodite. After the benediction service, a big nun swoops down upon the child and embraces her, "mashing the side of her face into the crucifix hitched onto her belt." The child has been imprinted by the image of the crucified Christ, as Flannery O'Connor explains to "A":

That one accepted embrace was marked with the ultimate all-inclusive symbol of love, and . . . when the child saw the sun again, it was a red ball, like an elevated Host drenched in blood and it left a line like a red clay road in the sky. Now here the martyrdom that she had thought about in a childish way (which turned into a happy sleeping with the lions) is shown in the final way that has to be for us all—an acceptance of the Crucifixtion [*sic*], Christ's and our own.[14]

Although the story's resolution leaves the child secure in her acceptance of her own peculiar nature as divinely justified, a central, troubling theme has been left dangling. She remains a *girl* who will grow into a woman. She is not a double-sexed freak like the hermaphrodite. The identification of this child with the freak therefore evades her female sexuality, leading us to ask why the question of sexual identity and its relation to courtship is such a dominant issue in most of the story, if it is ultimately to be discarded as irrelevant. The answer to this question is found in O'Connor's ambivalence about sexuality and a closely related attitude toward adolescence. Within the religious terms of the plot's unfolding, there is ample sanction for courtship, so that we might expect O'Connor to resolve the plot in some harmony with it. The farm boys woo the cousins with hillbilly hymns, and the usually silly girls respond by singing a Latin hymn by St. Thomas Aquinas. Even these adolescents behave inadvertently as if they are engaged in something holy, and O'Connor wrote "A" that although relations between the sexes is a category lacking in her stories, "I identify it plainly with the sacred." "But there is also the fact," she goes on to say, "that it being for me the center of life and most holy, I should keep my hands off it until I feel that what I can do with it will be right." In spite of this feeling, she did not manage to keep her hands off the subject entirely. Readers will recall, for instance, that Joy-Hulga tries to seduce the Bible salesman in "Good Country People" but is instead violated by the theft of her wooden leg, and Mrs. May in "Greenleaf" is gored by a bull who buries his head in her lap like a tormented lover. O'Connor thought it very perceptive of writer and scholar Ben Griffith to remark that in her work "there was usually a strong kind of sex potential that was always turned aside and that this gave the stories some of their tension." Again and again this sexual material is resolved in spiritual terms, as in "A Temple of the Holy Ghost." Claire Katz maintains that the sexual dimension of O'Connor's work remains potent, indeed terrifying, in spite of its ultimate religious purpose, and that the motivating force behind it is regressive fantasy expressing infantile fears. While this Freudian plunge into O'Connor's psyche is rather extreme, it corresponds in a very general sense with some comments O'Connor made about herself to "A," comments which are directly relevant to the problems of adolescent identity in "A Temple of the Holy Ghost." "The things you have said about my being surprised to be over twelve, etc., have struck me as quite comically accurate," she wrote. "When I was twelve I made up my mind absolutely that I would

not get any older. . . . There was something about 'teen' attached to anything that was repulsive to me. I certainly didn't approve of what I saw of
people that age." "A" must have been probing a tender spot because the
problem continues as a subject for discussion in O'Connor's next letter to
her friend, when she emphasizes, "I never allowed myself to picture me as
an adult."[15] Even in her early thirties, her childhood reluctance to grow up
and her disgust with the behavior of teenagers remained intensely alive.

In the context of these remarks, she admitted the accuracy of her
friend's insights into another aspect of her inner life closely related to the
problems of adolescence. "What you say about there being two [sexes]
now brings it home to me. I've always believed there were two but generally acted as if there were only one."[16] It is in adolescence that the existence of two sexes becomes acutely obvious and a source of embarrassed
confusion. Trapped in changing bodies and driven by strange energies,
boys and girls are drawn to each other with a giddy clumsiness which
O'Connor captures in the antics of the simpering cousins and their farm-
boy suitors. If she generally behaved as if there were only one sex, she
must have succeeded in maintaining her own youthful determination not
to grow up and admit the sexual differences which make adolescent behavior so embarrassingly silly. She would have been naturally drawn to the
portrayal of Frankie Addams's terror of growing up and her desperate
efforts to ignore sexual differences in *The Member of the Wedding*. Unlike
McCullers, however, O'Connor does not force her twelve-year-old protagonist to accept "normal" femininity as her destiny. While Frankie's tomboy independence is destroyed by the end of McCullers's novel, O'Connor's child preserves her fierce individuality with the assurance that it is
God-given. Her identification with the freak whose body unites the two
sexes into one frees her from having to accept the future represented by
her silly cousins.

Read in light of its links with *The Member of the Wedding*, "A Temple of
the Holy Ghost" functions in part as a dialogue with Carson McCullers on
the question of the choices a girl must make as she emerges from childhood and begins to construct a sense of herself as an adult. Flannery
O'Connor insists through the religious imagery and resolution of her story
that the demeaning conditions of adolescent femininity can be avoided by
an independence which may be freakish in the eyes of the world but
which is sanctified by God in the ancient tradition of the Christian
martyrs.

"A Temple of the Holy Ghost" is an early story, and therefore if its
religious solution to the problem of feminine identity were fully satisfactory to Flannery O'Connor, we should not expect to hear of it again. But

that problem continues to be a source of difficulty within the mother-daughter pattern of the farm stories. Because the sexual issue is so power-ful, O'Connor's attempt to transform it in religious terms not only contrib-utes tension to the stories, as Ben Griffith suggested to her, but it also disrupts plot structure and leaves a profound residue of anxiety in the reader's mind after many of the stories have been laid aside. If we look closely at the repeated motifs in the mother-daughter stories, we will be-gin to see why they are troubling.

The major elements of the mother-daughter pattern appear in "Good Country People": "Every morning Mrs. Hopewell got up at seven o'clock and lit her gas heater and Joy's. Joy was her daughter, a large blonde girl who had an artificial leg. Mrs. Hopewell thought of her as a child though she was thirty-two years old and highly educated" (p. 271). In at least six of O'Connor's thirty-one published stories, the plot centers on a mother resembling Mrs. Hopewell and a daughter like Joy. The mother is a hard-working widow who supports and cares for her large, physically marred girl by running a small farm. The daughter is almost always bookish and very disagreeable. The mother is devoted to her nevertheless, but she is exasperated by her daughter's perversity. Most critics of O'Connor's fic-tion have noticed how often variations of this motif appear in the stories, but few commentators go beyond asserting that this material has auto-biographical sources.

Even the most extreme autobiographical explanations, such as Katz's psychoanalysis of O'Connor's infantile fears, seem to have been antici-pated by "A." We have seen that O'Connor admitted the acuteness of "A's" comments about sexuality, and in an intense series of letters running through 1956 the two women carried on a sort of debate about O'Connor's childhood, her relation to her father, sexuality, and feminism. Since we only have O'Connor's side of the correspondence, and not even that in unabridged form, it is necessary to infer most of what "A" wrote. Even so, O'Connor's letters are usually self-explanatory and allow us to see that "A" must have probed and probed the questions of O'Connor's status as a woman, her acceptance of maturity, and the sexual dimension of her sto-ries. That Flannery O'Connor was willing to consider these subjects and to grant the truth of many of "A's" insights shows her both candid and generous in her thinking. There were a few times when she balked, how-ever. One of these came in September of 1956, in an answer to a letter in which "A" apparently charged her with arrested development and with failing to notice or accept her gender. The issues must have been impor-tant ones to "A" because O'Connor realizes that she could be hurting her friend's feelings and tries to reassure her with the reference to the patter of baby rhino's feet:

If you are going to pass on the Luces and the *Bulletin*, I will pass on being Miss Delayed Development, though not without me [*sic*] inner groan. Anyway, I ain't going to wory about stomping over your ego: it's just the patter of little feet, even though it may be the little feet of the baby rhinoceros at the zoo. Once or twice people have written me that I have been barbarous or rude about one thing or another and all the time it will be something that I have been wondering if I have made even a slight impression about.

On the subject of the feminist business, I just never think, that is never think of qualities which are specifically feminine or masculine. I suppose I divide people into two classes: the Irksome and the Non-Irksome without regard to sex. Yes and there are the Medium Irksome and the Rare Irksome.[17]

Most of the characters in her stories are the comically irksome, but there are important differences between male and female in spite of O'Connor's disclaimers. Males are usually aggressive and vindictive, whereas females are rendered passive by punishment. There are exceptions—males like Tarwater or Parker or Mr. Head, who are punished—but females get by far the worst treatment.

In fully half the stories published in *A Good Man Is Hard to Find* and the posthumous *Everything That Rises Must Converge*, widowed or divorced mothers are central female characters who are tricked, deluded, or violently chastened. These stranded women have been left to raise bad-tempered sons or, more often, daughters, but they prove tough and resourceful in their dealings with the outside world and thus create modest little matriarchies where their sour children can lead comfortable lives. O'Connor satirizes the stinginess, smugness, wariness of strangers, and determination to see things in a cheerful light, which are the side effects of the widows' struggle. In most of these stories the mother's pride is ultimately smashed by a vindictive male force, perhaps most extremely in "Greenleaf," "The Comforts of Home," and "Everything That Rises Must Converge," where she dies under assault.

Daughters have the same outrage at their mothers' smugness and the same resentment of her authority that sons express, but there the similarity ends. Almost every son wants to punish his mother or "teach her a lesson." Two actually kill their mothers, and the Misfit of "A Good Man Is Hard to Find" could be said to have the same instinctive reaction in shooting the grandmother when she reaches out to him saying, "Why, you're one of my babies!" Daughters, on the other hand, usually end up as allies of their mothers, forced by male deceit and violence into humiliating defeat.

Bertram Wyatt-Brown confirms the historical reality behind the vulnerability which Flannery O'Connor describes for her widows and their daughters. Southern legal traditions made it difficult for women to control property in the nineteenth century, and widows who attempted to manage their own affairs were regarded as arrogant. The carnage of the Civil War produced many widows who had to support their families alone through the terrible decades of Reconstruction. Although most succeeded, they did so in a hostile masculine business and legal environment where "the widow had to struggle keenly against the presumption that she would be the loser in any sort of transaction."[18] O'Connor's stories show us a modern South where similar hardships exist for widows in muted form; her Mrs. Cope and Mrs. Hopewell, Mrs. MacIntyre, Mrs. May and Mrs. Crater all preserve a fear of disaster hovering just at the borders of consciousness. This fear is a defensive understanding of the predatory forces they have only narrowly survived.

These women have maintained homes for their children against great odds, and have sacrificed to give them a chance in life, yet neither sons nor daughters mature successfully. Sons grow up to be intellectual drones who live at home, sullenly resentful of their mothers but unable to break away. In "Why Do the Heathen Rage?" a son snarls at his mother, "A woman of your generation is better than a man of mine" (p. 485). He sees this as a shameful reversal of normal masculine superiority, and O'Connor intends it to demonstrate his bitter understanding of his own failure. The daughters' situations are more specifically hopeless because they are not only physically unappealing but also too intelligent, well educated, and sourly independent to ever assume "normal" roles as wives and mothers. Father James McCown said something similar about Flannery O'Connor herself: "She was incapable of being anything but herself, and the self she was would probably have frightened away any save a suitor of singular discernment."[19] Like O'Connor, the daughters of the stories are social misfits whom she is always contrasting to girls of both upper and lower classes who are immersed in courtship and reproduction. Nothing could be further from the beauty and grace of the Southern belle than the glasses, ugly braces, and extra pounds of O'Connor's twelve-year-old girls or the wooden legs, bad hearts, and fondness for ridiculous sweat shirts and Girl Scout shoes of her mature daughters.

In "A Circle in the Fire" we meet Sally Virginia Cope, "a pale fat girl of twelve with a frowning squint and a large mouth full of silver bands" (p. 181). At one point in the story, we find her wearing a pair of overalls pulled over her dress, a man's old felt hat pulled down so far on her head that it squeezes her face livid, and a gun and holster set around her waist. "Good Country People" provides a mature example of the type. At thirty-two, Joy Hopewell suffers from a bad heart and a resentful disposition which her mother blames on her wooden leg. In an act of typical perversity Joy changes her legal name to Hulga because of its ugly sound, and dresses "in a six-year-old skirt and a yellow sweatshirt with a faded cowboy on a horse embossed on it." All day she sits "on her neck in a deep chair," reading nihilistic philosophy. "Sometimes she went for walks but she didn't like dogs or cats or birds or flowers or nature or nice young men. She looked at nice young men as if she could smell their stupidity" (p. 276).

Mrs. Cope and Mrs. Hopewell have their hands full with such daughters. They try to be understanding and patient in the traditional ladylike style they are vainly attempting to instill in their daughters. Sometimes, however, their patience snaps, and they give way to despair. This happens when Sally Virginia dons her overalls and felt hat. "Mrs. Cope watched her with a tragic look. 'Why do you have to look like an idiot?' she asked. 'Suppose company were to come? When are you going to grow up? What's going to become of you? I look at you and I want to cry!'" (p. 191). Sally Virginia responds in a high, irritated voice. "Leave me be. Just leave me be. I ain't you." The child deliberately speaks in poor-white dialect as she defies her mother's efforts to make her conventionally feminine; she refuses to identify herself with her mother.

Such rebellion against the standards set by genteel mothers is typical for the daughters of the stories, and we may guess it was characteristic of Flannery O'Connor herself. If we wish to know why the daughters resist so fiercely, we need only turn to "The Life You Save May Be Your Own." The story opens with a mother and daughter who live in a perfect harmony symbolized by their bearing exactly the same name—Lucynell Crater. That is their only resemblance, however, and their grotesque differences provide a caricature of their relationship. The mother is a hard-bitten, leathery, and toothless country widow whose toughness has enabled her to survive but has taken its toll. The daughter is a moron whose vapid beauty is, in Martha Chew's words, "a parody of the pink and white looks and facade of sweetness required of Southern women."[20] She has long pink-gold hair and "eyes as blue as a peacock's neck." In contrast to most of O'Connor's daughters, Lucynell Jr. is absolutely docile, serving as a strange and distorted symbol of spiritual innocence.

Lucynell's speechless imbecility must be the reason for her sweet nature. Female intelligence is a curse in the world of these stories, for it creates profound discontent. Frustrated in a society of hillbillies, religious fundamentalists, and snuff-dipping tenant farmers, most of these bright fat girls snipe away at the pretension and stupidity around them. In "A Temple of the Holy Ghost," as we have seen, the twelve-year-old girl's proud and sour intelligence makes her see her cousins and their dates as "stupid idiots" and prevents her from participating in their normal adolescent activities. In "Revelation," the same kind of intelligence causes a rage of resentment verging on madness for the acne-faced college girl in the doctor's waiting room. Mary Grace grows more and more outraged as she listens to Mrs. Turpin's self-congratulatory remarks about her own virtuous place in Southern society. Although her genteel mother tries to placate her, the girl finally explodes, hurling her book across the room at Mrs. Turpin's head and then leaping after it and trying to strangle the object of her rage. She has to be forcibly restrained and finally drugged. The girl serves only as a vehicle to produce a humbling revelation for Mrs. Turpin. Yet the strange intensity of her hatred and the unexpected violence of her action leave us with a shocked curiosity. Intelligence seems a curse which has unbalanced her, but at the same time the story's resolution bears out the rightness of her negative judgment upon Mrs. Turpin's pride. Ultimately Mary Grace's presence in the story is too strong and troubling for the limited role she plays.

Most of O'Connor's daughters keep their intolerance under better control and try to maintain an aloofness from the world their mothers and people like Mrs. Turpin represent. Involvement with men eventually destroys their pretensions of independence, however, and forces them to share their mothers' vulnerability. Ruby Hill of "A Stroke of Good Fortune" is not bookish like most of the O'Connor daughters, but she tries just as strenuously to escape becoming like her mother. The feminine heritage her mother represents is the horrifying biological destiny of childbearing. At thirty-four Ruby is smugly pleased to have avoided ruining her life with motherhood. She constantly compares herself to her mother, who at the same age was gray-haired, sour, "like a puckered-up old yellow apple": "All those children were what did her mother in—eight of them: two born dead, one died the first year, one crushed under a mowing machine. Her mother had got deader with every one of them" (p. 97). Ruby counts on her husband Bill Hill to take care of the danger, and she smiles to think of how she has escaped being "the dried-up type" like her shriveled parents. "She was warm and fat and beautiful and not too fat because Bill Hill liked her that way. She had gained some weight but he hadn't noticed except that he was maybe more happy lately and didn't know why" (p. 99). By the end of the story, however, Ruby is forced to realize that Bill Hill's birth control methods have failed and that she is pregnant. Perhaps Bill was happier lately and *did* know why. Her palmist's prophecy of "a stroke of good fortune" now appears sardonic. Ruby's shock of recognition comes in an almost ludicrously Freudian setting—the cavernous stairwell of her apartment building which makes a "thin black rent in the middle of the house," and where she accidentally sits down on a little boy's toy pistol. As she sits on the steps in pain and feels a piece of her insides rolling over, she realizes with horror that the baby is just waiting to make her into an old woman.

> "Good fortune," she said in a hollow voice that echoed along all the levels of the cavern, "Baby."
> "Good Fortune, Baby," the three echoes leered.
> Then she recognized the feeling again, a little roll. It was as if it were not in her stomach. It was as if it were out nowhere in nothing, out nowhere, resting and waiting, with plenty of time. [p. 107]

The story ends here, with the leering mockery of the echoes in the stairwell. By now the title "A Stroke of Good Fortune" has come to symbolize O'Connor's heavily ironic but ambivalent attitude toward Ruby's situation. She intended the story to be a Catholic statement "about the rejection of life at the source,"[21] but instead the story presents an appalling picture of the physical cost of reproduction and one woman's realization that she has been tricked into paying it. No solution to Ruby's problem is offered; no clear religious symbolism is provided to suggest an alternative vision of her fate. Instead we leave the defeated woman slumped in her echoing stairwell, her mind paralyzed by the ghastly vision of an alien being "out nowhere in nothing," patiently waiting its time to destroy her.

A consistent pattern of masculine behavior emerges if we survey the mother-daughter stories. Bill Hill's remembered smile grows slyer and slyer as "A Stroke of Good Fortune" unfolds, so that by the end we know Ruby made a mistake in trusting him. Eudora Welty has Katie Rainey make a remark in *The Golden Apples* which could apply to the men in Flannery O'Connor's world: "Haven't you noticed it prevail, in the world in general? Beware of a man with manners."[22] She is thinking especially of King MacLain, the courtly seducer in the white linen suit who is Welty's incarnation of Zeus as a Southern Gentleman. We have seen that Welty is affectionately indulgent of King's promiscuous habits, seeing him as an agent of nature's potency. Flannery O'Connor's courtly "gentlemen" are of a far different order. Although they serve an ultimately beneficial purpose in the religious scheme of the stories, on a literal level they use their manners only to seduce women into relaxing their guard so that they can be exploited. The sexuality of these seductions is usually displaced or sublimated, but O'Connor admitted its presence in her fiction and knew that it was vindictive and destructive rather than erotic in at least one story.[23]

The most clearly but perversely sexual of these courteous seducers has the expressive name of Manley Pointer, and he is used in "Good Country

People" to administer a lesson in humility to the most famous of O'Connor's fictional daughters, Joy Hopewell. In a very revealing letter to "A," O'Connor talks about the relation of this story to her own life, presumably because "A" has claimed Hulga is like her creator in never having loved anybody before she meets young Pointer. After agreeing that Hulga is autobiographical, O'Connor writes an uncharacteristically vehement and muddled paragraph whose confusion mirrors in a small way the confusions of the story itself.

> That my stories scream to you that I have never consented to be in love with anybody is merely to prove that they are screaming an historical inaccuracy. I have God help me consented to this frequently. Now that Hulga is repugnant to you only makes her more believable. I had a letter from a man who said Allen Tate was wrong about the story that Hulga was not a "maimed soul," she was just like us all. He ended the letter by saying he was in love with Hulga and he hoped some day she would learn to love him. Quaint. But I stick neither with you nor with that gent here but with Mr. Allen Tate. A maimed soul is a maimed soul.[24]

The "gent" who wrote expressing his love for Hulga might as well have been Manley Pointer himself. As the author of the story defended by her Catholicism and the privacy of her actual life with her mother, Flannery O'Connor is able to remain aloof from his overtures. But in the same letter to "A," she said that "there was less conscious technical control in GCP than in any other story I've ever written." The difficulties of interpretation in the story could very well derive from that lack of conscious control. "Good Country People," like "A Temple of the Holy Ghost," is very close to O'Connor's life and is overwhelmed in a similar way by its courtship theme despite her efforts at the end to turn it to religious purposes.

The entire length of "Good Country People" is concerned with courtship, from the opening paragraphs where Joy is introduced and contrasted to Glynese and Carramae Freeman, caricatures of "normal" girls. "Joy called them Glycerin and Caramel. Glynese, a redhead, was eighteen and had many admirers. Carramae, a blonde, was only fifteen but already married and pregnant. She could not keep anything on her stomach. Every morning Mrs. Freeman told Mrs. Hopewell how many times she had vomited since the last report" (p. 272).

Mrs. Freeman, the tenant farmer's wife, is obviously proud of her successful daughters, while Mrs. Hopewell cannot live up to her name where her own daughter is concerned. Joy has never known the experiences of normal adolescence, and, as we have seen, she has deliberately made herself as ugly as possible. When she changed her legal name to Hulga at the age of twenty-one, she felt she had achieved her highest creative act. "One of her major triumphs was that her mother had not been able to turn her dust into Joy, but the greater one was that she had been able to turn it herself into Hulga." No wonder her mother thinks of her as a "poor stout girl in her thirties who had never danced a step or had any *normal* good times" and who would have been far better off without her useless Ph.D. "It seemed to Mrs. Hopewell that every year she grew less and less like other people and more like herself—bloated, rude, and squint-eyed" (pp. 275–76).

Manley Pointer is a skillful young Bible salesman who can adapt his manners to charm every customer, including even rude and squint-eyed Joy-Hulga. By flattering Mrs. Hopewell, pretending naive piety, and finally claiming to have a bad heart, he melts her skepticism and moves her to go so far as to invite him to dinner. This Uriah Heep act does not seem to be working on her daughter, for Joy-Hulga is deliberately rude to the young man all through the meal. "Mrs. Hopewell could not understand deliberate rudeness, although she lived with it, and she felt she had always to overflow with hospitality to make up for Joy's lack of courtesy" (p. 280). Still, she notices that the Bible salesman and her daughter have been watching each other intently and that they have a conversation outside the house as he is leaving. What the mother cannot hear is his courtly treatment of her large and clumsy "child." O'Connor tells us that when they talked he gazed at Joy-Hulga "with open curiosity, with fascination, like a child watching a new fantastic animal at the zoo," but what he says to her is, "You're a brave sweet little thing and I liked you the minute I seen you walk in the door." He continues his flattery by admiring her name and then inviting her to go with him on a picnic the next day. "I like to walk in the woods," he says, "and see what Mother Nature is wearing" (pp. 283–84).

When Joy-Hulga lies awake that night imagining she seduces him in the storage barn, she thinks of this as a way of transmitting her genius to an inferior mind and thus giving him a deeper understanding of life. She is not even vaguely aware of how sexual her reaction to him is or how vulnerable it makes her. The next day she is so preoccupied that she forgets to take any food when she goes to meet him. She is completely unprepared for the emotional tumult of lovemaking. When he first kisses her, she feels an extra surge of adrenaline and believes herself clearheaded and ironically detached from the experience. In fact, she is gradually falling under his power, returning his kisses, and unaware that he has taken her glasses and rendered her practically blind. The climax of the story comes when they embrace in the hayloft and he asks her to prove her love by showing where her wooden leg joins on. The artificial leg is like her sacred soul, private and secret, but he persuades her to let him take it off. When she agrees, she surrenders completely to him. "Without the leg she felt entirely dependent on him. Her brain seemed to have stopped thinking altogether and to be about some other function that it was not very good at" (p. 289). Indeed she is not very good at this function; she is completely disabled. When Pointer opens a hollow Bible to reveal a flask of whiskey, obscene playing cards, and contraceptives, Joy-Hulga is stunned. "Aren't you just good country people?" she pleads, exposing a naivete equal to her mother's. "Yeah," Pointer sneers, "but it ain't held me back none." Disgusted to learn that she is as gullible and innocent as her mother, he scoops his entertainments back into his suitcase with her glasses and wooden leg and disappears down the ladder, leaving his victim completely devastated (pp. 290–91).

Joy-Hulga's surrender to Manley Pointer is described in one sentence intended to parody the believer's surrender to Christ: "It was like losing her own life and finding it again, miraculously, in his" (p. 289). Thus O'Connor meant us to see that when the Bible salesman steals the wooden leg, "he has taken away part of the girl's personality and has revealed her deeper affliction to her for the first time." This is true in part, but in her commentary on the story, O'Connor also insists on the primacy of the literal level of the plot. On that level, the story is a grotesque courtship rite in which the Bible salesman uses sexual seduction for a perverse theft, and Joy-Hulga falls prey to his advances. "If a writer is any good," O'Connor said in a talk to a college audience, "what he makes will have its source in a realm much larger than that which his conscious mind can encompass and will always be a greater surprise to him than it can ever be to his reader."[25] What might have been a surprise to her was the profound symbolic material she provided in "Good Country People" for an understanding of rape.

Joy-Hulga's sexuality is essential to her identity, though she is completely unaware of it. The part of her personality which the Bible salesman takes away by stealing her wooden leg is her sour independence as a female who refuses to accept the submissive role her Southern world has dictated for her. In trying to live an independent intellectual life, Joy-Hulga fails to realize the power of sexual differences and her needs as a woman. Thus her apparent toughness is brittle and her wooden leg an apt symbol for her independence.

Manley Pointer seems to understand this at once. He is fascinated by her perverse uniqueness and tells her that the leg is "what makes you different. You ain't like anybody else." Joy-Hulga thinks he appreciates her bravery and her defiance of life's attempt to cripple her. "This boy, with an instinct that came from beyond wisdom, had touched the truth about her." But we learn that his instincts are entirely predatory. He delights in sexual conquests of crippled women, snatching away as trophies their artificial eyes and legs—the manufactured props which make them whole. When he has persuaded Joy-Hulga to let him remove her wooden leg, she is overwhelmed by her helplessness and pleads to have the leg restored. "Leave it off for a while," he says. "You got me instead" (p. 289). So he says, but he will violate her trust and her physical and emotional integrity more completely by stealing her leg than the normal physical rape could ever have done. O'Connor has taken the significance of rape to a symbolic extreme in the picture of this man who preys sexually on women and literally leaves them crippled.

Recently Frederick Asals has shown how the maternal contours of the landscape Joy-Hulga sees from the barn loft are connected with the child-like quality of the Bible salesman's lovemaking and Hulga's motherly response.[26] All this is merely a ploy, as we know, but because Pointer's virtual rape is intended to serve the beneficial purpose of awakening the heroine to her spiritual needs, O'Connor transforms the landscape into a green lake over which Joy-Hulga sees him depart like a mock Christ walking on water. Something similar happens in "The Life You Save May Be Your Own," for here too the maternal is associated with a daughter's sexuality, and both mother and daughter are violated by a "Christlike" seducer. This is a puzzling story which seems to promise a typical O'Connor come-uppance for a miserly widowed farm owner, but instead turns into an indictment of the hypocritical robber bridegroom Tom T. Shiftlet and an exposure of his misogyny. Mr. Shiftlet is a lower-class parody of the Southern gentleman who courts the maiden of the story—retarded Lucynell Crater, Jr.—only to exploit her mother.

John Desmond sees Mr. Shiftlet's character change as the plot unfolds, but if we look closely at Shiftlet's behavior when he first arrives on Mrs. Crater's farm, we will see that from the beginning his gallantry and his quaint piety are only a disguise to hide his desire for the old car in the widow's garage.[27] Arriving in the Craters' front yard at sunset, the one-armed stranger sets down his box of tools and tips his hat at retarded Lucynell Jr. as if she were perfectly normal. Then he turns to the mother and sweeps his hat completely off in greeting. Rather than answering her "Good evening," however, he performs a strange ritual.

> He turned his back and faced the sunset. He swung both his whole and his short arm up slowly so that they indicated an expanse of sky and his figure formed a crooked cross. . . .
>
> He held the pose for almost fifty seconds and then he picked up his box and came on to the porch and dropped down on the bottom step. "Lady," he said in a firm nasal voice, "I'd give a fortune to live where I could see me a sun do that every evening." [p. 146]

His resemblance to "a crooked cross" should be taken literally—he is crooked, no matter how reverent he seems. As they introduce themselves and begin a guarded conversation, Shiftlet presents himself as an eccentric country moralist and patriotic veteran of the "Arm Service" who is not interested in money and reveres virtuous women. All the while, however, he has been eyeing the car he had noticed the moment he arrived. While he talks about the mysteries of the human heart, he is mentally calculating the age of the car, so that when he comes to the subject of the retarded Lucynell we would be fools not to suspect his motives.

> "Is she your baby girl?" he asked.
> "My only," the old woman said, "and she's the sweetest girl in the world. I would give her up for nothing on earth. She's smart too. She can sweep the floor, cook, wash, feed the chickens, and hoe. I wouldn't give her up for a casket of jewels."
> "No," he said kindly, "don't ever let any man take her from you."
> "Any man come after her," the old woman said, " 'll have to stay around the place." [p. 149]

This passage quivers with dramatic irony, for the old widow has just stated her terms for marriage while Shiftlet declares his reverence for the girl at the same time that he focuses his eye in the darkness on "a part of the automobile bumper that glittered in the distance." He will reluctantly agree to marry Lucynell Jr. so that he can have the car, and one hundred miles after he has driven his bride away from her tearful mother, he will abandon her in a roadside diner.

Although Shiftlet has nothing but disgust for his moron bride, the boy behind the counter at the diner has a genuine reverence for her which shows up the cynicism of her departing husband. As she sleeps in her seat, the boy stares at her pink-gold hair and murmurs, "She looks like an angel of Gawd" (p. 154). Even Tom T. Shiftlet must have been affected by her innocence, because he feels increasingly depressed as he drives towards Memphis after abandoning her. To assuage his conscience, he picks up a suspicious young hitchhiker and begins a pious recital of his mother's virtues. His language reveals that he has identified Lucynell with the image of his mother, and it also sounds like a twisted echo of the overblown reverence for womanhood which was such a central feature of rhetoric in the antebellum South. "It's nothing so sweet as a boy's mother. She taught him his first prayers at her knee, she give him love when no other would, she told him what was right and what wasn't, and she seen that he done the right thing. Son, . . . I never rued a day in my life like the one I rued when I left that old mother of mine" (p. 155). By this time the latter-day

Henry Grady is almost overcome with his own rhetoric, and the car slows to a crawl as he exclaims, "My mother was a angel of Gawd. He took her from heaven and giver to me and I left her." The boy turns angrily toward Shiftlet and cries, "My old woman is a flea bag and yours is a stinking pole cat!" With that, he jumps out of the car, leaving a stunned Tom T. Shiftlet to absorb his insult. Shiftlet recovers his composure, raises his arm, and prays, "O Lord! Break forth and wash the slime from this earth" (p. 156). A guffawing peal of thunder and the crash of raindrops on his car are the answer to his prayer; he himself is the slime to be washed from the earth.

This is the only one of O'Connor's mother-daughter stories in which the patriarchal God behind the natural world defends the betrayed women. Usually the women need to be chastened for their pride, and the gentlemanly invader serves as a strangely diabolical agent for the robust O'Connor brand of divine grace. As Asals explains, O'Connor learned to use the natural world, particularly landscape, sun, moon, and sky, with increasing symbolic richness as her career progressed.[28] The transformation he observed in "Good Country People," from maternal earth to domain of the male god after feminine defeat, recurs in more complicated form elsewhere, revealing an inversion of traditional patterns of landscape imagery in myth and literature.

Chapter Seven

O'Connor's
Sacred Landscapes

N o one can enter the world of Flannery O'Connor's fiction without sensing at once the strange power of its landscapes and skies.
The raw earth gapes orange, red, and purple; but where it is
cultivated neat little farms sit dreaming uneasily under swollen suns and
glaring skies, their fertile pastures protected by dark sentinel lines of gaunt
woods. Sunsets are bruised purple or bloody red, bathing woods and
meadows in livid light. Although readers have learned to see religious
mystery in these landscapes and have become familiar with O'Connor's
use of the traditional opposition between urban corruption and pastoral
wholeness,[1] such explosive forces slumber in her woods or menace from
her skies that the effect is anything but familiar. We must all share the little
boy's response in "The River" as he enters the woods for the first time,
walking carefully and "looking from side to side as if he were entering a
strange country." If we look carefully we can see landmarks from our
mythic past which cast disturbing shadows in the stories very different
from the warm and lifegiving mythic shapes in Eudora Welty's fiction.

In one after another of O'Connor's stories we find ourselves in woods
and pastures that are sacred precincts for the enactment of violent rituals
intended to batter her characters into an awareness of their helplessness

before God. A family is shot to death in a grove of trees beside a country road, a girl is beaten by her father and grandfather in the woods, a boy is raped by a homosexual among the trees, and woods are the setting for retributive arson and groveling ceremonies of prayer healing. In pastures a woman is gored to death by a bull, a little boy drowns himself in an orange stream, and the Bible salesman steals Joy-Hulga's wooden leg. These conjunctions of action and setting are unique to O'Connor's fiction, but the places themselves are very old, as we learned when exploring the bayou wood and the Mound Field of *Delta Wedding*. Flannery O'Connor knew that sacred groves and meadows or pastures were symbolic locations in the oldest of myths, and she deliberately exploited the ancient connections. Her library included not only the Bible but also Bulfinch's *Mythology*, the Greek tragedians, Homer in Robert Fitzgerald's translations, and works in comparative mythology.[2] Thus she knew not only the Garden of Eden and the pastures of the Old Testament patriarchs and Jesus's parables, but also the meadows where Persephone and Europa were stolen away, the pastures where the Bacchants worshipped Dionysos in their frenzy, and the groves sacred to Artemis but fatal to Adonis. In echoing the old pagan material, however, O'Connor wrenched it from its original associations to destroy the power of the mother identified with the land and the woods.

The Edenic, restorative quality of O'Connor's rural settings has been amply demonstrated by Michael Cleary, but within that general context woods serve distinctly different functions from pastures or cultivated lands, and both are closely associated with the women of the stories. Cleary sees the countryside as a sanctuary in the sense of a refuge for prophet figures like old Tarwater, but it also serves as a sanctuary for worship such as Mrs. Greenleaf's prayer-healing in the woods and the Reverend Bevel Summers's baptism service in the river running through a wood-encircled meadow. More often, however, meadows are presented as vulnerable gardens. Woods or "sentinel lines of trees" protect them from the menace of the outside world, but by a terrible kind of irony these sacred groves harbor uncontrollable forces which some have likened to the explosive, irrational powers which Hawthorne located in the forest.[3] In *The Violent Bear It Away*, for instance, Old Tarwater's farm is protected from citified invaders by a thick tangle of trees and undergrowth, but at the end of the story his nephew is raped in its outskirts near the road. At the end of "The Artificial Nigger" Nelson and Mr. Head escape from the infernal city and return to their mysteriously moonlit countryside where treetops fence the clearing around their railroad junction "like the protecting walls of a garden." The word "garden" is a deliberate hint toward the Edenic significance of this place, especially as the train which returns the boy and his grandfather to their home is described as a frightened serpent. Here the serpent-train represents corrupting urban forces which do not belong in the tranquil garden. The most typical garden settings of the stories, however, are the farms—those cultivated landscapes ringed by protective woods and almost always ruled by women. Mrs. Cope and Mrs. Hopewell are only two of the most familiar of O'Connor's legion of farm owners whose husbands are conveniently dead or long-divorced, leaving them in full control. As we saw in the previous chapter, there are at least nine stories dominated by such women, and almost all their farms have flourished because of the qualities suggested by the names "Cope" and "Hopewell."

But the prosperity of these female domains is insecure. Mrs. Cope's constant fear of fire in her woods is symbolic of the danger which lurks just outside every farm and which, as we have noticed, usually materializes in the form of an invading male. Not surprisingly, the intruder in the garden is often likened to a snake. Mr. Shiftlet of "The Life You Save May Be Your Own" stretches "like a weary snake waking up by a fire," Mrs. Cope reacts to Garfield's cigarette in "A Circle in the Fire" as if "a snake had been slung in her path," and Mr. Greenleaf in the story "Greenleaf" is described as a snake striking in one of his conversations with Mrs. May. Flannery O'Connor meant these serpent references to suggest parallels to the Genesis story of Eve's seduction by Satan, so that her female gardeners suffer a fortunate fall which destroys their complacent materialism and opens their eyes to ultimate spiritual values. Close attention to the sexual dynamics of the stories, however, reveals that the serpent's invasion of the garden is only presented as an ultimately positive event if the garden is dominated by a woman. If it is a male preserve, as in "The Artificial Nigger" or *The Violent Bear It Away*, violations of pastoral sanctity are seen as negative intrusions by representatives of the corrupt city. In the stories about women farm owners, O'Connor seems to be demonstrating that independent female authority is unnatural and must be crushed by male force. Most of these women are mothers, and the unnaturalness of their authority is reflected most clearly in the impotence of their adult children who have never managed to leave home.[4]

O'Connor's close identification of these mothers with their land is coupled with sexual imagery implying that male incursions amount to a kind of rape, even in stories where the erotic theme is more subtle than the seduction patterns so clearly visible in "Good Country People" and "The Life You Save May Be Your Own." Sexual symbolism has been a traditional Catholic vehicle for describing God's intervention in human affairs, and one critic speaks of O'Connor's emphasis on "the penetration by the divine" through the complacency of her characters' minds, male as well as female, so that they may be opened to the action of grace.[5] But repeated emphasis on the vulnerable womanhood of the farm-owning mothers and the predatory malice of their male adversaries sets the stories apart from traditional use of the lyric eroticism of the Song of Songs to describe the relation of the Bridegroom Savior to his Beloved Virgin Mother, to the Church, and to individual worshipers.

The pattern and tone of action in O'Connor's farm stories is much closer to the archetypal rape images of Greek mythology, especially familiar in the stories of Persephone and Europa. O'Connor deliberately echoed Europa's rape in "Greenleaf," and it is hard to imagine that she never noticed similarities between pagan mother/daughter motifs and the situations in many of her other stories. Her childhood imagination had been nourished by the Greek and Roman mythology in her copy of the children's encyclopedia *The Book of Knowledge*, and Robert Fitzgerald's translations of Homer and the Greek tragedians introduced her to the stark power of some of the primary sources and affected her revisions of *Wise Blood*. Whether reading Greek tragedy renewed her childhood interest in myth, or whether she had always maintained it, by the time she came to write "Greenleaf" she was well acquainted with fertility myths and interested in their relation to Christianity.[6] She sought consciously in "Greenleaf" to draw the old patterns of suggestion into the service of her Christian vision, but they are peculiarly retentive of their integrity, and she seems to have been ambivalent about them. In the other farm stories where masculine invasion less consciously echoed myths of rape than in "Greenleaf," there are similarly disturbing inversions of the myths. A brief review of their evolution from Neolithic times will help to show why their persistence creates tensions in the stories which O'Connor's craft cannot resolve.

The oldest known symbols of divinity are female. Most of us are familiar with the corpulent "Venuses" recovered from Paleolithic caves in southern Europe, and recent archaeological work emphasizes the predominance of such artifacts all over northern Europe as well, reaching as far east as Siberia. In *The Roots of Civilization*, Alexander Marshack links these obvious fertility symbols with sophisticated systems of lunar notation and cave art recording careful observation of animal and vegetable fertility in proper seasonal contexts. Soviet archaeologist Z. A. Abramova summarizes prevailing scientific opinion in the USSR that connects the female figurines not only with the fertility of the earth and influence of the moon but also with ancient hunting myths which revered woman as guardian of animals and owner of forests.[7] It seems clear that the Earth Mother governed wild nature and the seasonal cycles of life and death in religious thought as long ago as 25,000 B.C.

Although the end of the Ice Age stimulated the gradual development of agriculture and brought profound cultural changes, Neolithic peoples continued to think in the basic religious terms of their ancestors. They simply elaborated the old symbolic forms to correspond to the new conditions of their lives. Massive accumulations of archaeological evidence from Neolithic cultures as old as 7,000 B.C. in the Near East, the Balkans, and all over the USSR are typified by votive figurines of the Mother Goddess which share many of the formal characteristics of the Paleolithic artifacts. In her various aspects, the Great Goddess appears with emphasis on her pregnancy, with her child, with snakes symbolizing water and rebirth, with a bird's head, or flanked by wild animals. For these agriculturists and domesticators of animals, however, bulls' horns became a particularly central emblem of the divine *Magna Mater*. As Mircea Eliade explains, "Wherever they are to be found in Neolithic cultures, either in iconography, or as parts of idols in the form of oxen, they denote the presence of the Great Goddess of fertility. And a horn is always the image of the new moon" because of its similar crescent shape. The serpent is also an epiphany of the moon and serves with the bull as male complement to the Mother's power. These figures appear in two main symbolic settings: either the hearth where grain is ground and sacrificial animals are cooked, or a stylized garden where the Mother is enthroned beside a tree of life.[8]

Robert Graves has earned the reputation of a crank for his voluminous attempts to prove that ancient female powers once reigned supreme in mythology and even after patriarchal suppression have continued to exert a pervasive influence on human thought. But more and more scholars— and not only the Jungians—have come to agree that the Indo-European migrations into Europe displaced and subverted the mother-worship of earlier peoples, introducing dominant male divinities but never wholly destroying the power of the old forms. The old worship survived almost into historic times with the Minoan civilization of Crete and its Mycenaean Greek imitators. Some of the old material has been transmitted in muted form through Homer's *Odyssey,* and in our own century the Minoan-Mycenaean scholar Martin Nilsson established the survival of the Minoan goddesses in post-Homeric Greek worship of Artemis, Athena, and Demeter.[9]

With Greek mythology we are back on familiar ground, where no one would contest the predominantly masculine emphasis in symbols of divine power. But even here, the fruitful earth continued to be the realm of Mother Demeter, as we have seen in chapter 3. And Artemis's dominion over the forests, wild creatures, and the fertility of human females was never challenged. According to Eliade, "In every kind of phenomenon to which the epiphany of the soil has given rise . . . we can discern the activity of motherhood, of an inexhaustible power of creation." Art historian Vincent Scully argues that Greek sacred architecture was always carefully placed within particular symbolic contours of Mother Earth so that the landscape performed a function as essential as that of the human structure in worship. Forests, pastures, and cultivated fields remained women's places whose identification with the female body is attested etymologically as well as through religious-mythological imagery. "Europa," for instance, is not only the name of a mythological maiden seduced by Zeus in the form of a bull; it was also the name of the Greek homeland which later was expanded to denote all of the known world of Western civilization. In Sophocles's *Oedipus* a common Greek term for tilled or arable land, ἄρουρα, is used as a metaphor for woman.[10] This metaphor reflects a traditional association of the land with woman. And, more particularly, we should remember that the meadow is associated with the circular dancing-ground as an erotic locus where rapes occur.

The iconography of the Virgin Mary is the Christian repository of many traditions related to the ancient goddesses, although as with all pagan customs and beliefs absorbed into the Church these were reshaped and subordinated to the patriarchal theology of Father, Son, and Holy Spirit. Even so, the power and richness of the Virgin's cult is greatly disproportionate to the place of Jesus's mother in the scriptures. Many of the symbols which came to be emblematic of Mary's power have nothing at all to do with her attributes in Biblical narrative but seem rather to embody the persistent force of older forms of belief. The Virgin of the Apocalypse, for instance, stands on the horned moon and treads a serpent or dragon beneath her feet. Or the Virgin appears with her babe atop the tree of Jesse, recalling the Neolithic imagery of the Goddess enthroned in her garden beside the tree of life. She is often pictured as the bride or consort of Christ. Sometimes she is shown as the central figure crowned by the figures of the Trinity. Or we see statues of her which open out to reveal the Trinity enclosed within her body.[11]

Flannery O'Connor was well aware of the Virgin Mary's associations with pagan fertility rites, as we know from her characterization of Mrs. May in "Greenleaf." She probably was not familiar, however, with the extensive history of the Great Mother's worship as I have sketched it, because much of the archaeological evidence has been discovered and publicized in the years since her death. In any case, her emphasis was always on the power of God the Father through His Son and the Holy Spirit, never through the intervention of the Virgin. O'Connor's religious vision was patriarchal, much in harmony with the Protestant fundamentalism she used in her fiction as symbolic of passionate faith. In the few stories where Catholic practice occurs, a priest is the usual representative of the Church, and the Virgin Mary is never addressed in prayer. Female symbolism of place in her farm stories is therefore curiously detached from the spiritual contexts where it could have served legitimate functions according to Catholic traditions. Why then do woods and meadows recur again and again as central locations for spiritual drama? Why is the mother condemned for her careful stewardship of the land? The two stories where the issue seems most fully developed are "Greenleaf" and "A Circle in the Fire," and more is at stake than spiritual revelation or the punishment of pride.

Frederick Asals and John Shields have explained how O'Connor fused fertility motifs from pagan mythology with erotic Christian imagery in "Greenleaf" to dramatize Mrs. May's violent conjunction with her Christian destiny.[12] The grim little widow is spiritually barren, although her name suggests her potential in its obvious associations with the celebrated month of spring fertility, the name of the primitive Italian earth goddess, and the name of the Virgin Mary. The paradox of Mrs. May's sterility is reinforced by the prosperity of her farm and O'Connor's emphasis on the green rubber curlers that "sprout" from her head at night. Genuine fertility in the overall pattern of the story stems naturally from Christian faith and appears in the unconscious harmony with natural forces of Mrs. May's tenant farmer Mr. Greenleaf and his uncouth family. On the first page of the story, a personification of these forces confronts Mrs. May in the form of a scrub bull who has invaded her farm. He belongs to Mr. Greenleaf's twin sons, but he is not a creature they can control. O'Connor invokes this universal symbol of masculine creative power in terms which recall the sacrificial bulls of ancient fertility rites, Zeus's metamorphosis in his courtship of Europa, and Jesus with his crown of thorns. He appears "silvered in moonlight" outside Mrs. May's bedroom window, "like some patient god come down to woo her," and his horns are garlanded with a hedge-wreath like the flowery crown Europa placed on her lovely bull in Ovid's *Metamorphoses*. But after he lowers his head in tribute to his ironic Lady May, the wreath slips down to the base of his horns where it looks "like a menacing prickly crown" (pp. 311–12). All the rest of the story is prefigured in the language of this passage. The bull's menacing courtship will be consummated as he is sacrificed like Jesus to release Mrs. May's rejuvenated soul in death.

As preparation for the climax of the story, O'Connor develops the bull's full significance by carefully paralleling and contrasting Mrs. May and her sons to the Greenleaf family, whose fecund piety is associated with the bull. Although they live at home, Mrs. May's resentful bachelor sons have no connection with the land. Instead of helping their widowed mother in her struggle to run the farm, they spend their time mocking her and carping maliciously at each other. Both follow parasitic occupations, one as a sour professor of a useless subject at a nearby university and the other as a salesman of "nigger insurance." If Mrs. May's farm prospers, it is only because she wages a precarious battle against the weather and the dirt—a battle against nature. The Greenleafs, on the other hand, live "like lilies of the field," flourishing without apparent toil and spontaneously expressing the full meaning of their springlike name. Mr. Greenleaf knows that his boys "would have cut off their right arm" before they would have allowed their mother to do farm work. They are exemplars of peaceful harmony with the earth, who never quarrel and are prosperously married and busy producing children.

The source of Greenleaf success is their piety, expressed most fully in Mrs. Greenleaf's daily prayer-healing ceremony in the woods. Unlike Mrs. May, with her neat little figure and energetic habits, Mrs. Greenleaf is a huge sloven who seems to have no other occupation than grotesque worship.

> Every day she cut all the morbid stories out of the newspaper—the accounts of women who had been raped and criminals who had escaped and children who had been burned and of train wrecks and plane crashes and the divorces of movie stars. She took these to the woods and dug a hole and buried them and then she fell on the ground over them and mumbled and groaned for an hour or so moving her huge arms back and forth under her and out again and finally just lying down flat and, Mrs. May suspected, going to sleep in the dirt. [pp. 315–16]

When Mrs. May accidentally surprises Mrs. Greenleaf at the climactic point in this curious ritual, she is shocked by its obscenity. As she marches through her woods carrying a stick to use against snakes, she comes upon Mrs. Greenleaf, a human mound writhing in the dirt and shrieking, "Jesus, stab me in the heart!" Mrs. May is a woman who thinks that "the word Jesus should be kept inside the church building like other words inside the bedroom," and so she is repelled by the sexuality of the spectacle before her—Mrs. Greenleaf lying "with her legs and arms spread out as if she were trying to wrap them around the earth." Whenever Mrs. May worries later about the contrast between her own sons and the successful Greenleaf twins, she needs only "to think of Mrs. Greenleaf sprawled obscenely on the ground, and say to herself, 'Well, no matter how far they *go*, they *came* from that'" (p. 317). She means that the twins were produced by their disgusting mother, but the language of the passage invites us to understand symbolically that they are the offspring of their mother's sprawling embrace with the potent earth.

By the end of the story we realize that the mate whose penetration Mrs. Greenleaf begs when she cries for Jesus to stab her in the heart is the same suitor who finally succeeds in impaling Mrs. May. The connection is foreshadowed in the passage describing Mrs. Greenleaf's worship, for when Mrs. May first hears the groans of "Jesus, Jesus!" in the woods, the sound is so "piercing" (O'Connor's word) that Mrs. May feels "as if some violent unleashed force had broken out of the ground and was charging toward her." This clearly masculine force is identified not only with the bull but with snakes and with far wider natural forces embodied in the sky. Mrs. May was wary of snakes when she entered the woods and was pierced by Mrs. Greenleaf's cries to Jesus. Mr. Greenleaf, who is compared once to a snake striking and whose face is described as "a rough chalice," is also compared to the weather, for Mrs. May has learned to read his face as other country people read sunrises and sunsets. He comes to serve as a priest in the final scene, officiating at the union of Mrs. May and her sacred lover. The night before this event she dreams a prophetic dream in which the sun is a swollen red ball trying to burn through the protective tree line around her rolling pastures. As she stands watching, the sun narrows and pales until it becomes a bullet which bursts through the tree line as the bull will do the next day, and races down the hill toward her. The noise of the burning sun in her dream is actually the bull munching the hedge outside her window in the night. The imagery can now be seen to form a coherent pattern with God represented by sky and sun and His earthly embodiment Jesus identified with the earth upon which Mrs. Greenleaf writhes. Jesus's active energy is associated with the bull but also with snakes. Mr. Greenleaf, as priest for the strange ritual in the sacred round meadow, naturally reflects these divine emblems.[13] He drives the bull out of the woods, and the formerly "patient god" charges into the green arena where Mrs. May sits waiting, burying his head in her lap "like a wild tormented lover" (p. 333). Then Mr. Greenleaf sacrifices the bull by shooting him four times, the shots perhaps representing the four points of the crucifix. Jesus has stabbed Mrs. May in the heart, and as she dies we are told she has "the look of a person whose sight has been restored but who finds the light unbearable."

For O'Connor this revelation fulfills Mrs. May's destiny, but there are problems both in the imagery and in the characterization of Mrs. May which prevent a wholly satisfactory resolution of the story. The crucial imagery of place is contradictory. In the scene where Mrs. Greenleaf performs her prayer-healing in the woods, the earth is presented as a potent masculine entity whose active force charges out of the ground when Jesus is invoked. The bull is the obvious incarnation of this force. But in passages describing Mrs. May's farm, the land is female. The farm is Mrs. May's garden, a cultivated area of gently rolling pastures which had been run-down before the widow came to restore it to productive order. Her hard work has transformed the place into a symbol of her own being. O'Connor tells us that whenever she looks out any window of her house, Mrs. May is soothed to see the reflection of her character in the pastures. Here, as in so many of the farm stories, the widow's domain is fenced in from the threatening sky by a wall of trees. In the final scene, the precarious integrity of this female place is violated in symbolic rape as the bull, who has paradoxically become the epiphany of sun and sky, breaks through the protective, encircling woods into the "green arena" which symbolizes Mrs. May's own being as well as her hard-won garden. Here we have undeniably returned to the χορός—the ancient circular meadow of rape in Greek religion, always the province of feminine powers. But Flannery O'Connor cannot have it both ways; the earth cannot be both male and female in the story, unless she wants us to see Mrs. May's domain as an unnatural female blot on an essentially male earth. If she does, she violates the traditional Catholic complement of female earth associated with the pure but fertile Virgin and the Heavenly Father whose earthly agent is Jesus the Bridegroom of the Canticles. The final scene of the story is a grim inversion of the popular medieval emblem of this relationship— the Virgin seated in a flowery meadow with a unicorn symbolizing Jesus kneeling gently to rest his horn in her lap. The magic beast is always her willing thrall, never her attacker.

Presenting Mrs. May's garden as a travesty also inverts the more ancient mythological patterns echoed in the story. Europa, for instance, is not destroyed by Zeus's seduction. Her identification with the earth is never challenged in the old stories. In Asals's view of "Greenleaf" as a deliberate parallel to Dionysian traditions, Mrs. Greenleaf is the properly reverent Maenad orgiastically worshiping Dionysos in his epiphany as bull, while Mrs. May is a Pentheus figure representing the sterile forces of rationality opposed to intuitive, emotional harmony with the natural world. But anyone familiar with Euripides's *Bacchae* should realize at once that Pentheus cannot be represented by a woman. Dionysos is a woman's deity whom many scholars see as descended from the annually slain consort of the mother goddess. Whatever his origins, in Euripides's play his worship is the celebration of the maternal nourishing forces of the earth and wild nature. The Maenads wander through the pastures outside Pentheus's city in a peaceful ecstasy of natural harmony. As we have seen, they nurse lion cubs, dandle snakes, and play with gazelles. Wherever they touch the earth with their staves, milk and honey and wine flow forth. It is only when males dare to spy on these mysteries that the orgy turns violent. When the shepherds and later Pentheus intrude upon the worship, Maenad ecstasy turns to murderous rage, and the women tear animals and men to pieces, gorging themselves on raw flesh. The earth and its pastures are women's places. Male invasion is punished with the most horrible finality. Mrs. May's clear femininity and her identification with her pastures make it inappropriate for her to function as Pentheus did in denying the maternal fruitfulness of the earth. The problem is complicated by the fact that O'Connor's "Maenad," Mrs. Greenleaf, worships a male, not a female, earth.

Even if we could accept Flannery O'Connor's paradoxical imagery of place, we should still be troubled by the lack of interior development in Mrs. May's character to prepare her for the spiritual revelation she is supposed to experience in the final scene. Never are we shown that she has the slightest understanding of Greenleaf reverence or the bull's significance. She simply fears the social and economic mobility of the Greenleafs, is horrified by Mrs. Greenleaf's obscene form of worship, and is afraid the bull will ruin her herd of cows because he is not purebred. In a literal sense all that transpires is that she is killed by the bull because none of the men around her will help her control it. We are told that she has a vision of unbearable light as she dies, but all its significance comes from outside her, in the author's manipulation of symbols which have no reflection in her mind. In her final vision, her protective tree line is a "dark wound in a world that was nothing but sky"; her green pasture, her farm, her very self, have been obliterated.

"A Circle in the Fire" moves inexorably toward a similar destruction of female control over the land. Mrs. Cope's identification with her farm is not as explicit as Mrs. May's, but her ownership and her authority are the central issues challenged by the invading teenaged boys from the city. Here, once again, a widow's farm is a vulnerable garden menaced by a blank sky that looks as if it is trying to break through the fortress wall of woods surrounding it. The swollen red sun which Mrs. May dreamed was trying to burn through her trees becomes a literal fire for Mrs. Cope when the triumphant boys serve as priests of destruction after a ritual of baptism and the tracing of magic circles in another sacred meadow.

No deliberate adaptation of pagan mythology is visible in "A Circle in the Fire," but the story employs a general mother-daughter motif which appears in three of O'Connor's other stories and seems to hearken back to very old patterns of association with the earth. In "Good Country People" and "The Life You Save May Be Your Own," a deceptively polite but mysterious male appears unexpectedly, lulls the widowed farm owner's suspicions, and violates her daughter. Manley Pointer steals Joy-Hulga Hopewell's wooden leg rather than her virginity, and Mr. Shiftlet abandons the retarded Lucynell Crater in a diner before his marriage can be consummated. But in each case the action involves an obscene intrusion upon the peaceful order of the mother's farm and amounts symbolically to rape. The daughter in "A Temple of the Holy Ghost" is disturbed by the more general question of sexuality itself when her cousins tell her about their dates with two pious farm boys who take them to see a hermaphrodite at the county fair. The problem is only indirectly treated here, but, as in the other two stories, males introduce a sexual threat. All these stories echo Hades's disturbing foray into Demeter's garden and his theft of Persephone. We must remember that the myth dramatizes the sanctity of the land as female and the power of mother earth to deny fertility when a male invades her dominion. Whether or not Flannery O'Connor meant to reiterate the underlying pattern of the Demeter-Kore myth, it is the only literary precedent which can illuminate the obsessive theme of masculine invasion in the mother-daughter farm stories. "A Circle in the Fire" is the fullest exposition of the theme, revealing parallels to the myth which are at least surprising.

A triad of females is established as the essential population of the farm at the opening of the story. Mrs. Cope works vigorously in her flower bed as Mrs. Pritchard, her ally and the tenant farmer's wife, looks on and chats about a woman who died having a baby in an iron lung. Twelve-year-old Sally Virginia Cope spies on the two women from an upstairs window. In a very general way the group parallels the Eleusinian trinity of Mother Demeter, Kore, and Hecate the dark goddess of death, all guardians of earth's mysteries in the famous Greek cult.[14] Mrs. Cope is custodian of the land and guardian of her daughter; Mrs. Pritchard's fascination with disease and funerals allies her with the gloomy deity who led initiates to symbolic death in Demeter's awesome rites.

Weeding the invading nut grass from her flower bed as if the plants "were an evil sent directly by the devil to destroy the place," Mrs. Cope is suddenly confronted by much more serious agents of destruction in the form of three thirteen-year-old boys who will claim the farm as their own and wreak havoc in defiance of the "damn women" whose province it has been. For Powell Boyd, the leader of the invading trio, the farm is a paradise, lost when his tenant farmer father moved the family to Florida. Powell has brought his friends from his new home in an Atlanta slum to see the place he wants to go when he dies, a heaven of horses to ride and open pastures to roam. O'Connor equates these hungry children with suffering European refugees and clearly intends to dramatize and finally punish Mrs. Cope's lack of real Christian charity towards them. But from the outset the boys' claim on the farm is so relentless and coldly misogynist that no possible kindness offered by Mrs. Cope could disarm their determination to have the whole place for themselves. The first thing we learn about Powell is that his gaze seems to come "from two directions at once as if it had [Mrs. Cope and Mrs. Pritchard] surrounded." All three boys have "white penetrating stares," and Powell's seems to pinch Mrs. Cope like a pair of tongs (p. 180). Their arrival is an assault which becomes more and more obvious as Mrs. Cope tries politely but vainly to keep them under control. When she refers to "her" woods, one boy echoes her in a sarcastic mutter. The next morning when she tells them she expects them to behave like gentlemen, they stand looking away from her as if waiting for her to leave. "After all," she says in a voice strained with anxiety, "this is my place!" In response to her authority they turn their backs on her and walk away (p. 186).

The boys' resentment of women in general and Mrs. Cope's claim to the farm in particular is twice made very clear. Sally Virginia has been fascinated by her mother's increasingly exasperated dealings with Powell and his friends. Red in the face with excitement which gradually turns to rage, she peers down on the unfolding drama from the safety of an upstairs window and finally crosses her eyes, sticks out her tongue, and says, "Ugggghhrhh." The large boy looks up and stares at her. "Jesus," he growls, "another woman." "She dropped back from the window and stood with her back against the wall, squinting fiercely as if she had been slapped in the face and couldn't see who had done it" (p. 185). Later Mrs. Pritchard reports that the boys have been disputing Mrs. Cope's ownership of the farm in a conversation with Mr. Pritchard. "She don't own them woods," one boy said. The same boy who had insulted Sally Virginia complained, "I never seen a place with so many damn women on it, how do you stand it here?" (p. 186).

The farm is under a siege whose sexual danger Mrs. Cope senses. At Mrs. Pritchard's suggestion that the boys might want to spend the night, she gives a little shriek and exclaims, "I can't have three boys in here with only me and Sally Virginia" (p. 181). Repeatedly she warns her daughter to stay away from the visitors, but she won't say why. O'Connor does, explaining to her friend "A" that Sally Virginia risks sexual attack if she goes near the boys. "They would do it because they would be sharp enough to know that it would be their best revenge on Mrs. Cope; they would do it to humiliate the child and the mother, not to enjoy themselves."[15] Sexual violence is the most potent form of masculine assault, whose ominous potential Mrs. Pritchard describes when she tells Mrs. Cope, "You take a boy thirteen year old is equal in meanness to a man twict his age. It's no telling what he'll think up to do. You never know where he'll strike next" (p. 186).

Sally Virginia finally disobeys her mother's protective warnings and marches off to confront the boys in the woods where the climactic scene of destruction takes place. Flannery O'Connor told "A" that the boys' attack takes another form than the sexual one Mrs. Cope fears, but the woods they destroy are so closely identified with the child that the effect is almost the same. Sally Virginia adopts male dress to stalk her enemy, but the overalls she wears over her dress and the toy pistols she waves in the air are ridiculously inadequate defense. She comes upon the boys performing a curious rite in the back pasture behind the woods, and she hides behind a pine tree to watch. They are bathing in the cow trough which O'Connor likens to a coffin so that we will not miss the significance of their baptismal rebirth in the symbolically female meadow. Their conversation is a litany of claims for possession of the place. The biggest boy says the farm "don't belong to nobody," and the smallest boy chimes in, "It's ours." At that signal Powell jumps out of the water and begins a celebratory race around the pasture, tracing its boundaries in a circular path. As he passes the trough again, the other boys leap from the water to follow him. Their long naked bodies glint in the sun, and their masculinity must be obvious in its simplest form to the frightened girl behind the tree. The side of her face is so closely pressed against the trunk that "the imprint of the bark [is] embossed red and white" upon it (p. 192). When the boys dress and move into the woods to set them on fire, we should remember that earlier in the story Sally Virginia had registered the big boy's contemptuous "Jesus, another woman" as if she had been slapped in the *face*. Her face carries the mark of her humiliated femininity just as it carries the imprint of the tree that identifies her with the ravaged woods.

Although Sally Virginia symbolically shares Kore's fate as object of male assault, the attackers' motivations differ profoundly in the Greek myth and in O'Connor's story. Like Kore, Sally Virginia is wandering outside her mother's protection when the violation of the garden occurs; the attack in both cases circumvents the mother's power. But while Plutos or Hades is motivated by positive desire for Demeter's daughter as his mate, Flannery O'Connor's boys hate women and seek revenge rather than sexual union. Demeter herself makes the land barren in retaliation against her daughter's rape; her authority is never challenged. In contrast, as we have seen, that kind of authority is exactly the object of male retribution in

"A Circle in the Fire." By burning Mrs. Cope's woods, O'Connor's boys humiliate the daughter and her mother, bringing the fiery devastation Mrs. Cope has feared throughout the story and destroying the female integrity of the land. For O'Connor, the boys are agents of divine retribution, prophets dancing in the fiery furnace, "in the circle the angel had cleared for them." Thus the story ends, with Mrs. Cope's pride humbled by a God who forces her to share the homeless misery of European refugees, Negroes, and hungry children.

In the special world of the farm stories, the force of destructive retribution is commensurate with the power of the mother and her closeness to the land. Thus it is more violent in "Greenleaf" and "A Circle in the Fire" than in "Good Country People" or "The Life You Save May Be Your Own." Final reckoning is also violently destructive in "A View of the Woods," where the female is only a girl but one fiercely protective of her *daddy*'s woods. Here the odd twist is the legitimacy of her position, for she shares the author's attitude toward the sanctity of the pastoral landscape and an acceptance of male authority. Even so, she is literally murdered by her grandfather for this allegiance. One is forced to conclude that the sex of the person close to the land is the determinant of her fate. Females connected with the land will be assaulted, whereas males like Mr. Head and Old Tarwater will be vindicated in their claim of ownership.

This pattern would not be necessarily disturbing if it were supported by consistent imagery and coherent reasons in the fiction for the illegitimacy of female authority. But we have seen the ambivalence created by the presence of strong mothers and the powerful mythological echoes which accompany their identification with the land. O'Connor's use of myth is deliberate in "Greenleaf," but she could not fully control the old forms which came to life under the surface of the story: hovering presences recalling the Virgin Mary, the medieval unicorn kneeling before her with his head in her lap in a meadow full of flowers, Europa and her gentle white bull, and behind them all the primordial Earth Mother, source and protectress of all life. Landscape imagery in "Greenleaf" is confused, reflecting the conflict between the power of the old myths and the patriarchal God who finally works His violent will. Although the land is masculine at the beginning of the story, by the end we are returned to the oldest female associations of the earth, only to have their value apocalyptically denied in a scene that is shocking rather than gratifying in the sense Flannery O'Connor intended. With "A Circle in the Fire," there appears to be no conscious attempt to refer to mythology, but in the vivid realization of mother and daughter's association with their farm O'Connor intensifies the pattern of fate familiar from the myth of Demeter and Kore. So much emphasis is placed upon the terrified inability of mother and daughter to prevent disaster that the failure of charity which O'Connor wants us to accept as justification for the boys' vengeance is simply not sufficient cause.

The source of the sense of disjunction in these stories is implied in the Biblical garden imagery suggested by O'Connor's frequent mention of snakes. The serpent in the Garden of Eden was unequivocally depicted as a wicked invader of the paradise ruled by the patriarchal Hebrew God. But in Flannery O'Connor's farm stories, the serpent performs an ambiguous double role both sinister and benign. We should remember that Mr. Greenleaf is likened to a snake but also that his face is "a rough chalice," a vessel for the incarnate essence of Christ. The marauding boys in "A Circle in the Fire" are also like snakes, yet by the end of the story they are prophets in a fiery furnace. These serpentine males are evidence that the demonic, as John Hawkes pointed out long ago, is strangely allied to the divine and often uncomfortably close to the author's stance.[16]

What is the ordinary reader to do with such paradoxes and with their central function in the repeated theme of rape? As I said at the beginning of our journey into Flannery O'Connor's world, the greatest of her stories achieve the profound spiritual purpose she intended, showing the mystery of God's grace at work in human life and at the same time satirizing our fallen manners with relentless comic accuracy. In three of the greatest of these—"A Good Man Is Hard to Find," "The Artificial Nigger," and "Revelation"—the feminine is associated with actions of grace that are not only shocking but ultimately positive. The grandmother who has been selfish and annoying during most of "A Good Man Is Hard to Find" is shocked by the extremity of her danger into a sudden transcendence of herself in reaching out to accept the Misfit as her child. The enormous black woman in "The Artificial Nigger" becomes a sort of Beatrice figure of solace for Nelson in his Dantesque journey through the Atlanta slums, and when he and his grandfather return to their pastoral home, they step off the train into a silvery landscape calmed by the moon, which has always been a symbol of femininity and which in Catholicism is associated with the Virgin Mary.[17] Finally, in "Revelation" it is the explosion of violent outrage from the college girl with the significant name of Mary Grace which wakens Mrs. Turpin from her complacency, and the great sow in the pigpen at the end of the story, who pants with a secret life, becomes the catalyst for Mrs. Turpin's heavenly vision. These feminine figures are anything but conventional, yet they are powerful agents of a good which the central characters understand and which we can therefore see at work in their lives.

By contrast, in the preceding pages we have been most closely examining stories where problems of female sexual identity twist plots away from their intended shapes and where feminine assertion is continually punished by masculine assaults which distort ancient mythic patterns associating women with the landscape. The victims of these attacks do not seem to understand any spiritual message, but are merely devastated by their experiences. Flannery O'Connor admitted that many of the daughter-figures who suffer such humiliation are like herself; and the Mrs. Mays and Mrs. Hopewells bear an unmistakable resemblance to Regina Cline O'Connor, the deceptively frail little widow who devoted her life to making a safe and comfortable home for her gifted invalid daughter. While it is true that O'Connor's fictional women are proud and complacent, their autobiographical dimensions suggest some explanations for what seems a disproportionate violence in the lessons administered by their masculine assailants. Critics like Josephine Hendon, Claire Katz, and Clara Claiborne Park go too far when they claim that O'Connor lived a fiction and wrote the dark truth about her life in her stories, or that the violence of the fiction expresses a pathological rage, or that the letters are her positive achievement and her stories failures.[18] Nevertheless, these commentators are struggling to explain many of the same difficulties that have been our concern throughout these pages. Placing the fiction and the facts of O'Connor's life in their Southern context helps to suggest some less negative ways of accounting for these problems.

We may remember O'Connor's grim description of her dancing lessons at age twelve and her determination to resist efforts to make her graceful and ladylike. The stories similarly reject traditional standards of femininity which were particularly exaggerated in the South. As Ellen Moers suggests, the emphasis on feminine beauty can well be seen as a contributing cause to what she calls the "female gothic" in literature. In this regard it is interesting to compare O'Connor's use of the grotesque with Diane Arbus's freakish photographs, which Susan Sontag has described as "reactive— reactive against gentility, against what is approved" in the world of fashion photography where Arbus earned her living working for *Vogue*. O'Connor said she herself used the grotesque to shock people into recognizing both spiritual and physical ugliness which they had been taking for granted, and she liked to quote Wyndham Lewis's statement, "If I write about a hill that is rotting, it is because I despise rot." Yet she clearly delighted in the grotesque elements of popular American culture, admiring the work of Nathanael West and writing to Sally and Robert Fitzgerald that "at times I feel that a feeling for the vulgar is my natural talent and don't need any particular encouragement. Did you see the picture of Roy Rogers's horse attending a church service in Pasadena?"[19] Unlike Arbus, whose treatment of vulgarity and freakish human beings is static and rather horrifying, O'Connor's grotesquery is full of vitality and humor so that we feel she really enjoys and sympathizes with her characters. She seems to have felt herself one of them and shared in their antics to deny genteel Southern standards of grace and politeness, for she said again and again that she loved characters like Hulga and Nelson and that she was like them in many ways.

Flannery O'Connor needed to escape from the Southern ideal of the lady if she ever wanted to succeed as a writer, and yet the chief influence pressuring her to accept those feminine standards was the mother with whom she lived her entire life, except for the five years of her Northern sojourn after college. Mrs. O'Connor's view of her daughter's status is comically clear in a letter Flannery wrote to Robert Lowell a year and a half after lupus sent her back to Milledgeville for good: "Harcourt sent my book to Evelyn Waugh and his comment was: 'If this is really the unaided work of a young lady, it is a remarkable product.' My mother was vastly insulted. She put the emphasis on *if* and *lady*. Does he suppose you're not a lady? she says. WHO is he?"[20]

One could plausibly argue that the chastisement of many of the widowed and divorced mothers in O'Connor's stories is a complement to the grotesque as a way of setting the author apart from certain "feminine" requirements represented by her mother. She was probably quite pleased that Waugh had trouble believing her work to be that of "a young lady," despite her mother's indignant reaction.

Ultimately, however, we have seen that the resentful daughters of the stories are also punished for their pride and are forced to accept their feminine alliance with their mothers. Josephine Hendin offers a perceptive suggestion when she says that "the very act of writing was itself a redemptive process for her. It may have been the only, and perhaps unconscious, way she could express all the contradictions within her." Claire Katz contributes a related hypothesis when she claims that O'Connor simultaneously confirmed and escaped the repugnant feminine role by identifying in her authorial power with the divine masculine authority which punishes people like herself who try to deny their femininity. Such comments are reminiscent of Eudora Welty's remarks about D. H. Lawrence: "Those who write with cruelty, and Lawrence is one, may not be lacking in compassion but stand in need to write in exorcisement."[21] These are plausible explanations, but if nothing more than the author's psychic or spiritual exorcisement is accomplished in this fiction, reading it would be merely a kind of voyeurism.

Clearly O'Connor's fiction is an achievement of the first order in literary terms, and at its best it provides the mysterious and exalting experience of all great art. In her complex and troubling presentation of mothers and daughters in the farm stories, Flannery O'Connor has inadvertently presented a poignant and often excruciating picture of the problems these women have in living together, of female self-loathing, powerlessness, and justified fear of masculine attack. She presents fictional doubles of herself, as Sandra Gilbert and Susan Gubar have shown so many women writers to have done, doubles who express the rage and frustration which is too dangerous for women to admit in ordinary life. O'Connor allows these doppelgängers to act their defiance, just as Charlotte Brontë and George Eliot and Carson McCullers do, but then, like the others, she punishes them with a finality which restores a balance with the dominant values of the world in which we all must live.

Chapter Eight

Place, Freedom, and Feminine Identity

With Eudora Welty, Carson McCullers, and Flannery O'Connor, Southern women have gained strong contemporary voices which define their condition as it has never before been understood. The power to be drawn from traditional feminine life in alliance with men has been richly celebrated in Welty's novels and stories, restoring the forgotten continuity between our own culture and the long centuries dominated by fertility religions before recorded history. Welty has made a remarkable intuitive leap in her connection of Southern matriarchal traditions with these old and long-suppressed cultural foundations. She has also been aware, however, that the gracious Southern life celebrated in *Delta Wedding* and wistfully reexamined in *The Optimist's Daughter* is dying. The New Women of the South are already emerging in *Delta Wedding*, impatient of their mothers' heritage and searching for wider and more active destinies. Virgie Rainey of *The Golden Apples* and Laurel Hand of *The Optimist's Daughter* have forged independent, clearly feminine identities, but they are rendered exiles and solitary wanderers by their choices. No community sustains them; no comrades share their new worlds. In fact, Welty does not seem able to dramatize their independent life at all. We leave Virgie Rainey literally sitting on a fence after her mother's death, musing about the meaning of her life. We know nothing of what she will do with her future, only that she will go away from her Mississippi home. Laurel Hand has long ago transplanted herself when *The Optimist's Daughter* begins, and references to her career assure us that she has made a success. All we see, however, is her awkward reunion with her dying father and then her grieving temporary return to her childhood home. There she merely lays to rest the remnants of a long-dead self and revises her understanding of her parents. When the novel ends we are as ignorant of her adult life in Chicago as we were at the beginning.

Other autonomous women characters do exist on the edges of Welty's fiction—characters such as Partheny and the maiden aunts of *Delta Wedding*, Miss Eckhart of *The Golden Apples*, and the occasional schoolteacher like Miss Julia Mortimer of *Losing Battles*. But those whose lives we see very closely seem to be ultimately disappointed. Miss Eckhart ends as a pitiful derelict in the county home, whose prize pupil Virgie Rainey will not even acknowledge her presence when she passes her on the sidewalk. She will never know of Virgie's final gratitude for her teacher's gift. Miss Julia Mortimer dies feeling that she has lost her long battle to educate the Banner community.

A far more drastic problem of identity confronts us in the fiction of Carson McCullers and Flannery O'Connor. Adolescent unwillingness to renounce childhood freedom and accept the entrapment of adult femininity is a painful, even horrifying, reality for Mick Kelly of *The Heart Is a Lonely Hunter*, Frankie Addams of *The Member of the Wedding*, Sally Virginia Cope of "A Circle in the Fire," and the unnamed twelve-year-old of "A Temple of the Holy Ghost." Neither McCullers nor O'Connor could really manage to envision any positive, active life for women of her own generation. When McCullers tried, she created Miss Amelia Evans—a grotesquely mannish Amazon whose solitary authority and refusal to play even the physical part of a woman in her brief marriage to Marvin Macy brings ultimate destruction from a punishing male alliance. All of Flannery O'Connor's adult daughters are paralyzed wards of controlling mothers. These young women in their thirties are intelligent, with the exception of the idiot Lucynell Crater, but instead of asserting themselves they seethe with resentment at the inane social world of the rural South where they find themselves trapped.

The imagery of clothing reveals the problem of sexual identification very clearly. All of Welty's major women characters wear conventionally feminine dresses and skirts, from the girlish frocks of Laura and India to Shelley's fashionable middies and pleated skirts and party gowns, Virgie's homemade dresses, and Laurel's suits. Whatever their activities may be, these women accept the emblematic clothing of their kind. Welty seems to delight in fabrics and all the flounces and swirls of women's dress almost as much as she does in the cornucopia of Southern foods which make the tables groan during the many festivities of her novels. There is an especially giddy scene at Shellmound where all the Fairchild girls snatch up the freshly arrived wedding dresses from their boxes and whirl in filmy pastel clouds around George and Ellen.

The clothing of McCullers's tomboys provides a marked contrast to Welty's lyrical catalog of frocks. Both Mick and Frankie swagger through their towns barefooted and crop-headed, wearing boys' shorts and undershirts of questionable cleanliness to match their tough nicknames. Miss Amelia is almost always clad in overalls and swamp boots appropriate to her activities of rural finance, hog butchery, carpentry, and moonshine distillery. On the rare occasions when these "boyish" characters appear in a dress, it is a deliberate and very awkward capitulation to social demands for conformity. Mick looks ridiculous in her sister's party dress, makeup, and high heels. This costume makes her feel alien to herself and painfully trips her up when she tries to run outdoors. Once she begins wearing dresses, she loses her physical freedom. Similar clothing leads Frankie Addams unwittingly close to rape. When she puts on "her most grown and best, the pink organdie," and parades around town all morning telling everyone she meets about her plan to join her brother and his bride on their honeymoon, she does not understand that her feminine looks make her sexual prey. The bold speech she uses with the soldier would have struck no erotic chord in him if she had been wearing her shorts and B.V.D. undershirt. But her dress and lipstick, party shoes and purse mark her as female; the soldier takes her boldness as an invitation to seduction. Miss Amelia is similarly ignorant of the message flashed to Marvin Macy by her dead mother's yellow satin wedding gown as she strides down the aisle to marry him. When her new husband tries to make love to her that night, she is just as indignant as Frankie is when the soldier attempts the same thing with her. Amelia, however, is physically strong enough to drive Macy away when he insists on his conjugal rights.

Upon Macy's vengeful return to town at the end of the novel, Miss Amelia once more wears a dress, but this time a red one and in full cognizance of the danger in which it places her. She will defy Marvin Macy even as she wears the clothing of a sex object he can never enjoy. After her near victory in the wrestling match has been upset by Cousin Lymon and she is left beaten almost to death, it is the unmistakable body of a woman we see lying on the floor of the cafe, for the red dress makes her a symbol of her sex, with all its attendant connotations of menstrual blood and the suffering of childbirth. The preferred clothing of Mick, Frankie, and Amelia shows their fundamental identification to be masculine. Wearing dresses seems to destroy the freedom achieved by that identification and to make them vulnerable.

Flannery O'Connor's women stand between the extremes represented by the very "feminine" clothing of Eudora Welty's women and the masculine shorts and overalls of McCullers's tomboys. The mothers of the stories always wear conventional clothing which the daughters seem to mock with their ugly sweat shirts and Girl Scout shoes. They will submit in general to their mothers' code of ladylike dress, but small acts of defiance and clumsiness will continually make them failures by the standards applied to the Southern belle. They have been dragged into femininity kicking and refuse to embrace their "proper" role.

Place is ultimately more important than clothing as an index of feminine identity in this fiction. That is partly because of the profound regional consciousness of Southerners and their deeply rooted love of their land, but it is also due to the ancient patterns of meaning which Welty exploits so richly in *Delta Wedding*. She is surely far more aware than McCullers and O'Connor were of the long association between the female and the land. Such habits of thought go back as far as we can trace the human imagination through art—back at least twenty thousand years to the Paleolithic periods which led gradually to the great Neolithic agricultural civilizations whose worship of fertility goddesses can still be traced in ancient Greek religion and survives in tribal cultures all over the world. Such attitudes were not invented by either sex but seem to have been held in common through the centuries, by simple analogy of woman's reproductive power to that of the earth. Thus the passage graves in Brittany and the British Isles are burial wombs in the Great Mother's body, where bones of the dead can be buried like seeds to sprout again into life. Perhaps also, as Vincent Scully suggests, the temples of classical Greek civilization nestled in crucial spots on the landscape so that breastlike mountains dominated the horizon along the proper axis of the building. And in the Homeric Hymns, the Earth is the oldest deity of all, whose daughters dance like the flowers and grasses in her meadows. Freud and Jung confirm the profundity of these traditions in their own psychoanalytic theory, though both men place them at the periphery of their masculine perspective. We should remember that both Freud and Jung were saturated with mythology, drawing many of their central insights from it. If we can assume, as G. R. Levy and Alexander Marshack do, that at deep levels of signification human culture is an unbroken continuum from our earliest thinking ancestors to the present, we must see why people everywhere continue to think of the earth as a mother and of its contours as sacred. No matter how unconscious individual women may be of these associations, their attitudes towards their sex is naturally related to their feelings about landscape.

This is clearly true for Eudora Welty, whose fertile Delta cotton fields, baptismal rivers of life and sexuality and death, mysterious bayou woods, and carefully tended flower gardens all glow with feminine sacredness. These Mississippi places define and nourish the lives of her characters, and we are told that the Delta really belongs to the women. To a degree unusual in fiction, Welty's women move freely and comfortably across the landscape, at the center of a world which affirms them and denies male pretensions of control.

Surprisingly for a writer who created girls as bold and active as Mick Kelly and Frankie Addams and an Amazon as fearless as Amelia Evans, Carson McCullers's fictional geography is very limited. Mick and Frankie are stifled in blazing hot Southern towns, and because we never see Miss Amelia anywhere else, we also tend to picture her in her airless hamlet. The girls explore their towns by traveling the sidewalks, but only Mick goes out beyond them and into the countryside. Her trip begins as an idyllic picnic by a creek of cool, swift water in a deep wood where the only sounds come from the water and a breeze high in the pines. Her swimming with Harry can be symbolically interpreted as a baptismal portent of the sexual initiation which occurs just afterward, but it is not a positive scene of feminine sexuality like Robbie and George's Bacchic tumble into the Yazoo or even Dabney's fascinated gazing into the mysterious bayou whirlpool. Mick's experience turns from pleasure to fright as she stares into the sun and desperately counts "something in her mind" to distract herself from what Harry's body is doing to hers.

Neither Miss Amelia's woods nor her farmland is ever pictured in *The Ballad of the Sad Café*, though we are told she visits them regularly. The only green landscape described in *The Member of the Wedding* is the backyard where Frankie and Berenice and John Henry see the line of adolescent girls in fresh dresses transfigured by the golden evening sun. Frankie herself has been exiled from this happy childhood garden by her entrance into puberty, and she is not yet ready for a temporary return to it in the new form which the older girls have already achieved. For all three of McCullers's tomboy heroines, the landscape is a scene of freedom glimpsed but then denied by masculine forces which demand submission to the restricted sphere they have created for feminine sexuality.

Flannery O'Connor's farm-owning mothers and their daughters are naturally very conscious of the pastures and cultivated fields that surround them, but the traditional patterns identifying those garden settings with the feminine are denied in story after story. Mrs. Cope, Mrs. May, and Mrs. Hopewell see their livelihood and very being reflected in their threatened land and woods, worrying constantly about fire and other forces of invasion. The message that the fiction conveys again and again is that God owns the land, "Gawd owns them woods," and only males are fit guardians. In some stories the land actually seems to be masculine. The earth appears symbolically to be a masculine lover in Mrs. Greenleaf's obscene prayer-healing ceremony, as she grovels spread-eagled upon it and begs, "Jesus, stab me in the heart!" Appearing to be walking across the water in the first paragraph of "A View of the Woods," the trees seem to be the incarnation of Christ. Later, when old Mr. Pitts has announced his determination to sell off part of his farmland and obscure his family's view of the woods, he looks out at them in the evening, "and the gaunt trunks appeared to be raised in a pool of red light . . . as if someone were wounded behind the woods and the trees were bathed in blood" (p. 348). Flannery O'Connor's vision could not countenance a feminine landscape controlled by the strong mother figures of the farm stories, for her world was ruled by a patriarchal authority which guarded His pastoral landscape as the Yahweh of the ancient Hebrews watched over Eden and the pastures of the Old Testament.

The fiction of Welty, McCullers, and O'Connor seems to confirm Ellen Moers's suggestions in *Literary Women* that open, sweeping landscapes are places for feminine assertion while enclosed, claustrophobic places mirror anxieties about the confinement which has been woman's traditional lot in our society. Eudora Welty's wide, glowing Delta allows free movement for heroines who confirm human unity with the rest of animate and inanimate nature by performing age-old rituals in its sacred precincts. Perhaps because the land is so hospitable, the Fairchild houses are open and welcoming rather than forbidding or confining. No one is trapped in the big house at Shellmound, where children and servants and pets and visitors tumble freely in and out the open doors. Visiting Aunt Tempe is always distressed by the clutter of the house and the incessant untidy motion of its life, but it is a place full of laughter where bounteous meals never fail to appear at the needed time, new babies are born with regularity, and an affectionate family community thrives. The Grove is quieter and better ordered, a "dove-gray box with its deep porch turned to the river breeze." It may serve as a little temple for antiques and memories, but here too the visitor finds immediate welcome. By the end of the novel we know that George and Robbie are planning to move in and open it up to rougher and fresher airs. The Grove is bordered by the shadowy Yazoo on one side and banks of flowers and mint on another; it merges modestly with its setting. Marmion is more stately, more beautiful, and more mysterious, dreaming beside the Yazoo like a hypnotized swamp butterfly but haunted by the death of its builders. It is wide open to weather, animals, and human explorers. When Laura and Roy join Aunt Studney there for her ritual of bees, however, we see that the house is an organic part of the landscape that can flower afresh as new life flows into it.

Even in *The Golden Apples* and *The Optimist's Daughter*, where the principal houses decline as their owners age or die, life flows in and out the open doors and windows. Virgie Rainey and Bucky Moffitt make love upstairs in the derelict MacLain house while Miss Eckhart enters her old quarters below and sets them on fire, only to be intercepted by two old men who climb in a window to stop her. Next door Loch Morrison, supposedly confined to his room by malaria, escapes out a window into a tree and eventually drops to the ground to snatch up the metronome tossed out of the fire. His sister Cassie and then his mother and the maid pour out the front door as the confusion increases. In death these houses are opened for processions of mourners laden with gifts of food which turn the funerals into something like celebrations. Both Virgie Rainey and Laurel Hand preside over such gatherings and watch in some amazement as the community of friends surges in and out through the doors.

Carson McCullers's most memorable houses are ultimately claustrophobic. Most of *The Member of the Wedding* occurs in the hot, stale kitchen where Berenice guides tomboy Frankie through her transformation into giddy adolescent Frances. The walls are covered with John Henry's grotesque childish drawings which give the room "a crazy look like that of a room in the crazy-house." The same conversations and the same card games are played maddeningly over and over by the three inhabitants of Frankie's domestic world so that the time passes like a sick dream. This world is a living freak show peopled by a transvestite boy, a black cook with a left eye of bright blue glass, and a gangling tomboy. It is a horrifying prison for Frankie, who moves into a completely new house at the end of the novel, leaving her freakish past behind.

Such an escape may be possible because she submits to conventional demands for femininity. The opposite resolution comes in *The Ballad of the Sad Café*. Whereas Miss Amelia's cafe had formerly been her fortress and treasure-house, and then under Cousin Lymon's influence had opened up to become a warm center for the town's social life, the destruction of Amelia's power transforms the cafe into a prison. Boarded up, painted only on one side, and leaning crazily to the right, it expresses the state of Miss Amelia's life. Sometimes when the heat is at its suffocating worst at the end of the day, a terrible face appears from behind the shutter of the one window left unboarded. Because she would not submit to her biological destiny, Miss Amelia has been left a sexless recluse, enclosed in her old house and only rarely looking out "with two gray crossed eyes which are turned inward so sharply that they seem to be exchanging with each other one long and secret gaze of grief."

Flannery O'Connor does not use houses to represent psychological states as McCullers does or to play such a defining role for social life as Welty does. But the houses in her farm stories are as threatened as the vulnerable pastures surrounded by their fortress lines of trees. They are similarly guarded by worried mothers who suspiciously intercept visitors like Tom T. Shiftlet of "The Life You Save May Be Your Own," the marauding boys of "A Circle in the Fire," and Manley Pointer of "Good Country People." Always the invaders succeed in breaking through the widows' defenses, though none goes so far as to actually inhabit her house. Sally Virginia Cope insults Powell Boyd and his friends from what she thinks is the safety of her mother's house, but their disgusted response easily reaches her ears through her upstairs window and hurts her feelings as much as it would have if she had been on the lawn with them. Ultimately, in all these stories, houses are no refuge from the humiliating lessons the mothers and daughters receive.

Occasionally an interior setting has a symbolic function, as we saw in the case of Ruby Hill's grim journey up the echoing stairwell of her apartment. There she is forced to identify herself with motherhood in a place resembling the very channel of birth. The unnamed child in "A Temple of the Holy Ghost" paces back and forth in her darkened bedroom where a shaft of light from the fair wanders over the walls. Like her private, darkened soul, the room is the scene of a questioning search for illumination. Finally, an inverted sort of new vision coincides with entrapment in the storage barn for Joy-Hulga Hopewell in "Good Country People." Unable to get out of the barn because Manley Pointer has stolen her wooden leg, Joy-Hulga lies astonished in the hayloft. She has been reduced to a female whose inadequate body literally cannot take her anywhere. Without her glasses, all she can see are blurs on the landscape, though O'Connor tells us that this new way of seeing forces the "girl" to understand her essential weakness and need for God.

Why do Carson McCullers and Flannery O'Connor punish and confine the female characters most like themselves, when Eudora Welty is able to affirm women's freedom to move? Why are Welty's landscapes so wide and joyous, when O'Connor's are threatened, beaten, and bleeding and McCullers's barely even exist? Welty embraces her femininity through her women characters—all kinds of them. She sees the world through their eyes, lovingly, reaffirming the old female powers of the land as she re-affirms the fruitful alliance of male and female humans and celebrates their domestic arrangements. McCullers and O'Connor, on the other hand, only grudgingly accept a female status that their fiction pictures as a trap, a paralysis, a diminishment. The problems they have articulated are not limited to the South, but because of the Southern tradition of the lady, the difficulties of defining a positive feminine self can be felt more intensely there. The ghosts, the myths, and the prejudices articulated by Eudora Welty, Carson McCullers, and Flannery O'Connor may speak with a Southern accent, but they are closely akin to those which all women must confront.

Notes

Introduction

1. Linda Kuehl, "The Art of Fiction XLVII: Eudora Welty," 72–97.
2. Moers, *Literary Women;* Showalter, *A Literature of Their Own.*
3. Allen, "Eudora Welty: The Three Moments," 12–21.
4. Fiedler, *Love and Death in the American Novel,* 481–82.
5. Woolf, *A Room of One's Own,* 70.

Chapter One. The Blight of Southern Womanhood

1. Wyatt-Brown, *Southern Honor,* 228.
2. Anne Firor Scott surveys the historical situation of upper-class Southern women in *The Southern Lady: From Pedestal to Politics, 1830–1930,* and in *Tomorrow Is Another Day* Anne Goodwyn Jones presents a catalog of historical trends and recent theories of their causes in her explanation of attitudes toward women which must have affected those in the South who became writers between 1859 and 1936. Since Scott and Jones have paved the way so thoroughly, I need not repeat their exhaustive documentation. Instead I shall emphasize what seem to me the crucial problems in Southern cultural ideology about women.
3. Mims, "The Southern Woman: Past and Present," 3.
4. Cash, *The Mind of the South,* 86–87.
5. See Paul Gaston, *The New South Creed,* 40–41; Lawrence J. Friedman, *The White Savage,* 61; and Rollin G. Osterweis, *The Myth of the Lost Cause,* 24–29.
6. See Friedman, *The White Savage,* 171–72, and Leslie Fiedler, *The Inadvertent Epic,* 43–57.

7. Dixon, *The Clansman*, 362. All further citations of this work will be from this edition; page numbers will be indicated parenthetically in my text.

8. See, for example, Leo Marx, *The Machine in the Garden*, and Annette Kolodny, *The Lay of the Land*.

9. Barlowe, quoted in Richard Hakluyt's *The Principall Navigations of the English Nation*, 728; Rolfe, *A True Relation of the State of Virginia*, 3; Bradford, *Of Plymouth Plantation*, 62.

10. Quoted in Annette Kolodny, "'Stript, Shorne and Made Deformed': Images on the Southern Landscape," 58–59.

11. See Marx, 75–88.

12. Beverley, *The History and Present State of Virginia*, 296–97.

13. Simms, quoted in Kolodny, "'Stript, Shorne and Made Deformed,'" 67; Dabney, *A Defence of Virginia*, 5; anonymous poem from *Southern Voices*, quoted in the *Southern Review* 11 (July 1872): 44.

14. Grady, *Orations and Speeches of Henry W. Grady*.

15. *The Inadvertent Epic*, 45–49.

16. See Jacquelyn Dowd Hall's recent analysis of the rape complex, *Revolt Against Chivalry: Jessie Daniel Ames and the Women's Campaign Against Lynching*, 145–57.

17. This connection between the rape of white women and the destruction of civilization during Reconstruction was also made by the popular novels of Thomas Nelson Page. See Friedman, *The White Savage*, 67.

18. "'Stript, Shorne and Made Deformed,'" 55.

19. Ransom, *I'll Take My Stand*, 10–11.

20. Scott, 4–14.

21. Quoted in "The Southern Woman," 6–7.

22. Scott, 16–21.

23. King, *A Southern Renaissance*, 34–35.

24. Quoted in Scott, 17.

25. *Southern Review* 8 (October 1870): 406, 418–19; 8 (July 1870): 52; 5 (April 1869): 303, 315.

26. See Scott, chapter 7, "The Right to Vote."

27. Quoted by Clement Eaton, in "Breaking a Path for the Liberation of Women in the South," 187.

28. Scott, 170–209.

29. *Southern Review* 9 (October 1871): 941–42.

30. See also William R. Taylor's excellent discussion of the fear of insubordination which underlay the sentimental plantation myth in *Cavalier and Yankee*, 165–76, and Marie Stokes Jemison, "Ladies Become Voters," 48–59.

31. Marjorie Stratford Mendenhall, "Southern Women of a 'Lost Generation,'" 351. See also Scott, 98–102.

32. Quoted in Mendenhall, 353.

33. Mims, *The Advancing South*, 254–56.

34. *The Advancing South*, 233–34.

35. Taylor, 165.

36. Chesnut, *Mary Chesnut's Civil War*, 59, 261–62, 279; see also 15, 23, 29–30, 172, 180–81.
37. Jemison, 53–54.
38. See Leslie Fiedler's "Uncle Tom as White Mother," in *The Inadvertent Epic*, 29–41, for a provocative bit of reconstructive surgery which bears on this issue.
39. Cash, 85–86; Tannenbaum, *Darker Phases of the South*, 33; Smith, *Killers of the Dream*, 119–34, 138–39.
40. Bierce, *Travels in the Southland*, 78, 99–100.
41. Stampp, *The Peculiar Institution*, 350–57; Genovese, *Roll, Jordan, Roll*, 413–31; Dabney, *A Defence of Virginia*, 281, 285.
42. Scott, 52–54; Chesnut, 30–31, 72. See Mrs. Chesnut's argument with British journalist William Howard Russell of the London *Times* on the subject, pp. 168–70, and the story she reports "a la Stowe," pp. 347–48. See also C. Vann Woodward, *American Counterpoint*, 72–77.
43. Quoted by Clement Eaton, "Breaking a Path," 193.
44. Porter, *The Collected Stories of Katherine Anne Porter*, 337.
45. Smith, 114–37.
46. Dollard, *Caste and Class in a Southern Town*, 136–37, 138–43.
47. See Anne Jones's discussion of Glasgow's life and work, pp. 225–70.
48. Glasgow, *The Woman Within*, 97–98.
49. Jones, 230.
50. Glasgow, *Virginia*, 83. All further citations of the novel are from this edition; page numbers will be indicated parenthetically in my text.
51. Jones, 245–47.
52. Cash, 46–47.
53. Faulkner, *Go Down, Moses*, 294. All further citations of this work are from this edition; page numbers will be indicated parenthetically in my text.
54. Fiedler, *Love and Death in the American Novel*, 51, 320, 321.
55. Faulkner, *Absalom, Absalom!*, 114. All further citations of this work will be from this edition, and page numbers will be indicated parenthetically in my text.
56. Jones, 362.

Chapter Two. Growing Up in the Modern South

1. Woolf, "American Fiction," in *The Moment and Other Essays*, 116; Tate, "The New Provincialism," 272.
2. *Faulkner in the University*, 1, 6.
3. King, 8–9.
4. Leslie Fiedler goes even further in *Love and Death in the American Novel* (p. 321), claiming that Faulkner punished the New Woman for her rebellion in *Sanctuary* by having Temple Drake brutally raped with a corncob.
5. Grady, "The South and Her Problems," in *The New South and Other Addresses*, 89. For a discussion of the social and political background of his appeal, see

William R. Taylor, "Holding the Wolf by the Ears: The Plantation Setting and the Social Order," in *Cavalier and Yankee*; Friedman, *The White Savage*; Gaston, *The New South Creed*; F. Garvin Davenport, *The Myth of Southern History*; and Osterweis, *The Myth of the Lost Cause*.

6. Dixon, *The Leopard's Spots*, 247, 468–69.
7. Taylor, *Cavalier and Yankee*, 148.
8. Hall, 149–66; Smith, 144–46.
9. Hall, 165–67.
10. Jan Nordby Gretlund, "An Interview with Eudora Welty," 194.
11. King, *Southern Ladies and Gentlemen*, 54.
12. *One Writer's Beginnings*, 18–19.
13. "Welty Rites," Jackson *Clarion-Ledger*, January 22, 1966; *One Writer's Beginnings*, 45–58; Elizabeth Evans, *Eudora Welty*, xi, 3–4; Gretlund interview, 195.
14. Virginia Spencer Carr, *The Lonely Hunter: A Biography of Carson McCullers*, 8–22.
15. Carr, 4–5, 16–17, 128–33, 195, 417.
16. Sally Fitzgerald, Introduction to *The Habit of Being*, xii, hereafter cited as *Habit*.
17. Welty, "A Sweet Devouring," in *The Eye of the Story*, 279–85; Porter, Introduction to Welty, *A Curtain of Green and Other Stories*, xiii; Carr, 26–28; McCullers, "How I Became a Writer," in *The Mortgaged Heart*, 249–50; Lorine M. Getz, *Flannery O'Connor: Her Life, Library and Book Reviews*, 7.
18. *Habit*, 167–68; O'Connor's youthful burlesque of Proust, "Recollections of My Future Childhood," unpublished ms. in the O'Connor Collection, Anna Dillard Russell Library, Georgia College, Milledgeville.
19. Moers, 108.
20. Carr, 38.
21. *Habit*, 145–46; Interviews with Miriam Johnson, December 2, 1975, and June 1982; O'Connor, *The Complete Stories*, 242; Margaret Inman Meaders, "Flannery O'Connor: 'Literary Witch'," 378. One of O'Connor's schoolmates, Mrs. Ann Park, recalls that O'Connor took pet chickens to the high school on several other occasions and sometimes sat on the porch swing of the Cline House with one or two beside her (conversation with the author, September 22, 1983, Milledgeville).
22. Glasgow, *Virginia*, 22; Richardson, 126–29; Woolf, *A Room of One's Own*, 25–26.
23. "Fulbright and Welty Distinguish 88th Commencement," 2.
24. Gretlund interview, 199.
25. See Porter, Introduction to *A Curtain of Green*, xii; Ruth Vande Kieft, *Eudora Welty*, 13–16; Evans, xi, 1–4.
26. See Carr, 26, 32, 42–64, 569–70; McCullers, *The Mortgaged Heart*, 250–51.
27. Getz, 12–14; *Habit*, 224, 230.
28. *Habit*, 522, 525–26; Robert Fitzgerald, Introduction to *Everything That Rises Must Converge*, xiv.
29. *The Mortgaged Heart*, 279.

30. Gilbert and Gubar, *The Madwoman in the Attic*, 4–11.
31. Evans, 4.
32. See *Habit*, 158, 170–71.
33. See Porter, xiv, and Gretlund, 203.
34. See Welty, *The Eye of the Story*.
35. *The Mortgaged Heart*, 250–78.
36. *Habit*, 98–99.
37. Woolf, *A Room of One's Own*, 82.
38. *Habit*, 98.
39. For a full exploration of this problem, see Judith Fetterley, *The Resisting Reader*.
40. *The Madwoman in the Attic*, 48, 69.
41. Flaubert said of his artistic struggles, "Women will never experience any of this." Quoted by James Atlas in a review of *The Letters of Gustave Flaubert, 1857–1880*, 3.
42. *Jane Eyre*, 141.
43. Woolf, *A Room of One's Own*, 70.
44. *Jane Eyre*, 349–50.
45. Moers, 66.
46. Kuehl interview, 75.
47. Michael Kreyling discusses links between Woolf's novel and *The Optimist's Daughter* in *Eudora Welty's Achievement of Order*, and Marcia McGowan touches upon echoes of Woolf's novel in *Delta Wedding* in her dissertation "Patterns of Female Experience in Eudora Welty's Fiction" (Rutgers, 1977), 73–86.
48. Woolf, *A Room of One's Own*, 87.
49. Kuehl interview, 83.
50. Carr, 115–56, 158, 175, 197, 161–62.
51. *The Mortgaged Heart*, 266–73.
52. *Habit*, 98–99, 446, 550. See Getz for a list of the writers in O'Connor's personal library; also see Robert Fitzgerald, Introduction to *Everything that Rises Must Converge*, xv–xvi.
53. *Habit*, 25, 95, 98.
54. Carr, 111, 156–57.
55. Kuehl interview, 83; Carr, 433–34; *Habit*, 246, 402–403, 446, 546, 550.
56. Fiedler, *Love and Death in the American Novel*, 481–82.

Chapter Three. The Enchanted Maternal Garden of *Delta Wedding*

1. Jean Todd Freeman, "Eudora Welty," *Conversations with Writers II*, 294. See also Charles T. Bunting, "The Interior World: An Interview with Eudora Welty," 718. For a discussion of particular differences between the novel and the original short story, see Kreyling, *Eudora Welty's Achievement of Order*, 52–61.
2. Welty, quoted in Kuehl interview, 75; Welty, *The Eye of the Story*, 191; Ransom, "Delta Fiction," *Kenyon Review*, 505.

3. Bunting interview, 716; Gretlund interview, 2001; "Images of the South: Visits with Eudora Welty and Walker Evans," 13.

4. Welty, *The Eye of the Story*, 7, 63; Gretlund interview, 200, 207.

5. Moers, 42–62; Bunting interview, 726.

6. Woolf, *The Diary of Virginia Woolf*, vol. 2, 68–69, 195–96, 199–200, 322; vol. 3, 7. See also Maria DiBattista, *Virginia Woolf's Major Novels: The Fables of Anon*, 23, 29.

7. Marcus, paper presented at the MLA Convention, 1982; and *Jacob's Room*, 3–4.

8. *Diary of Virginia Woolf*, vol. 2, 14, 199.

9. *Diary of Virginia Woolf*, vol. 2, 317, and vol. 3, 18–19; *To the Lighthouse*, 58–60. All further citations of this novel will be indicated parenthetically by page number in my text.

10. Ruth Vande Kieft discusses the family network at length in her *Eudora Welty* (p. 94). Critics such as Peggy Prenshaw and John Allen have previously commented on allusions to the myth of Demeter and Kore. See Prenshaw, "Woman's World, Man's Place: The Fiction of Eudora Welty," 70–72, and Allen, "The Other Way to Live: Demigods in Eudora Welty's Fiction," 40–41.

11. *Delta Wedding*, 63. All further references to the novel will be to this edition and will be cited by page number in my text.

12. George's dependence on Robbie is also described during the wedding of Dabney and Troy (pp. 212–13). There has been much critical discussion of George's function as heroic fulcrum of attention. See, for instance, Vande Kieft, 95–96; Lucinda H. MacKethan, "To See Things in Their Time: The Act of Focus in Eudora Welty's Fiction," 264–66; and John Allen, "The Other Way to Live," 28–29. In two later novels, *The Ponder Heart* and *Losing Battles*, a similar adoring focus is placed upon Uncle Daniel Ponder and Jack Renfro.

13. Kuehl interview, 84; Bunting interview, 721.

14. Vande Kieft (p. 107) and Kreyling, in *Eudora Welty's Achievement of Order* (p. 61), have commented on the symbolic meaning of the name "Shellmound," but specific historical information can be found in the Mississippi Department of Archives and History. The geographical distribution of the mounds is discussed in the subject file "Indian Mounds," which also includes an essay, "Indian Mounds of Mississippi," explaining Choctaw legends concerning them. Annie H. Dixon presents a detailed history of the mound Welty placed in *Delta Wedding*, in File 610: "Shellmound, Leflore County."

15. Many critics have discussed the mythic elements in these stories. See, for instance, Vande Kieft, 57–67; Prenshaw, "Woman's World, Man's Place," 60–61; Allen, "The Other Way To Live," 29–31; F. Garvin Davenport, "Renewal and Historical Consciousness in *The Wide Net*," in *Eudora Welty: Critical Essays*, 189–200; and Kreyling, *Eudora Welty's Achievement of Order*, 20–31.

16. Hardy, "*Delta Wedding* as Region and Symbol," 397–417, especially 400.

17. Young, *The Heart's Forest*, 20, 29–31.

18. Lewis, *The American Adam*; Marx, *The Machine in the Garden*; Fiedler, *Love and Death in the American Novel*; unpublished talk given by Fiedler at Oregon State University in the spring of 1977.

19. Kolodny, *The Lay of the Land*.
20. Prenshaw, "Woman's World, Man's Place," 60–61; Neil D. Isaacs, *Eudora Welty*, 33–36.
21. Gretlund interview, 203; Welty, *One Writer's Beginnings*, 4–9.
22. Kirk, *The Nature of Greek Myths*, 249–53; Jaan Puhvel, "Eleuthēr and Oinoâtis: Dionysiac Data from Mycenaean Greece," in Emmett L. Bennett, Jr., ed., *Mycenaean Studies*, 161–69; *The Bacchae of Euripides*, trans. G. S. Kirk, 28, 81–83; Robert Briffault, *The Mothers*, 371–78; and C. Kerényi, *Eleusis*, 18–25, 30–41.
23. Deborah Dickmann Boedeker, *Aphrodite's Entry into Greek Myth*, 45–53; see Sophocles's *Oedipus, Sophoclis Fabulae*, ed. A. C. Pearson, line 1497; and Hesiod, *The Homeric Hymn and Homerica*, trans. H. G. Evelyn-White, 457.
24. Moers, 257–62.
25. Later in the novel Robbie remembers the whirlpool as a place where she and George have swum together at night, immersing themselves as married lovers in the erotic waters (p. 144).
26. Kerényi describes the *omphalos* in the temple of the Mysteries at Eleusis, (p. 80), and he also presents evidence from vase paintings that the *omphalos* is associated with Dionysos (pp. 159–62). See also *The Oxford Classical Dictionary*, 324, 484, 850.
27. Kerényi, 34–35, 356–69; George E. Mylonas, *The Hymn to Demeter and Her Sanctuary at Eleusis*, 3.
28. Allen, "The Other Way To Live," 29.
29. Puhvel, 165; Martin P. Nilsson, *The Mycenaean Origin of Greek Mythology*, 75; Kerényi, 25–40; Briffault, 372–77; Erich Neumann, *The Great Mother*, 362–65.
30. Kreyling, *Eudora Welty's Achievement of Order*, 72–76.
31. Prenshaw, 50; "Woman's World, Man's Place," 50; Welty, *The Eye of the Story*, 119–20.
32. Moore, "Aunt Studney's Sack," 593; Neumann, 262–67.
33. Allen, "The Other Way to Live," 40–41.
34. Prenshaw, "Woman's World, Man's Place," 51.

Chapter Four. Venturesome Daughters

1. See Hardy, "*Delta Wedding* as Region and Symbol," 404.
2. This tradition is provocatively explored by Bertram Wyatt-Brown in *Southern Honor*, but even Wyatt-Brown's careful treatment of the idea cannot disguise its character as an elaborate form of masculine pride.
3. See John Edward Hardy, "Marrying Down in Eudora Welty's Novels," 93–119, and Albert J. Devlin, *Eudora Welty's Chronicle*, 110–11.
4. See Devlin, 107.
5. Hardy, "*Delta Wedding*," 415. See also Devlin, 109.
6. Vande Kieft, 139, 145–46.
7. *The Collected Stories of Eudora Welty*, 434. All further citations of *The Golden Apples* will be to this edition and will be indicated by page number in my text.

8. Jeanne Rolfe Nostrandt, "Fiction as Event: An Interview with Eudora Welty,"
32.

9. See Allen, "Eudora Welty: The Three Moments," 16.

10. Devlin, 204.

11. John Griffin Jones, *Mississippi Writers Talking: Interviews with Eudora Welty,
Shelby Foote, Elizabeth Spencer, Barry Hannah, Beth Henley*, 27.

12. Jones interview, 27.

13. *The Optimist's Daughter*, 102–103. All further page references to the novel will
be from this edition and will be indicated parenthetically in my text.

14. See John F. Desmond, "Pattern and Vision in *The Optimist's Daughter*," in Desmond, ed., *A Still Moment*, 131, and Devlin, 178.

15. Jones interview, 26.

16. Gretlund interview, 195. See *One Writer's Beginnings*, 46–60, for Welty's recollections of childhood visits to West Virginia.

17. This experience must be very close to Welty's own, for her grandmother An-
drews kept pigeons on her West Virginia mountain farm and offered some to
her granddaughter, just as Laurel's grandmother does. The letters from Laurel's grandmother to her mother clearly echo the letters Welty quotes from her
own grandmother in *One Writer's Beginnings*, pp. 55–57.

18. See Kreyling, *Eudora Welty's Achievement of Order*, 168–69, Devlin, 180–82.

19. Jones interview, 28. For an introduction to the problem of tradition and social
order in the novel, see Thomas Daniel Young, "Social Form and Social Order:
An Examination of *The Optimist's Daughter*," in Prenshaw, ed., *Eudora Welty:
Critical Essays*, 367–85.

20. See Desmond, "Pattern and Vision," 136–37; Kreyling, *Eudora Welty's Achievement of Order*, 172–73. Walter Sullivan describes the ultimate effect of this
novel as a reflection of the fragmentation of Southern culture into mean-
inglessness (Sullivan, *A Requiem for the Renascence*, 52–58). I disagree with his
view that Laurel achieves no more than an uneasy peace here.

Chapter Five. Tomboys and Revolting Femininity

1. Jones, *Tomorrow Is Another Day*, 355; Heilbrun, *Reinventing Womanhood*, 106–
108; Karen Horney, *Feminine Psychology*, 54–70. For previous discussions of
sexual ambivalence in these works, see Fiedler, *Love and Death in the American
Novel*, 333, 484–85; Moers, *Literary Women*, 108–109; and Patricia S. Box,
"Androgyny and the Musical Vision: A Study of Two Novels by Carson Mc-
Cullers," 117–23.

2. Quoted in Wyatt-Brown, 231–33.

3. Chopin, *The Awakening and Other Stories*, 270; Jones, *Tomorrow Is Another Day*,
142–44.

4. Jones, *Tomorrow Is Another Day*, 144–45.

5. Woolf, "Professions for Women," in *The Death of the Moth and Other Essays*, 153.
Woolf's most famous description of the crippling difficulties women face is of

course *A Room of One's Own*, but she illustrated the assertions of that work in
the whole body of her essays and in her treatment of women characters like
Mrs. Ramsay and Lily Briscoe in her novels. For scholarly examination of the
presentation of these problems in women's writing since the early nineteenth
century, see Moers, *Literary Women;* Showalter, *A Literature of Their Own;* and
Gilbert and Gubar, *The Madwoman in the Attic.*

6. Mossberg, "Slant Truths and Bandaged Secrets: The Art of Deceit in Emily
   Dickinson and Gertrude Stein"; Mossberg, *Emily Dickinson: When a Writer Is a
   Daughter;* Gilbert, " 'My Name Is Darkness': The Poetry of Self-Definition,"
   443–57, and especially 446–47; Heilbrun, 72. See also Heilbrun, 105–24.
   Karen Horney is a notable exception, as Heilbrun points out (p. 99), but her
   daring resulted in ostracism by her professional colleagues.

7. Cather, *The Song of the Lark*, 140.

8. *The Heart Is a Lonely Hunter*, 17. All subsequent references to this work will be
   cited parenthetically by page number in my text.

9. See Karen Horney's classic assertion that female masochism is not innate, as
   Freud argued, but rather a response to cultural pressure which denies women
   the freedom to assert themselves (*Feminine Psychology*, 217).

10. Carr, 570–73.

11. McCullers, *The Mortgaged Heart*, 274.

12. Rubin, "Carson McCullers: The Aesthetic of Pain," 278–79; Carr, 110–29,
    157–85.

13. Robert Rechnitz, "The Failure of Love: The Grotesque in Two Novels by
    Carson McCullers," 460.

14. McCullers, *The Mortgaged Heart*, 269–70; Phillips, "Dinesen's 'Monkey' and
    McCullers's 'Ballad': A Study in Literary Affinity," *Studies in Short Fiction* 1
    (1963–64), 184–90. Phillips sees both stories in Freudian terms of father-
    daughter incest which renders the daughter unfit for heterosexual love.

15. Isak Dinesen, *Seven Gothic Tales*, 109–63. Subsequent references will be indi-
    cated parenthetically by page number in my text.

16. *The Ballad of the Sad Café and Other Stories*, 17. Subsequent references will be
    indicated parenthetically by page number in my text.

17. Millichap, "Carson McCullers's Literary Ballad," 334–35.

18. Panthea Reid Broughton, in "Rejection of the Feminine in Carson McCullers'
    The Ballad of the Sad Café," 34–43, argues that the dress is a symbol of Amelia's
    accessibility, but that interpretation is denied by all her actions. Rechnitz (p.
    461) thinks she is trying to lure Macy away from Cousin Lymon, but again,
    her behavior is the opposite of seductive.

19. *The Mortgaged Heart*, 280–81.

20. Moers, 109; *The Member of the Wedding*, 77–78. Subsequent references will be
    indicated parenthetically by page number in my text.

21. See Moers, 19–41.

22. Rich, "When We Dead Awaken" and "Snapshots of a Daughter-in-Law,"
    Adrienne Rich's Poetry, 95 and 12.

Chapter Six. Good Country People

1. O'Connor, *Mystery and Manners*, 52.
2. Conversation with Rebekah Poller regarding Hicks, June 28, 1983, Eugene, Oregon; *Habit*, 499, 202, 105–106.
3. *Habit*, 566; *Mystery and Manners*, 29; *Habit*, 522.
4. Louise Hardemon Abbot, "Remembering Flannery O'Connor," 3–25; Father James H. McCown, "Remembering Flannery O'Connor," 86–88.
5. Typescript donated to the O'Connor Collection by Rebekah Poller, possibly the one O'Connor gave her to show to Granville Hicks in 1957 or 1958.
6. The strongest treatment of the problem written during her lifetime, and one which she tries to counter a number of times in her letters, is John Hawkes's "Flannery O'Connor's Devil." She debated the issue with him for years and talks at some length about it in a letter to him in late 1961 (*Habit*, 455–57). See also *Habit*, 366, 486, 507. Later "heretical" criticism includes Josephine Hendin, *The World of Flannery O'Connor*; Martha Stephens, *The Question of Flannery O'Connor*; Claire Katz, "Flannery O'Connor's Rage of Vision"; Andre Bleikasten, "The Heresy of Flannery O'Connor"; and Clara Claiborne Park, "Crippled Laughter: Toward Understanding Flannery O'Connor."
7. *Habit*, 85, 416, 464, 490, 180, 149.
8. *Habit*, 363–64, 446, 546, 550.
9. Carr, 443.
10. Stephens, 155–56.
11. O'Connor, *The Complete Stories*, 239–40. All subsequent references to the stories will be indicated parenthetically by page number in my text.
12. *Habit*, 124.
13. *American Heritage Dictionary*, 850. See also the appendix of "Indo-European Roots" compiled by the distinguished Harvard linguist and classicist Calvert Watkins, p. 1529, meaning number 3 of *men-*[1]; and p. 637. David R. Mayer suggests this connection in "Apologia for the Imagination: Flannery O'Connor's 'A Temple of the Holy Ghost,'" 152.
14. *Habit*, 124.
15. *Habit*, 117–19; Katz, 57–64; *Habit*, 136–37, 141.
16. *Habit*, 136–37.
17. *Habit*, 176. Passing on the subject of the Luces and the *Bulletin* may be a reference to Time-Life Publications.
18. Wyatt-Brown, 240.
19. McCown, 87.
20. Martha Chew, "Flannery O'Connor's Double-Edged Satire: The Idiot Daughter Versus the Lady Ph.D.," 20. I obviously continue to hold the views I expressed in "Flannery O'Connor's Mothers and Daughters," in contrast to Chew's conclusion that there is ultiately little difference between the quality of Lucynell's life and Joy-Hulga's.
21. *Habit*, 85.
22. *The Collected Stories of Eudora Welty*, 264.

23. *Habit*, 118–20.
24. *Habit*, 171.
25. O'Connor, *Mystery and Manners*, 99, 83.
26. Asals, *Flannery O'Connor: The Imagination of Extremity*, 70–72.
27. Desmond, "The Shifting of Mr. Shiftlet: Flannery O'Connor's 'The Life You Save May Be Your Own,'" 55–59. In one early manuscript version of the story (Folder 156b, Flannery O'Connor Collection, Georgia College), the canny old widow tricks Shiftlet out of the car at the last minute. This manuscript reveals Shiftlet's close kinship with Manley Pointer, because Shiftlet entertains the old woman's daughter with almost the same grotesque joke about a two-day-old chicken that Pointer tells Joy-Hulga.
28. Asals, *Flannery O'Connor*, 65–94.

Chapter Seven. O'Connor's Sacred Landscapes

1. See Desmond, "Flannery O'Connor's Sense of Place," 251–59; Michael Cleary, "Environmental Influences in Flannery O'Connor's Fiction," 20–34; Sung Gay Chow, "'Strange and Alien Country': An Analysis of Landscape in Flannery O'Connor's *Wise Blood* and *The Violent Bear It Away*," 35–44; and Asals, *Flannery O'Connor: The Imagination of Extremity*, 65–94.
2. O'Connor's personal library is housed in the Flannery O'Connor Collection at the Ida Dillard Russell Library of Georgia College in Milledgeville, Georgia.
3. Cleary, "Environmental Influences"; George D. Murphy and Caroline L. Cherry, "Flannery O'Connor and the Integration of Personality," 96–98.
4. See Josephine Hendin's discussion of mothers and children in *The World of Flannery O'Connor*, 43, 72, 76, 97–130, and Claire Katz's Freudian analysis of infantile fantasies in "Flannery O'Connor's Rage of Vision," 54–67.
5. Marina Warner, *Alone of All Her Sex*, 121–33, 255–84; Desmond, "Flannery O'Connor's Sense of Place," 256.
6. *Habit*, 98; Robert Fitzgerald, Introduction to *Everything That Rises Must Converge*, xvi. O'Connor's personal library included Bulfinch, Eliade's *Patterns in Comparative Religion*, Guthrie's *The Greeks and Their Gods*, and Keeler's *Secrets of the Cuna Earthmother*. Another indication of O'Connor's interest is Asbury Fox's fascination with the myth of the dying god in "The Enduring Chill" (*The Complete Stories*, 375).
7. Quoted in Marshack, 337–38.
8. Gertrude R. Levy traces this evolution in *The Gate of Horn*. See Eliade, *Patterns in Comparative Religion*, 164–71; Marija Gimbutas, *Goddesses and Gods of Old Europe*, 67–88, 89–150, 236–38; Joseph Campbell, *The Masks of God*, 9–92; and James Mellaart, *The Neolithic of the Near East*, 106–109.
9. Gimbutas, 238; Nilsson, *The Mino-Mycenaean Religion and Its Survival in Greek Religion*, 415–513. See also Campbell, 9–92.
10. Eliade, 261; Scully, *The Earth, the Temple and the Gods*; *The Oxford Classical Dictionary*, 324, 421–22; Sophocles, *Oedipus, Sophoclis Fabulae*, lines 1256–57 and 1497.

11. Eliade, 280–90; Campbell, 42–45, 512–13; Warner, chapters 16 and 17.
12. Asals, "The Mythic Dimensions of Flannery O'Connor's 'Greenleaf'," 317–30. See also John C. Shields, "Flannery O'Connor's 'Greenleaf' and the Myth of Europa and the Bull," 421–31.
13. Shields comments interestingly on his relation to circles (p. 429).
14. Kerényi, 64, 92–93, 148–49.
15. *Habit*, 119–20.
16. Hawkes, "Flannery O'Connor's Devil."
17. Asals, in *Flannery O'Connor: The Imagination of Extremity*, discusses this story in related terms but sees the Negro woman as a symbol of passionate abandon of the rational life.
18. Hendin, 13; Katz, 54–67; Park, 249–57.
19. Moers, 107–110; Sontag, *On Photography*, 44; O'Connor, *Mystery and Manners*, 25–50; *Habit*, 16, 49.
20. *Habit*, 35.
21. Hendin, 17; Katz, 58–67; Welty, *The Eye of the Story*, 98.

Bibliography

Abbot, Louise Hardeman. "Remembering Flannery O'Connor." *Southern Literary Journal* 2 (Spring 1970): 3–25.

Allen, John Alexander. "The Other Way to Live: Demigods in Eudora Welty's Fiction." In *Eudora Welty: Critical Essays*, edited by Peggy Whitman Prenshaw. Jackson: University Press of Mississippi, 1979.

———. "Eudora Welty: The Three Moments." In *A Still Moment: Essays on the Art of Eudora Welty*, edited by John F. Desmond. Metuchen, N.J.: Scarecrow Press, 1978.

Allen, Suzanne. "Memoirs of a Southern Catholic Girlhood: Flannery O'Connor's 'A Temple of the Holy Ghost.'" *Renascence* 31 (Winter 1979): 83–92.

The American Heritage Dictionary of the English Language. New York and Boston: American Heritage Publishing Co. and Houghton Mifflin, 1969.

Asals, Frederick. *Flannery O'Connor: The Imagination of Extremity.* Athens: University of Georgia Press, 1982.

———. "The Mythic Dimensions of Flannery O'Connor's 'Greenleaf.'" *Studies in Short Fiction* 5 (Summer 1968): 317–30.

Atlas, James. "Art Is the Only True Thing in Life." Review of *The Letters of Gustave Flaubert, 1857–1880*, edited and translated by Francis Steigmuller. *New York Times Book Review*, October 17, 1982, 3, 48.

Bartlett, Irving H., and C. Glenn Cambor. "The History and Psychodynamics of Southern Womanhood." *Women's Studies* 2 (1974): 9–24.

Bennett, E. L., ed. *Mycenaean Studies.* Madison: University of Wisconsin Press, 1964.

Beverley, Robert. *The History and Present State of Virginia.* Edited by Louis B. Wright. Chapel Hill: University of North Carolina Press, 1947.

Bierce, Lucius Verus. *Travels in the Southland, 1822–1823: The Journal of Lucius Verus Bierce.* Edited by George W. Knepper. Columbus: Ohio State University Press, 1966.

Bledsoe, Albert Taylor. Articles in the *Southern Review* 5–11 (April 1869–July 1872).

Bleikasten, André. "The Heresy of Flannery O'Connor." In *Les Américanistes: New French Criticism on Modern American Fiction*, edited by Ira D. Johnson and Christiane Johnson. Port Washington, N.Y.: Kennikat Press, 1978.

Bloom, Harold. *The Anxiety of Influence.* New York: Oxford University Press, 1973.

Boedeker, Deborah Dickmann. *Aphrodite's Entry into Greek Epic.* Leiden, Netherlands: E. J. Brill, 1974.

Bolsterli, Margaret Jones. "Woman's Vision: The Worlds of Women in *Delta Wedding, Losing Battles* and *The Optimist's Daughter.*" In *Eudora Welty: Critical Essays*, edited by Peggy Whitman Prenshaw. Jackson: University Press of Mississippi, 1979.

Box, Patricia S. "Androgyny and the Musical Vision: A Study of Two Novels by Carson McCullers." *Southern Quarterly* 16 (January 1978): 117–23.

Bradford, William. *Of Plymouth Plantation, 1620–1647.* 1856. New ed. Edited by Samuel Eliot Morison. New York: Alfred A. Knopf, 1952.

Branston, Brian. *The Lost Gods of England.* New York: Oxford University Press, 1974.

Briffault, Robert. *The Mothers.* Abridged, with an introduction by Gordon Rattray Taylor. New York: Atheneum, 1977.

Brinkmeyer, Robert H., Jr. "Borne Away by Violence: The Reader and Flannery O'Connor." *Southern Review* 15 (Spring 1979): 313–21.

Brontë, Charlotte. *Jane Eyre.* Harmondsworth, England: Penguin Books, 1966.

Broughton, Panthea Reid. "Rejection of the Feminine in Carson McCullers' *The Ballad of the Sad Café.*" *Twentieth Century Literature* 20 (January 1974): 34–43.

Browning, Preston M. *Flannery O'Connor.* Carbondale: Southern Illinois University Press, 1974.

Bryant, J. A., Jr. *Eudora Welty.* Minneapolis: University of Minnesota Press, 1968.

Buckley, William F., Jr. "The Southern Imagination: An Interview with Eudora Welty and Walker Percy." *Mississippi Quarterly* 26 (Fall 1973): 493–516.

Bunting, Charles T. "'The Interior World': An Interview with Eudora Welty." *Southern Review* (Autumn 1972): 711–35.

Burns, Stuart. "Torn by the Lord's Eye: Flannery O'Connor's Use of Sun Imagery." *Twentieth Century Literature* 13 (October 1967): 154–66.

Campbell, Joseph. *The Masks of God: Occidental Mythology.* New York: Viking Press, 1971.

Carmer, Carl. *Stars Fell on Alabama.* New York: Farrar and Rinehart, 1934.

Carr, Virginia Spencer. *The Lonely Hunter: A Biography of Carson McCullers.* Garden City, N.Y.: Doubleday, 1975.

Cash, W. J. *The Mind of the South.* New York: Alfred A. Knopf, 1941.

Cather, Willa. *The Song of the Lark.* Boston: Houghton Mifflin, 1915.

Chaffee, Patricia. "Houses in the Short Fiction of Eudora Welty." *Studies in Short Fiction* 15 (Winter 1978): 112–14.

Chesnut, Mary. *Mary Chesnut's Civil War*. Edited by C. Vann Woodward. New Haven: Yale University Press, 1981.

Chew, Martha. "Flannery O'Connor's Double-Edged Satire: The Idiot Daughter Versus the Lady Ph.D." *Southern Quarterly* 19 (Winter 1981): 17–25.

Chopin, Kate. *The Awakening and Other Stories*. New York: New American Library, 1976.

Chow, Sung Gay. "'Strange and Alien Country': An Analysis of Landscape in Flannery O'Connor's *Wise Blood* and *The Violent Bear It Away*." *Flannery O'Connor Bulletin* 8 (1979): 35–44.

Cleary, Michael. "Environmental Influences in Flannery O'Connor's Fiction." *Flannery O'Connor Bulletin* 8 (1979): 20–34.

Cook, Martha E. "Flannery O'Connor." In *American Women Writers*, edited by Maurice Duke, Jackson R. Breyer, and M. Thomas Inge. Westport, Conn.: Greenwood Press, 1983.

Cook, Richard M. *Carson McCullers*. New York: Frederick Ungar, 1975.

Cooper, William J. *The South and the Politics of Slavery, 1828–1856*. Baton Rouge: Louisiana State University Press, 1978.

Coulthard, A. R. "The Christian Writer and the New South: or, Why Don't You Like Flannery O'Connor?" *Southern Humanities Review* 13 (Winter 1979): 79–82.

Dabney, Prof. Robert L. *A Defence of Virginia (and Through Her, of the South)*. 1867. Reprint. New York: Negro Universities Press, 1969.

Davenport, F. Garvin. *The Myth of Southern History: Historical Consciousness in Twentieth-Century Southern Literature*. Nashville: Vanderbilt University Press, 1970.

Desmond, John F. "Flannery O'Connor's Sense of Place." *Southern Humanities Review* 10 (Summer 1976): 251–59.

———. "The Shifting of Mr. Shiftlet: Flannery O'Connor's 'The Life You Save May Be Your Own.'" *Mississippi Quarterly* 28 (Winter 1974–75): 55–59.

———, ed. *A Still Moment: Essays on the Art of Eudora Welty*. Metuchen, N.J.: Scarecrow Press, 1978.

Detienne, Marcel. *Dionysos Slain*. Translated by Mireille Muellner and Leonard Muellner. Baltimore: Johns Hopkins University Press, 1979.

Devlin, Albert J. *Eudora Welty's Chronicle: A Story of Mississippi Life*. Jackson: University Press of Mississippi, 1983.

DiBattista, Maria. *Virginia Woolf's Major Novels: The Fables of Anon*. New Haven: Yale University Press, 1980.

Dinesen, Isak. *Seven Gothic Tales*. New York: Modern Library, 1934.

Dixon, Annie. "Shellmound, Leflore County." File 610. Mississippi Department of Archives and History, Jackson.

Dixon, Thomas, Jr. *The Clansman: An Historical Romance of the Ku Klux Klan*. 1905. Reprint. Lexington: University Press of Kentucky, 1970.

———. *The Leopard's Spots*. New York: A. Wessels Co., 1906.

Dollard, John. *Caste and Class in a Southern Town*. Garden City, N.Y.: Doubleday, 1957.

Dollarhide, Louis, and Ann J. Abadie, eds. *Eudora Welty: A Form of Thanks.* Jackson: University Press of Mississippi, 1979.

East, Charles. "The Search for Eudora Welty." *Mississippi Quarterly* 26 (Fall 1973): 477–82.

Eaton, Clement. "Breaking a Path for the Liberation of Women in the South." *Georgia Review* 28 (Summer 1974): 187–99.

———. *A History of the Old South: The Emergence of a Reluctant Nation.* New York: Macmillan, 1949.

Eliade, Mircea. *Myths, Dreams, and Mysteries.* Translated by Philip Mairet. New York: Harper & Row, 1967.

———. *Patterns in Comparative Religion.* New York: Meridian Books, 1966.

Evans, Elizabeth. *Eudora Welty.* New York: Frederick Ungar, 1981.

Farnham, James F. "The Disintegration of Myth in the Writings of Flannery O'Connor." *Connecticut Review* 8 (October 1974): 11–19.

Faulkner, William. *Absalom, Absalom!* New York: Modern Library, 1951.

———. *Go Down, Moses.* New York: Modern Library, 1942.

———. *The Sound and the Fury.* New York: Modern Library, 1946.

Faulkner in the University. Edited by Frederick L. Gwynn and Joseph L. Blotner. New York: Vintage Books, 1965.

Feeley, Sister Kathleen. *Flannery O'Connor: Voice of the Peacock.* New Brunswick, N.J.: Rutgers University Press, 1972.

Fetterley, Judith. *The Resisting Reader: A Feminist Approach to American Fiction.* Bloomington: Indiana University Press, 1978.

Fiedler, Leslie. *The Inadvertent Epic: From "Uncle Tom's Cabin" to "Roots."* New York: Simon & Schuster, 1979.

———. *Love and Death in the American Novel.* New York: Dell, 1969.

Fitzgerald, Robert. "The Countryside and the True Country." *Sewanee Review* 70 (1962): 380–94.

Freeman, Jean Todd. "Eudora Welty." In *Conversations with Writers II.* Conversations, vol. 3. Detroit: Gale Research Company, 1978.

Freud, Sigmund. *Collected Papers.* Vol. 5. London: Hogarth Press and the Institute of Psycho-Analysis, 1957.

Friedman, Lawrence J. *The White Savage: Racial Fantasies in the Postbellum South.* Englewood Cliffs, N.J.: Prentice-Hall, 1970.

Friedman, Melvin J., and Lewis A. Lawson. *The Added Dimension: The Art and Mind of Flannery O'Connor.* New York: Fordham University Press, 1966.

"Fulbright and Welty Distinguish 88th Commencement." *R-MWC Today* (Summer 1981), 2.

Gaston, Paul M. *The New South Creed: A Study in Southern Mythmaking.* New York: Alfred A. Knopf, 1970.

Genovese, Eugene D. *Roll, Jordan, Roll: The World the Slaves Made.* New York: Pantheon Books, 1974.

Getz, Lorine M. *Flannery O'Connor: Her Life, Library, and Book Reviews.* New York: Edwin Mellen Press, 1980.

Gilbert, Sandra M. "'My Name Is Darkness': The Poetry of Self-Definition."

Contemporary Literature 18 (Autumn 1977): 443–57.

Gilbert, Sandra M., and Susan Gubar. *The Madwoman in the Attic: The Woman Writer and the Nineteenth-Century Literary Imagination*. New Haven: Yale University Press, 1979.

Gimbutas, Marija. *The Goddesses and Gods of Old Europe, 7000 to 3500 B.C.* Berkeley: University of California Press, 1982.

Glasgow, Ellen. *Virginia*. Garden City, N.Y.: Doubleday, Page & Co., 1913.

————. *The Woman Within*. London: Eyre and Spottiswoode, 1955.

Gordon, Caroline. "Rebels and Revolutionaries: The New American Scene." *Flannery O'Connor Bulletin* 3 (1974): 40–56.

Gossett, Thomas F. "Flannery O'Connor's Opinions of Other Writers: Some Unpublished Comments." *Southern Literary Journal* 6 (Spring 1974): 70–82.

Goudie, Andrea. "Eudora Welty's Circe: A Goddess Who Strove with Men." *Studies in Short Fiction* 13 (Fall 1976): 481–89.

Grady, Henry W. *The New South and Other Addresses*. New York: Charles E. Merrill, 1904.

————. *Orations and Speeches of Henry W. Grady*. New York: Hinds, Noble, and Eldredge, 1910.

Grant, Michael. *Myths of the Greeks and Romans*. New York: Mentor, 1962.

Graver, Lawrence. *Carson McCullers*. Minneapolis: University of Minnesota Press, 1969.

Gray, Richard. *The Literature of Memory*. Baltimore: Johns Hopkins University Press, 1977.

Gretlund, Jan Nordby. "An Interview with Eudora Welty." *Southern Humanities Review* 14 (Summer 1980): 193–208.

Hakluyt, Richard. *The Principall Navigations of the English Nation*. London: Cambridge University Press, 1965.

Hall, Jacquelyn Dowd. *Revolt Against Chivalry: Jessie Daniel Ames and the Women's Campaign Against Lynching*. New York: Columbia University Press, 1979.

Hammond, N. G. L., and H. H. Scullard, eds. *The Oxford Classical Dictionary*. Oxford: Clarendon Press, 1970.

Hardy, John Edward. "*Delta Wedding* as Region and Symbol." *Sewanee Review* 60 (Summer 1952): 397–417.

————. "Marrying Down in Eudora Welty's Novels." In *Eudora Welty: Critical Essays*, edited by Peggy Whitman Prenshaw. Jackson: University Press of Mississippi, 1979.

Haskell, Molly. *From Reverence to Rape*. Baltimore: Penguin Books, 1974.

Hawkes, John. "Flannery O'Connor's Devil." *Sewanee Review* 70 (Summer 1962): 395–407.

Heilbrun, Carolyn G. *Reinventing Womanhood*. New York: W. W. Norton Co., 1979.

Heilman, Robert B. "The Southern Temper." In Louis D. Rubin, Jr., and Robert D. Jacobs, eds., *Southern Renascence: The Literature of the Modern South*. Baltimore: Johns Hopkins University Press, 1953.

Hendin, Josephine. *The World of Flannery O'Connor*. Bloomington: Indiana University Press, 1970.

Hesiod. *The Homeric Hymns and Homerica*. Translated by Hugh G. Evelyn-White. Cambridge: Harvard University Press, 1974.

Hicks, Granville. "A Writer at Home with Her Heritage." *Saturday Review*, May 12, 1962, 22–23.

Hoffman, Frederick J. *The Art of Southern Fiction: A Study of Some Modern Novelists*. Carbondale: Southern Illinois University Press, 1967.

Holman, C. Hugh. *The Roots of Southern Writing*. Athens: University of Georgia Press, 1972.

Horney, Karen. *Feminine Psychology*. Edited by Harold Kelman. New York: W. W. Norton Co., 1967.

Howard, Zelma Turner. *The Rhetoric of Eudora Welty's Short Stories*. Jackson: University Press of Mississippi, 1973.

Images of the South: Visits with Eudora Welty and Walker Evans. Introduction by Bill Ferris. Southern Folklore Reports 1. Memphis: Center for Southern Folklore, 1977.

"Indian Mounds." Mississippi Department of Archives and History, n.d.

Isaacs, Neil D. *Eudora Welty*. Austin: Steck-Vaughn, 1969.

James, E. O. *The Cult of the Mother-Goddess*. New York: Praeger, 1959.

Jemison, Marie Stokes. "Ladies Become Voters." *Southern Exposure* 7 (Spring 1979): 48–59.

Johnson, James Weldon. *The Autobiography of an Ex-Coloured Man*. Introduction by Carl van Vechten. New York: Alfred A. Knopf, 1927.

Jones, Anne Goodwyn. *Tomorrow Is Another Day: The Woman Writer in the South, 1859–1936*. Baton Rouge: Louisiana State University Press, 1981.

Jones, John Griffin, ed. *Mississippi Writers Talking: Interviews with Eudora Welty, Shelby Foote, Elizabeth Spencer, Barry Hannah, Beth Henley*. Jackson: University Press of Mississippi, 1982.

Jung, Carl. *The Psychology of the Unconscious*. New York: Moffat, Yard & Co., 1916.

Katz, Claire. "Flannery O'Connor's Rage of Vision." *American Literature* 46 (March 1974): 54–67.

Kazin, Alfred. *Bright Book of Life: American Novelists and Storytellers from Hemingway to Mailer*. New York: Delta, 1974.

Kerényi, C. *Eleusis: Archetypal Images of Mother and Daughter*. Translated by Ralph Manheim. New York: Schocken Books, 1977.

King, Florence. *Southern Ladies and Gentlemen*. New York: Stein and Day, 1975.

King, Grace. *Memories of a Southern Woman of Letters*. New York: Macmillan, 1932.

King, Richard H. *A Southern Renaissance: The Cultural Awakening of the American South, 1930–1955*. New York: Oxford University Press, 1980.

Kinney, Arthur F. "In Search of Flannery O'Connor." *Virginia Quarterly Review* 59 (Spring 1983): 271–88.

Kirk, G. S., trans. *The Bacchae of Euripides*. New York: Cambridge University Press, 1979.

———. *Myth: Its Meaning and Functions in Ancient and Other Cultures*. Cambridge: Cambridge University Press, 1974.

———. *The Nature of Greek Myths*. New York: Penguin Books, 1980.

Kolodny, Annette. *The Lay of the Land: Metaphor as Experience and History in American Life and Letters*. Chapel Hill: University of North Carolina Press, 1975.

———. "'Stript, Shorne and Made Deformed': Images on the Southern Landscape." *South Atlantic Quarterly* 75 (Winter 1976): 55–73.

Koon, William. "'Hep Me Not To Be So Mean': Flannery O'Connor's Subjectivity." *Southern Review* 15 (Spring 1979): 322–32.

Kreyling, Michael. *Eudora Welty's Achievement of Order*. Baton Rouge: Louisiana State University Press, 1980.

———. "Life with People: Virginia Woolf, Eudora Welty and *The Optimist's Daughter*." *Southern Review* 13 (Spring 1977): 250–71.

Kuehl, Linda. "The Art of Fiction XLVII: Eudora Welty." *Paris Review* 14 (Fall 1972): 72–97.

Levy, G. R. *The Gate of Horn: A Study of the Religious Conceptions of the Stone Age, and Their Influence upon European Thought*. London: Faber and Faber, 1948.

Lewis, R. W. B. *The American Adam*. Chicago: University of Chicago Press, 1955.

MacKethan, Lucinda H. "To See Things in Their Time: The Art of Focus in Eudora Welty's Fiction." *American Literature* 50 (May 1978): 258–75.

Manning, Carol S. "Little Girls and Sidewalks: Glasgow and Welty on Childhood's Promise." *Southern Quarterly* 21 (Spring 1983): 67–76.

Marcus, Jane. "'A Rose for Him to Rifle, A Cloak for Him to Trample': The Feminist Critic and the Centenaries." Paper presented at the MLA convention, Los Angeles, December 1982.

Marshack, Alexander. *The Roots of Civilization*. New York: McGraw-Hill, 1971.

Marx, Leo. *The Machine in the Garden: Technology and the Pastoral Ideal in America*. New York: Oxford University Press, 1978.

May, John R. *The Pruning Word: The Parables of Flannery O'Connor*. Notre Dame: University of Notre Dame Press, 1976.

Mayer, Charles W. "The Comic Spirit in 'A Stroke of Good Fortune.'" *Studies in Short Fiction* 16 (Winter 1979): 70–74.

Mayer, David R. "Apologia for the Imagination: Flannery O'Connor's 'A Temple of the Holy Ghost.'" *Studies in Short Fiction* 11 (Spring 1974): 147–52.

McCown, James H. "Remembering Flannery O'Connor." *America* (September 1979): 86–88.

McCullers, Carson. *The Ballad of the Sad Café: The Novels and Stories of Carson McCullers*. Boston: Houghton Mifflin, 1951.

———. *Clock Without Hands*. Boston: Houghton Mifflin, 1961.

———. *The Mortgaged Heart*. Edited by Margarita G. Smith. Boston: Houghton Mifflin, 1971.

———. *The Square Root of Wonderful: A Play*. Boston: Houghton Mifflin, 1958.

McDowell, John Patrick. *The Social Gospel in the South*. Baton Rouge: Louisiana State University Press, 1971.

McFarland, Dorothy Tuck. *Flannery O'Connor*. New York: Frederick Ungar, 1976.

McGowan, Marcia. "Patterns of Female Experience in Eudora Welty's Fiction." Ph.D. dissertation, Rutgers University, 1977.

McKenzie, Barbara. "Flannery O'Connor Country: A Photo Essay." *Georgia Review* 29 (Summer 1975): 329–62.

———. *Flannery O'Connor's Georgia.* Athens: University of Georgia Press, 1980.

Meaders, Margaret Inman. "Flannery O'Connor: 'Literary Witch.'" *Colorado Quarterly* 10 (Spring 1962): 377–86.

Mebane, Mary E. *Mary.* New York: Viking Press, 1981.

Mellaart, James. *The Neolithic of the Near East.* New York: Charles Scribner's Sons, 1975.

Mendenhall, Marjorie Stratford. "Southern Women of a 'Lost Generation.'" *South Atlantic Quarterly* 33 (1934): 334–53.

Millichap, Joseph R. "Carson McCullers's Literary Ballad." *Georgia Review* 27 (Fall 1973): 329–39.

Mims, Edwin. *The Advancing South: Stories of Progress and Reaction.* Garden City, N.Y.: Doubleday, Page, 1926.

———. "The Southern Woman: Past and Present." *Bulletin* of Randolph-Macon Woman's College (July 1915): 3–17.

Moers, Ellen. *Literary Women.* New York: Doubleday, 1976.

Montgomery, Marion. "The Artist as 'A Very Doubtful Jacob': A Reflection on Hawthorne and O'Connor." *Southern Quarterly* 16 (Winter 1978): 95–103.

———. "Flannery O'Connor: Prophetic Poet." *Flannery O'Connor Bulletin* 3 (1974): 79–95.

Moore, Carol A. "Aunt Studney's Sack." *Southern Review* 16 (Summer 1980): 591–96.

Morris, Harry C. "Eudora Welty's Use of Mythology." *Shenandoah* 6 (Spring 1955): 34–40.

Mossberg, Barbara Clarke. *Emily Dickinson: When a Writer Is a Daughter.* Bloomington: Indiana University Press, 1982.

———. "Slant Truths and Bandaged Secrets: The Art of Deceit in Emily Dickinson and Gertrude Stein." Paper presented at the MLA convention, New York, December 1978.

Mowry, George E. *Another Look at the Twentieth-Century South.* Baton Rouge: Louisiana State University Press, 1973.

Muller, Gilbert H. *Nightmares and Visions: Flannery O'Connor and the Catholic Grotesque.* Athens: University of Georgia Press, 1972.

Murphy, George D., and Caroline L. Cherry. "Flannery O'Connor and the Integration of Personality." *Flannery O'Connor Bulletin* 7 (1978): 85–100.

Mylonas, George E. *The Hymn to Demeter and Her Sanctuary at Eleusis.* St. Louis: Washington University Studies, 1942.

Neumann, Erich. *The Great Mother.* Translated by Ralph Manheim. Bollingen Series 47. New York: Pantheon Books, 1955.

Newman, Frances. "The State of Literature in the Late Confederacy." *Books,* August 16, 1925.

Nilsson, Martin P. *The Minoan-Mycenaean Religion and Its Survival in Greek Religion.* London: Oxford University Press, 1927.

———. *The Mycenaean Origin of Greek Mythology.* Berkeley: University of California Press, 1932.

Nostrandt, Jeanne Rolfe. "Fiction as Event: An Interview with Eudora Welty." *New Orleans Review* 7 (1979): 26–34.

Oates, Joyce Carol. "The Visionary Art of Flannery O'Connor." *Southern Humanities Review* 7 (Summer 1973): 235–46.

O'Connor, Flannery. *The Complete Stories*. New York: Farrar, Straus and Giroux, 1972.

———. *Everything That Rises Must Converge*. Introduction by Robert Fitzgerald. New York: Farrar, Straus and Giroux, 1965.

———. *The Habit of Being*. Edited by Sally Fitzgerald. New York: Farrar, Straus and Giroux, 1979.

———. *Mystery and Manners: Occasional Prose*. Selected and edited by Sally and Robert Fitzgerald. New York: Farrar, Straus and Giroux, 1967.

———. *Three by Flannery O'Connor*. New York: New American Library, 1962.

Orvell, Miles. *Invisible Parade: The Fiction of Flannery O'Connor*. Philadelphia: Temple University Press, 1972.

Osterweis, Rollin G. *The Myth of the Lost Cause, 1865–1900*. Hamden, Conn.: Archon Books, 1973.

Park, Clara Claiborne. "Crippled Laughter: Toward Understanding Flannery O'Connor." *American Scholar* 51 (Spring 1982): 249–57.

Percy, William Alexander. *Lanterns on the Levee*. New York: Alfred A. Knopf, 1941.

Petty, Jane Reid. "The Town and the Writer: An Interview with Eudora Welty." *Jackson Magazine*, September 1977, 29–35.

Phillips, Robert L., Jr. "A Structural Approach to Myth in the Fiction of Eudora Welty." In *Eudora Welty: Critical Essays*, edited by Peggy Whitman Prenshaw. Jackson: University Press of Mississippi, 1979.

Phillips, Robert S. "Dinesen's 'Monkey' and McCullers' 'Ballad': A Study in Literary Affinity." *Studies in Short Fiction* 1 (Spring 1964): 184–90.

Porter, Katherine Anne. *The Collected Stories of Katherine Anne Porter*. New York: Harcourt, Brace and World, 1965.

Prenshaw, Peggy Whitman, ed. *Eudora Welty: Critical Essays*. Jackson: University Press of Mississippi, 1979.

———. "Woman's World, Man's Place: The Fiction of Eudora Welty." In *Eudora Welty: A Form of Thanks*, edited by Louis Dollarhide and Ann J. Abadie. Jackson: University Press of Mississippi, 1979.

Presley, Delma Eugene. "Carson McCullers and the South." *Georgia Review* 28 (Spring 1974): 19–32.

Puhvel, Jaan. "Eleuthér and Oinoâtis: Dionysiac Data from Mycenaean Greece." In *Mycenaean Studies*, edited by Emmett L. Bennett, Jr. Madison: University of Wisconsin Press, 1964.

Randisi, Jennifer Lynn. *A Tissue of Lies: Eudora Welty and the Southern Romance*. Washington, D.C.: University Press of America, 1982.

Ransom, John Crowe. "Delta Fiction." *Kenyon Review* 8 (Summer 1946): 503–507.

——— et al. *I'll Take My Stand: The South and the Agrarian Tradition*. New York: Harper & Brothers, 1930.

Rechnitz, Robert M. "The Failure of Love: The Grotesque in Two Novels by Carson McCullers." *Georgia Review* 22 (Winter 1968): 454–63.

Rich, Adrienne. *Adrienne Rich's Poetry.* New York: W. W. Norton Co., 1975.

Richardson, Eudora Ramsay. "The Case of the Women's Colleges in the South." *South Atlantic Quarterly* 29 (April 1930): 126–39.

Rolfe, John. *A True Relation of the State of Virginia.* Edited by Henry C. Taylor. Charlottesville: University Press of Virginia, 1971.

Rout, Kathleen. "Dream a Little Dream of Me: Mrs. May and the Bull in Flannery O'Connor's 'Greenleaf.'" *Studies in Short Fiction* 16 (Summer 1979): 233–35.

Rubin, Louis D., Jr. "Carson McCullers: The Aesthetic of Pain." *Virginia Quarterly Review* 53 (Spring 1977): 265–83.

———. "The Golden Apples of the Sun." In *The Faraway Country: Writers of the Modern South.* Seattle: University of Washington Press, 1963.

———. *William Elliott Shoots a Bear: Essays on the Southern Literary Imagination.* Baton Rouge: Louisiana State University Press, 1975.

Ruddick, Lisa. *The Seen and the Unseen: Virginia Woolf's "To the Lighthouse."* Cambridge: Harvard University Press, 1977.

Scott, Anne Firor. *The Southern Lady: From Pedestal to Politics, 1830–1930.* Chicago: University of Chicago Press, 1970.

Scouten, Kenneth. "The Mythological Dimensions of Five of Flannery O'Connor's Works." *Flannery O'Connor Bulletin* 2 (1973): 59–72.

Scully, Vincent. *The Earth, the Temple, and the Gods.* Rev. ed. New Haven: Yale University Press, 1979.

Segal, Charles. *Dionysiac Poetics and Euripides' "Bacchae."* Princeton: Princeton University Press, 1982.

Shields, John C. "Flannery O'Connor's 'Greenleaf' and the Myth of Europa and the Bull." *Studies in Short Fiction* 18 (Fall 1981): 421–31.

Showalter, Elaine. *A Literature of Their Own: British Women Novelists from Brontë to Lessing.* Princeton: Princeton University Press, 1977.

Sieveking, Ann. *The Cave Artists.* London: Thames and Hudson, 1979.

Simpson, Lewis P. *The Dispossessed Garden: Pastoral and History in Southern Literature.* Athens: University of Georgia Press, 1975.

———. "Southern Fiction." In *The Harvard Guide to Contemporary American Writing,* edited by Daniel Hoffman. Cambridge: Harvard University Press, 1979.

Singal, Daniel Joseph. *The War Within: From Victorian to Modernist Thought in the South, 1919–1945.* Chapel Hill: University of North Carolina Press, 1982.

Smith, Lillian. *Killers of the Dream.* New York: W. W. Norton Co., 1949.

Sophocles. *Oedipus, Sophoclis Fabulae.* Edited by A. C. Pearson. Oxford: Oxford University Press, 1964.

Sontag, Susan. *On Photography.* New York: Dell Publishing Co., 1977.

Stampp, Kenneth. *The Peculiar Institution: Slavery in the Ante-bellum South.* New York: Alfred A. Knopf, 1965.

Stephens, Martha. *The Question of Flannery O'Connor.* Baton Rouge: Louisiana State University Press, 1973.

Sullivan, Walter. *Death by Melancholy: Essays on Modern Southern Fiction.* Baton Rouge: Louisiana State University Press, 1972.

———. *A Requiem for the Renascence: The State of Fiction in the Modern South.* Athens: University of Georgia Press, 1976.

Tannenbaum, Frank. *Darker Phases of the South.* New York: Putnam, 1924.

Tate, Allen. "The New Provincialism." *Virginia Quarterly Review* 21 (Spring 1945): 262–72.

———. "The Profession of Letters in the South." In *Essays of Four Decades.* Chicago: Swallow Press, 1968.

Taylor, William R. *Cavalier and Yankee: The Old South and American National Character.* New York: George Braziller, 1961.

Vande Kieft, Ruth M. *Eudora Welty.* New York: Twayne, 1962.

Walker, Alice. "Beyond the Peacock: The Reconstruction of Flannery O'Connor." *Ms.* 4 (December 1975): 77–79, 102–106.

———. "Eudora Welty: An Interview." *Harvard Advocate* 106 (1973): 67–72.

Walters, Dorothy. *Flannery O'Connor.* New York: Twayne, 1973.

Warner, Marina. *Alone of All Her Sex.* New York: Pocket Books, 1976.

Warren, Robert Penn. "The Love and Separateness in Eudora Welty." *Kenyon Review* 6 (Spring 1944): 246–59.

Welty, Eudora. *The Collected Stories of Eudora Welty.* New York: Harcourt Brace Jovanovich, 1980.

———. *A Curtain of Green and Other Stories.* New York: Harcourt, Brace, 1941.

———. *Delta Wedding.* New York: Harcourt, Brace, 1946.

———. *The Eye of the Story.* New York: Random House, 1978.

———. *Losing Battles.* Greenwich, Conn.: Fawcett, 1970.

———. *One Writer's Beginnings.* Cambridge: Harvard University Press, 1984.

———. *The Optimist's Daughter.* Greenwich, Conn.: Fawcett, 1972.

———. *The Ponder Heart.* New York: Harcourt, Brace, and World, 1954.

"Welty Rites Today." Jackson *Clarion-Ledger,* January 22, 1966.

Westling, Louise. "Carson McCullers' Amazon Nightmare." *Modern Fiction Studies* 28 (Autumn 1982): 465–73.

———. "Carson McCullers's Tomboys." *Southern Humanities Review* 14 (Fall 1980): 339–50.

———. "Flannery O'Connor's Mothers and Daughters." *Twentieth Century Literature* 24 (Winter 1978): 510–22.

———. "The Perils of Adolescence in Flannery O'Connor and Carson McCullers." *Flannery O'Connor Bulletin* 8 (1979): 88–98.

Wikborg, Eleanor. *Carson McCullers' "The Member of the Wedding": Aspects of Structure and Style.* Göteborg, Sweden: Acta Universitatis Gothoburgensis, 1975.

Wilson, Edmund. *Patriotic Gore: Studies in the Literature of the American Civil War.* New York: Oxford University Press, 1962.

Woodward, C. Vann. *American Counterpoint: Slavery and Racism in the North-South Dialogue.* New York: Oxford University Press, 1983.

———. *The Burden of Southern History.* Rev. ed. Baton Rouge: Louisiana State University Press, 1968.

Woolf, Virginia. *The Death of the Moth and Other Essays.* London: Hogarth Press, 1942.

———. *The Diary of Virginia Woolf.* Vols. 2 and 3. New York: Harcourt Brace Jovanovich, 1978 and 1980.

———. *Jacob's Room.* New York: Harcourt, Brace, 1930.

———. *The Moment and Other Essays.* New York: Harcourt, Brace, 1948.

———. *A Room of One's Own.* Harmondsworth, England: Penguin Books, 1965.

———. *To the Lighthouse.* New York: Harcourt, Brace, 1927.

Wright, Richard. *Black Boy.* Cleveland: World Publishing Co., 1945.

Wyatt-Brown, Bertram. *Southern Honor: Ethics and Behavior in the Old South.* New York: Oxford University Press, 1982.

Young, David P. *The Heart's Forest: A Study of Shakespeare's Pastoral Plays.* New Haven: Yale University Press, 1972.

Young, Marguerite. "Metaphysical Fiction." *Kenyon Review* 9 (Winter 1947): 151–55.

Young, Thomas Daniel. *The Past in the Present: A Thematic Study of Modern Southern Fiction.* Baton Rouge: Louisiana State University Press, 1981.

Zoller, Peter T. "The Irony of Preserving the Self: Flannery O'Connor's 'A Stroke of Good Fortune.'" *Kansas Quarterly* 9 (Spring 1977): 61–66.

Index

DATE DUE

SEP 1 9 1994		
OCT 1 8 199		
OCT 3 0 2003		
FEB 1 3 2009		